# I Talk of Dreams

# I Talk of Dreams

Reflections on Adolescence, Theatre,
and Performing Shakespeare

Edited by
Andrew Garrod, James Rice, and Andrew Nalani

Foreword by Mike Leigh
Afterword by David Barnet

**Rock's Mills Press**
Rock's Mills, Ontario • Oakville Ontario
2024

Published by
**Rock's Mills Press**
www.rocksmillspress.com

The editors are grateful to the owners of the photographs reproduced beginning on page 277 for their kind permission to use them in this book: Ian MacEachern for the photographs of Gail Taylor (p. 288); Andrew Garrod as the proprietor of the photographs taken by Ken Woods of the other Canadian productions (pp. 277–282, pp. 284–286, pp. 289–292, pp. 299–302, pp. 307–310); and Andrew Garrod (pp. 283, 287, 297, 298, 315, 317), Alex Payne (pp. 313, 316), Gordan Stojkić (p. 314), Ken Taggart (pp. 303, 304, 306), Chewy Lin (p. 294), Hilary Hosia (p. 293), Tony Dujmovic (pp. 305, 311), and Gentrit Syla (pp. 295, 296), for the photographs of the various international productions. Special acknowledgement is made to Ken Woods, who so thoroughly documented the productions at Saint John High School in the 1960s and 1970s while working at the school.

For information, including permissions information and information about trade, library, and bulk orders, please contact the publisher at customer.service@rocksmillspress.com

*This book is dedicated to our eloquent and courageous contributors, willing to share their experiences of acting on stage with a wide audience.*

*It is also dedicated to former students and faculty actors and helpers who have died:*

| | |
|---|---|
| Susan Bate | Michael Davis |
| Christopher Kipping | Elizabeth Foster Chase |
| Norman Casey | Peter Chipman |
| Jennifer Brittain | Jeremy Gadd |
| Dale Peters | Amy Fleming |
| Michael Hovey | Christine Duplessis |
| Helen Buck | Elaine Logan |
| Jim Oram | Lyle Isaacs |
| Peter Somerville | Donald Laidlaw |
| Lowell Boyle | Kim Fullerton |
| David MacKenzie | Liz Janes |
| Joanne Kee | Linda Moore Keirstead |
| Bruce Campbell | George Fry |
| Richard Green | Robert Edwards |
| Peter Hayward | Edgar Moore |
| Gordon Moffitt | Leslie Newton |
| Naomi Macleod | Bud Crandall |
| David MacPherson | Alan Michelson |
| Geoff Foss | Bill Seeley |
| Ian McLean | Dr. Mark Sadler |
| John Morgan | Patricia Murray |
| Susan Crandall | Timothy Colwell |
| Andrew Terris | |

# Contents

# Foreword

Mike Leigh

The provincial all-boys grammar school I attended in the north of England in the 1950s had an occasionally active dramatic society. Albert Finney had just left when I arrived—he had gone off to London to train at RADA (Royal Academy of Dramatic Art), where I was to follow him. So there was some enthusiasm, and I found myself in my time there in Hans Andersen and Chekhov one-act plays, Shaw's *Androcles and The Lion*, in which I played the eponymous quadruped, Gogol's *Government Inspector*, playing the lead, and a couple of musical shows including Gilbert and Sullivan's *Trial by Jury*, in which I gave my bridesmaid.

I was devastated not to be cast in *Treasure Island*—too much of a grotesque for Jim Hawkins, and too unbroken a voice for a pirate—and extremely disappointed when the headmaster, who sometimes directed (or "produced," as they then still called it), scrapped a promising *Importance of Being Earnest*. (What I thought was particularly promising was my putative Lady Bracknell.)

As might be expected, these shows were approached and rehearsed in an old-fashioned, externalised, plodding sort of way, and our amateurish performances were more concerned with the audibility than with truth or style. And they were further cluttered and obscured by the most cumbersome hired costumes and wigs, and by thick layers of very greasy greasepaint, administered ineptly by an army of volunteer mums, whose timid leader was the headmaster's entirely untheatrical wife. As the school Art Department was run by an uncharacteristically enlightened bloke, the set design was always far more sophisticated and "contemporary" than the production itself, and I would get as involved in painting and construction as rehearsals—and homework—would permit.

These shows were quite awful, very popular, undoubtedly educational, and great fun to be involved in. Our camaraderie, our high spirits, and our sense of achievement were terrific. And, despite the lamentable absence from the proceedings of young women, and the appalling convention of boys playing girls, it was all pretty healthy and wholesome. (Somebody must have been gay, but the prevailing sweaty heterosexual ethos of post-war industrial Lancashire prevented you from ever knowing it!)

The 1950s were, of course, the last decade of the Age of Innocence as we knew it. So any radical notions one might have harboured lay deep in the subconscious, buried under layers of provincial and suburban respectability and received ideas.

Had it been possible to flush it out, my own serious reservation would have been that what we were actually putting on the stage was somehow entirely unrelated to our lives.

Later, in the Glorious Sixties, as a young dramatist and director, this all became very clear to me. I began to develop a new kind of experimental theatre, which quite apart from the improvisational techniques deployed to create the material, was first and foremost about depicting our own world in a realistic way.

Although my primary concern was to work with professional actors (and, indeed, to make films), I was also compelled to take my ideas back to young people's theatre, to compensate, somehow, for my own school play experiences.

Working with youth theatre groups in Birmingham and later, in Manchester, I created several so-called "improvised plays," that is, finished pieces evolved from improvisation. *The Box Play* was about a family living in a box-like house and inter-reacting with the outside world, *My Parents Have Gone to Carlisle* concerned a disastrous teenage party, and *Big Basil* and *Glum Victoria and The Lad with Specs* were big-cast dramas with music, set in comprehensive schools and working-class homes.

I always include these shows on my CV alongside my best-known feature films. I am proud of them as plays, but above all, I cherish their memory as times of great creativity and sharing friendship. I have lost touch with nearly all the young people involved, but I am quite sure they all feel the same as I do.

Reading the moving Saint John High School essays gathered here by Andrew Garrod, it quickly becomes apparent that these kids experienced the best of what I am talking about—truly exploratory, personally fulfilling ensemble work with which they were able to connect.

I have often regretted that we didn't tackle Shakespeare at Salford Grammar School. But our worthy, if limited, schoolmaster-producers were no Andrew Garrods, with his special ability to make the work alive and relevant, so perhaps it is just as well.

Gail Taylor describes Andrew as "alert to the flux of formation that marked our adolescent rhythms," adding that "he seemed less bent on potential." And, in his creative writing class, she recalls that "playing with the discovery that even the chaotic experience was better let out than kept in, I was rehearsing without knowing it for my imminent infatuation with theatre."

Pure theatre—raw, basic, honest, truthful, motivated, organic, resonant with the stuff of real life, comic, tragic, and epic—is the most natural activity in the world for young people to experience as a part of their journey from adolescence to adulthood.

It is rich and special, and if you are lucky enough to get a dose, your life will be enhanced forever.

That is obviously the Saint John High School experience under Andrew Garrod, and reading this book is truly inspiring.

# Acknowledgements

For a project that spans sixty years and that embraces the words of Canadians from Saint John High School in New Brunswick in the 1960s and '70s, and from 2004 until the present day of international students from Bosnia and Herzegovina, Kosovo, Rwanda, and the Marshall Islands, there are many friends and associates to be thanked.

The set and costume designer for almost all the productions in Canada was the remarkable George Fry—bold and imaginative and always receptive to a genuine dialogue with me about the conception of the play. For the critical role of music director in our Broadway shows, I have two highly talented men to thank—David Carter and Bob Edwards, both of them originally British with expert training from their homeland in their respective instruments, the violin and the piano. Their professionalism and expertise set standards not often achieved by high school musicals. The choreographer for all the Broadway musicals we mounted was Judy Scott, a lecturer in modern dance at Columbia University, who had an uncanny ability to understand the strengths and vulnerabilities of unseasoned dancers and created dance steps that were fascinating, dynamic, and eminently watchable. The constructor of most of our sets was the carpenter supreme, Jon Simpson, who was able to build from George's designs powerful realizations of George's drawings and models. In charge of costume creation was the resourceful and talented Sandy Thorne, and for lighting the sets, we were indebted to Richard Thorne for his fine sense of theatricality. Amongst other contributors, I must mention Walter Glover, Leslie Newton, Barry Snodgrass, Gordon Clover, and Herb Foley. A special thank you to Helmer Bierman and Jo Anne Claus, art critics of the Saint John *Telegraph Journal* and the Fredericton *Gleaner*, respectively. Their love of drama and the significance they accorded to student theatre illuminated their dramatic reviews. Mike Leigh and David Barnet are owed a special thanks for their willingness to write the graceful foreword and afterword of this anthology. I owe a special debt to Marti Maraden and Nicholas Pennell of the Stratford Festival, and David Barnet who at that time was at the University of Alberta; they traveled to Saint John to run illuminating and compelling workshops for the benefit of our actors. Ken Woods was the masterful photographer of nearly all the pictures in this book. We are deeply grateful to his skills and kindness. The two photographs from *King Lear* reproduced in this anthology were taken by Ian MacEachern.

The international productions have been the recipients of great generosity from Anne Huebner Waller and Ross Waller, Sandra Irving, Andy Brown, Betsy Miller, and Dr. Anthony Riccio. These projects were assisted by a rotating group of helpers and theatre people often closely connected to Dartmouth College as well as by my own non-profit organization that aimed to mount dramatic productions in countries of the world that faced enormous challenges—Youth Bridge Global (YBG).

I need to acknowledge the Ministry of Education in the Marshall Islands and the succession of Presidents of the Marshall Islands for their most generous financial help in producing eight bilingual Shakespearean plays and eight bilingual Broadway musicals. For all these productions, I am indebted to the student directors from Dartmouth between 2004 and 2019 and to the principal choreographers for dances in the Shakespearean comedies, Asena Ketedromo, and in the Broadway musicals to Nina Roy, Marisa Clementi, and Ilona Bito. I was always grateful to Bonny Taggart, a boundlessly energetic, efficient, and loving woman who was our peerless producer in the Marshal Islands and in Kosovo, and to Mona Levi-Strauss, for her brilliant costume creations. Dody Riggs supplied essential editorial suggestions as manuscripts achieved their final forms, and former and present students at Dartmouth have served critical roles in the essays' preparation and the book's production. Critical to the introduction to this book were the invaluable contributions of Gail Taylor, Christina Gomez, and Dody Riggs; their comments and stylistic suggestions improved the readability of the introduction immeasurably. These students provided indispensable help: Yadira Montano Gonzalez, Zach Panton, Angel Pedro, Sumreet Sandhu, Sovi Wellons, Sereena Knight, Nathan

Syvash, and Noah Martinez—all have helped markedly to improve and edit the text. A heartfelt thanks to Sereena Knight for fine-tuning the text for publication with Rock's Mills Press.

Acknowledgement of our government sector partners in the Marshall Islands is vital: the Office of the President of the RMI (Kessai Note, the late Litokwa Tomeing, the late Jurelang Zedekaia, Christopher Loeak, Hilda Heine, David Kabua); the Ministry of Education, especially Wilbur Heine, Hilda Heine and Kittilang Kabua, Kanchi Hosia, Cassiano Jetnil; the late Jerre Bennett, the late Evelyn Konou, Ned Jabwill, and Kathy Digno of the Marshall Islands High School; Mayor Ladie Jack, Majuro Atoll Local Government; Tony Wase and Rocky Harry of the RMI's International Conference Center; and the U.S. Ambassadors to the Marshall Islands (Clyde Bishop, Martha Campbell, Thomas Armbruster, Karen Stewart, Roxanne Cabral). Our business supporters included Colette and Ramsey Reimers of Robert Reimers Enterprises; Larry Hernandez, Do It Best Hardware; Hirobo Obeketang, Marshall Islands Resort; Giff Johnson and the late Joe Murphy of the Marshall Islands *Journal*; Patrick Chen, Bank of Marshall Islands; Liz Rodick, EZ Price Mart; Jerry and Daniel Kramer, Pacific International, Inc.; Mike Slinger, TSL Office Solutions; Imams Mataullah Joyia and Sajid Iqbal of the Ahmadiyya Mosque; Biram Stege of Assumption High School, and the late Monsignor Ray Sabio of Assumption Catholic Church. Other key supporters included Mona Levy-Strauss, Veronica Wase, Miram DeBrum, Ben Chutaro, Alson Kelen, Bryant Zebedy, Milner Okney, Save Filolita, Scott Stege, Ben and Monique Graham, Dennis and Daisy Momotaro, Robbie Chutaro, Jack Niedenthal, Mark Stege, Becky and Willard Lathrop, Brian Tidwell (front of house), Cheta Anien, Yshiwata Lomae, Hilary Hosia, Wilbert Alik, Allen Tareo, Chewy Lin, Hanty Kaishi and William Apo Leo.

For our Shakespearian production in Pristina, Kosovo, we gratefully thank the executive director of TOKA Jehona Gjurgjeala, and her former program manager Renea Behluli. We also honor members of the production team, especially the Co-Director of Youth Bridge Global Ray Rochester and the producer Bonny Taggart. The contributions of the following people were essential: Agnes Nokshiqi, Jessica Swale, Alex Payne, Butrint Pasha, Tyler Malbreaux, Mentor Berisha, Alma Krasniqi, Gentrit Syla, Doruntina Hoti, and Sara Linsey.

The production of *Romeo and Juliet* in Rwanda is deeply grateful to our partner organization Ishyo Arts Center and its director Carole Karemera who also served as our producer. We would also like to thank the following individuals and organizations: SOS Children's Village and its Director Mr. Kiba, Dida Nihagwire, Liliane Nsengiyumva, Jean de Dieu Kamel, Omar Selekene, Fawe Girls School, Oscar Gasigwa, and Alexis Nshimiyimana; Assistant Directors Heidi Lansburgh, Aidan Nelson, and Ray Rochester; Production Coordinators Charlotte Pfeffer, Tess Page, and Kayley Reed; Translator into Kinyarwanda Manou Emmanuel and into French Jean-Michel Déprats; Choreographers Kevin Nyayiha and Ray Rochester; Vocal Coach James Rice and Music by Daniel Ngarukiye; Lighting Design by Roman Kanobana and Positive Productions; Light and Sound Technical Director Raoul Rugamba and Light and Sound Technical Assistant Vincent de Paul Kwizera; Set Design/Construction by Ray Rochester, Jean de Dieu Kamel and Omar Selekene; Costume Design by Jacques Sindabye, Costume Assistants Charlotte Pfeffer and Heidi Lansburgh, and Props Mistress Kayley Reed; House Manager Tess Page and Poster/Program Art by Patrick Ruganimtwali. Majors donors include Sandra and Arthur Irving, Ann Huebner Waller and Ross P. Waller, Gabrielle Krengel, Professor Nancy Frankenberry, Professor Jonathan Crewe, Dr. Robert Kilkenny, Philip and Diane Dowd, William Levin, Sonia Reed, Harte and Ann Crow, Ellyn Lindsay, Katherine Lindsay, and Allan Klinge.

The seven Shakespearean projects in Mostar, Bosnia and Herzegovina spanning from 2006 to 2016 are most grateful to the following individuals for their assistance over the years: Michael Markin, Anesa Markin, Ivan Rozic, Marko Rozic, Anita Krtalic, Ilija Pujić, Mustafa Stupac, Heidi Rice, Annie Considine, Alex Payne, Barbara Cule, Diana Markotic, Peter Sutoris, Tomislav Papac, Filip Pastelek, Denan Behmen, Emina Tojaga. We wish to honor also: Selma Ridanovic, Lora Savonovic, Iana Rebac, UWC in Mostar—direktorica Valentina Mindoljevic, Hotel Ero, Mostar, and Sef Hajrusi. Amongst the donors were: Hickory Ginsburgh, David Yorio, Dr. Emil Chynn, Professor Peter Travis, Professor Jamie and Nancy Horton, Vincent Ng, and Dr. Robert Kenny.

A heartfelt thank you to two remarkable friends—Dr. Geoff Fox, previously of Exeter University, who has been a lifelong influence and participant in many, many conversations on youth theatre; and Jessica Swale, whose gifted artistry has enriched many of my productions on which she has worked. And a final tribute to my former high school student and lifelong friend of 62 years, Gail Taylor. Her wisdom, persistence, and encouragement have been critical to my efforts to complete this book project. Her gifts as a writer and editor, so evident in her essay "The Leave to Stop Posturing," have proved essential to the successful publication of this anthology.

The editors of *I Speak of Dreams: Reflections on Adolescence, Theatre, and Performing Shakespeare*, particularly want to recognize *all* the adults and students who worked with such industry, openness, and courage to bring their stories from the realm of strictly private into more public view. Those who do not show up here have given no less generously of themselves. We would also like to thank particularly all those adults and students who assisted in the plays' productions and in the realization of this book.

# Introduction
# "Who Is It that Can Tell Me Who I Am?"

Andrew Garrod

## Beginnings

"You're just the sort of chap we're looking for," said the Prince Philip–like headmaster of Marlborough College in Wiltshire, England, jabbing his spittled pipestem at me as we patrolled the spacious school grounds—he with one hand clasped in the other behind his back; me anxious to impress but vaguely uneasy. He eyed me watchfully as he said, "There are absolutely bags of opportunity for you here."

However, my mind was already made up: I would teach abroad for perhaps two years and then return to Britain. I was just finishing my diploma in education at Oxford University. My parents, adamant that I owed it to the state to teach in a British school as a form of thank you for funding my Oxford degree, could not dissuade me from my decision. Though I was moved by my father's recitation of a few lines from *Macbeth* as we said our goodbyes at Newton Abbot Railway Station, I was unpersuadable.

I boarded a Trans-Canada Air Lines flight via Halifax to Saint John, Canada, on a cold fall day in 1962. Sitting beside me was a bejeweled woman of a certain age—she was probably thirty years younger than I am now—who seemed riveted by why this young Englishman was coming to Canada. "Is it Toronto or Montreal or Vancouver that you are on your way to?" she queried. I replied, "It's Saint John, New Brunswick, where I will be teaching English at Saint John High School." "Oh," she responded with a slight sigh, "I thought a likely young man like you would be going to the big city."

While big cities have their charms, to my everlasting gratitude, this "likely young man" chose the port city of Saint John as his destination.

I hadn't exactly stumbled into this posting; in fact, I had been offered three teaching posts in North America, one in California, one in Upstate New York, and the third in Saint John. But it was the letter from Saint John that captivated me. "You will have the opportunity to hunt bear in the forests of New Brunswick," it claimed. No other job posting included this possibility—how could I turn down such a whimsical offer?

I came to theatre not by professional training as an actor, nor by having acted extensively in school plays in my youth. Despite minimal engagement in theatre at a young age, I had an intense interest in acting and possibly directing, but I initially was fearful of taking a bold step in this direction. What ultimately brought me to theatre was my strong interest in the psychology of character—characters I met and whom we read about in novels and plays I taught in my English class at Saint John High School. Through teaching Shakespeare in the classroom and novels—analyzing characters' motivations, values, dilemmas, moral choices, and relationships—I acquired a foundation in directing theatre. Over the course of sixteen years, I produced nine Shakespeare plays (*Macbeth, Hamlet, King Lear,* and many comedies), fifteen musicals (*West Side Story, Fiddler on the Roof, Guys and Dolls, My Fair Lady*), and nine more modern plays (American classics such as *The Crucible* and *The Glass Menagerie*). Over this time, I shifted from a prescriptive approach to directing to a more developmental one.

In my early productions at Saint John High School (SJHS), I worked with the actors to create my personal vision of a play, but the more I worked with teenagers, the more I came to trust and respect their individual values, quirks, and experiences, as well as how their distinctive characteristics could enhance the play. My goal then became to work with each actor to help them realize their potential and make their character come alive.

The first play I directed at SJHS was *Twelfth Night,* in 1963; I went on to direct three plays a year. The plays were mounted on two stages. One was in a converted classroom that sat 100 people, which provided an intimate experience for both the actors and the audience. The other was in the school auditorium, which had an elaborate proscenium arch and a seating capacity of around 900. My aim in having these vastly different venues was to ensure that the actors learned to play under very different conditions that gave them very different relationships with their audiences. I worked at SJHS (until 1978) to make theatre both acceptable to and a vital form of development for every student—not just the "artsy" students but also the athletes. These castings were instrumental in changing school norms, and theatre did become an activity for many students, not just a select few.

## Evolutions

After sixteen years of teaching and directing at SJHS, I decided to seek an advanced degree in education at Harvard University. After I completed my doctorate, I had two short teaching stints in the educational psychology departments of the University of Victoria and the University of Manitoba. In 1985 I accepted a position in the education department of Dartmouth College in New Hampshire, where I taught for twenty-five years and served as Chair and Director of Teacher Education. As I entered my third decade of teaching, I felt the urge to re-create the kind of experience that directing theatre at Saint John had provided me. I particularly wanted to offer an experience that would duplicate the warmth of the people I had worked with and the extraordinary opportunities I had been given. The notion of producing plays abroad came to me serendipitously when I was invited to direct bilingual Shakespeare productions in Majuro, the capital of the Marshall Islands. This opportunity followed from an earlier project in the Marshall Islands, where I had instituted the Dartmouth Volunteer Teaching Program. The program brought Dartmouth undergraduate and graduate students to teach in this central Pacific island nation for one term or one full school year. The institution of this program provided a double benefit. First, it exposed the Marshallese students to competent native English speakers while supporting an under-resourced education system. Second, the program fulfilled my dream of offering Dartmouth students the opportunity to study and teach abroad while being immersed in a culture that would challenge their assumptions about the United States and open their minds to what it means to be a global citizen (Nalani, Gómez, and Garrod, 2021). My theatre work in Saint John gave me the idea of mounting a yearly Shakespearean production with the Marshallese students—an idea that was initially met with skepticism but later, after they had experienced the delights of performing in *A Midsummer Night's Dream*, was fully embraced.

I was soon given another opportunity to work abroad, this time in 1998 in Mostar, Bosnia-Herzegovina, where a genocidal war had recently drawn to a close. The invitation came from my brother, Sir Martin Garrod, who at the time was the EU administrator of Mostar. He supported my ongoing research project, which involved looking at the effects of war on children and adolescents, specifically their attitudes about forgiveness, punishment, and morality (Thomas and Garrod, 2002). Motivated by a desire to give back to the Bosnian community in a tangible way, I initiated the production of a series of Shakespeare plays, which were to be performed by students from all sides of the cultural divide—Bosniaks. Croats, and Serbs—in the ruins of the old university library in Mostar. The productions would tour Bosnia-Herzegovina, Croatia, and Montenegro.

My research work in Bosnia and my teaching program in the Marshall Islands confirmed my intention to work with communities and students worldwide to further moral education and personal development through dramatic involvement. This intention led me to co-found Youth Bridge Global (YBG) with David Yorio in 2004. YBG is a nonprofit organization that provides dramatic opportunities for youth from countries facing unusual challenges, such as ethnic conflict and the dramatic effects of climate change. As of 2023, YBG has mounted productions in Bosnia-Herzegovina, Kosovo, Rwanda, and the Marshall Islands.

YBG's international team aims not to parachute into communities abroad to put on isolated productions. We want to teach the players to mount future local productions, thereby generating ownership while enriching their own communities. Our vision is that these productions will include not only the young cast members who have come to recognize the social value of theatre but also adults who have the ability and technical know-how to help the young people mount a production.

These principles undergird our dramaturgical process at each stage—from choosing the language of production to taking the final bows. We recruit producers, choreographers, composers, costume designers, and event hosts from the local population as best we can, adults as well as youth. When first mounting productions in the Marshall Islands, I saw that the model we were using could be applied in countries facing even greater challenges. Moreover, the program seemed complementary to the Dartmouth Volunteer Teaching Program, also within my purview, which fostered bilingual competence in Marshallese and English.

My ultimate goal is manifested in my belief that education represents not the endorsement of a system of privilege or class but the liberation and development for all. I like to think that the motivations, concerns, and decisions that mark my teaching career reflect my interest in privilege and class, justice, and fairness. In Shakespeare's *Hamlet,* the prince observes that "the play's the thing wherein I'll catch the conscience of the king." For me, the play's not *quite* the entire thing. While it is vitally important that any production is the best it can be—after all, the performers' joy in the productions is bound up with its success—the play is essentially a vehicle for meeting other goals. In a world riddled with religious conflict, ethnic division, racial disparities, political upheaval, gender violence, and income inequality, can we doubt that we all have a major obligation to pitch in? For me, theatre became my primary way of pitching in.

This book's goal is to be a testimonial to the experiences of theatre students and the transformational possibilities that exist when youth are allowed to take risks in a space that allows for creativity and growth. Drama requires imagination, discipline, and fearlessness—which, I dare say, we all need more of. My hope in sharing these stories is that the reader will come away inspired and aware of the potentialities of the arts in a world that has slowly eliminated many creative programs, particularly in under-resourced schools and communities. Consequently, this book will interest those who work with adolescents (in the arts and other spaces), teachers in general, and school boards that fund student programs in the arts. Creating theatre with young people has book-ended my career, beginning with SJHS and ending with YBG. It has helped me find my own voice and purpose in life. My desire in "doing" theatre has always been to help students discover who they are—to find their "forward voice" and the "good in everything."

## Staging
### *"Come, sit down, every mother's son, and rehearse your part"*
In producing the YBG plays, many decisions had to be made and some difficult choices, given where the productions were taking place. Below

I briefly summarize some issues that arose while producing the plays and how the YBG team handled them.

### CHOICES

All the youth I worked with were of a similar age and they had some of the same personal issues. However, working with international students posed distinctive challenges. For example, all my students had experienced a search for identity, a lack of self-confidence and resources, a sense of hopelessness about the political situation in their home countries, and many other issues, but most of my international students also had childhoods traumatized by war. Thus I had to pay particular attention to their home nations' histories and political contexts. Language added another difficulty for my international students, as none spoke English as a first language and none of my YBG team spoke the local languages fluently.

### AUDITIONS

One of YBG's goals is to build friendships across ethnic, racial, religious, class, and gender lines. Therefore, we enroll as many students as possible from all parts of the communities where we mount our plays. We test applicants for their ear and singing voice, dance ability, and acting potential. Because of the wealth of talent among these young people, we often double-cast parts so that each cast performs half of a play's run; this gives many more young people a chance to perform.

### LANGUAGE

Due to our desire to honor and respect the performers' local languages, all of YBG's Shakespeare productions are presented bilingually. Most of our actors are expected to move between two or three languages, English and their local tongues. Our Marshall Islands productions, for example, are performed in both Marshallese and English. Many older Marshall Islanders speak only limited English, so critical turns in the plot and much of the humor would be lost to them if the plays were performed entirely in English. In Bosnia-Herzegovina, language is one of many politicized elements, and the government recognizes three distinct languages—Croatian, Bosnian, and Serbian. We used a Serbo-Croat text, which all the players understood readily.

Language was a particular challenge when we mounted a production in Kosovo. Many of our Albanian-speaking actors had a limited command of English, and some none at all. Therefore, in our performances of *A Midsummer Night's Dream,* we had to decide carefully which parts of Shakespeare's verse we would present in English. The girls who played Queen Titania performed in different languages— one in Albanian, the other entirely in Shakespeare's verse. (All young people's names have been changed to ensure anonymity.) The youth who played King Oberon alternated between the two languages.

## REHEARSALS

Before rehearsals we engage in theatre games to encourage teamwork and build actors' confidence, with the help of Jessica Swale, the Olivier Award–winning writer and director. A vital part of these activities is to honor what each student brings to the occasion and validate their life experiences. The fact that most of the YBG team is not fluent in the language(s) where we produce plays inevitably creates problems. For the initial rehearsals, the ensemble uses the "No Fear" version of Shakespeare in English. The translated text is not introduced until the director is convinced that the players understand the plot and their characters.

Creating the final version of a scene is a collaborative effort between the director and the actors, to which the students bring the vitality of their own life experiences. One poignant example is a young Rwandan man who played the prince in YBG's production of *Romeo and Juliet* in Kigali. He had seen his mother murdered during the genocide that took place in the 1990s; this tragedy perhaps enabled him to bring particular urgency to his role.

## COSTUMING

We attempt to localize our Shakespearean productions as much as possible and adopt a mixture of traditional and modern attire. For instance, in our Marshall Islands production of *Romeo and Juliet,* members of the Capulet and Montague families were tattooed on the chest and arms with motifs of different fish, which identified each family. Costumes for the Rwandan production of *Romeo and Juliet* incorporated past and present African clothing; the older characters' costumes were inspired by traditional Rwandan dress, while the younger players wore street clothes accented with contemporary African patterns.

### Justifications: Why Shakespeare and Musicals?

Cultural sensitivity must always be considered when producing a Shakespearean play in any part of the world. "But why Shakespeare?" a skeptic may ask. "What about producing a play by a local writer that reflects the community?" To this, I respond that Shakespeare's analysis of human psychology is so rich and deep that it connects to the lives of people across time and space. In our experience, young people connect with the feelings that make the characters they are playing real and relevant. That said, the situation on the ground is sometimes so provocative that Shakespeare's message of reconciliation founders on the rocks of reality.

This reality came to light when YBG produced its first bilingual Shakespeare play in Bosnia. The genocidal war among the Orthodox Bosnian Serbs, Catholic Croats, and the Muslim Bosniaks had been over for nine years, yet memories were still raw and animosities unmitigated. Thus our chosen play was, appropriately, *Romeo and Juliet*. I selected a Croatian girl to play Juliet and a Bosniak boy to play Romeo. Sadly, they never came to like or even respect each other. The production of *Romeo and Juliet* in Rwanda was similarly wrought with tension, but in this case, the cast drew its swords against the assistant director and me. YBG had traveled to Kigali at the invitation of Rwanda's minister of health, who had charged me thus: "The play you must put on is, of course, *Romeo and Juliet*." Once in Kigali, I was warned not to ask the actors if they were Hutu or Tutsi. I was told, "They are all Rwandans."

Within a week of rehearsals beginning, the cast threatened to quit when they learned that they would not be financially compensated. Although we fully understood that some of our actors needed to make money during the summer holidays, YBG has never paid its performers. This was a reminder to us that many foreigner-native relationships on the African continent have a historical legacy of imperialism characterized by plunder, divisiveness, and oppression. Some saw our production as another colonial project disguised as humanitarianism. I lament the cast members' perception that all foreigners are wealthy

North Americans who don't understand the Rwandans' plight. And maybe we don't, but I felt nonetheless that the experience we offered was about much more than money.

This experience led me to question further how we, as Westerners, can best approach the notion of reconciliation with our actors from former colonies. A strictly Anglicized interpretation of Shakespeare risks reproducing the colonial relationship. As we cannot know what experiential and psychological concerns our students bring to our project, we encourage the actors to use their personal experiences to shape their characters. Because we, as outsiders, cannot fully understand the trauma our players have experienced, we try to create a space in which a natural process of healing can occur through the context of the play. Our hope is that our young players will establish friendships across lines of difference through a shared commitment to a joint artistic project, and by celebrating the fact that their hard work enables them to contribute meaningfully to their communities.

It is important to note that YBG does not focus only on Shakespeare. To honor my Marshallese students' intense musicality, I decided to do an American musical with them. I have never heard a Marshallese student sing out of tune, and these young performers can easily harmonize even the most challenging musical line. The musicals attracted enormous audiences that could no longer be accommodated in the old banana grove in Majuro, where we had performed Shakespeare. Our performance drew record crowds. The YBG team saw considerable transformation among the students who participated in these ambitious musical performances, which helped them build confidence in mind and body. In my ongoing relationships with some of my actors, I have become aware that the life skills acquired while participating in our musicals helped them learn greater self-awareness and raised their personal and academic aspirations.

## Lives Looking Back

My decision of whom I would invite to contribute to this memoir was influenced in part by those who had a substantial role in my various theatre programs and who I believed had been affected by the experience. I received more rejections than acceptances, particularly from international students who didn't trust their written English skills (as conveyed to me in correspondence). The questions I posed included:

- What drew you to audition?
- What were you looking for?
- What did you find?
- What scenes were most rewarding for you?
- What did you take away from the play?

In this anthology, we, the editors, highlight the experiences of twelve Canadian and ten international actors (non-Canadians) who were selected because of the presumed commonalities of their dramatic experiences. Our aim in doing so is to demonstrate the contribution that participation in theatre can make to adolescent and adult development. This is evident in the essays written by international actors who are now ages eighteen to thirty and those from Canada, who were mainly in their forties at the time of writing. By combining essays from these two distinct timeframes, some only a few years away from their acting experience and others who are twenty or more years away, we hope to present a developmental perspective and show the powerful impact adolescent acting and engagement in theatre can have in later life. The ongoing effects that are expressed in these essays testify to the significance of art-making and the many direct and indirect repercussions their participation in theatre had in the authors' lives.

We have consistently observed that the process of autobiographical writing can have a profound transformative effect on the spiritual, moral, and emotional demands of a person's life. For many of our actor-authors, the process of putting their theatre experiences into words has acted as a catalyst for further self-reflection, and they have been overwhelmingly open to the invitation to make sense of these experiences. We have enjoyed guiding our student-actor-writers to a deeper level of self-understanding and helping them gain purchase on the world through self-analysis and articulation.

All the Canadian contributors to this book performed in productions I directed between 1962 and 1978; I also taught English literature to a number of them. I sought writers whose lives have taken distinctly different paths, and those I thought might profit from the act of reflection and enjoy putting their theatre experiences down on paper.

For the international students, I sought out actors who had played leading roles in the YBG productions and seemed likely to have been affected by their participation from 2004 to the present. Writing in a second language proved a daunting challenge for several contributors; some eventually dropped out. We ultimately are able to present twenty-two essays. We are deeply grateful for the diligent effort so many of our former students and actors made, whether or not their essays are included in this book.

## Plan of the Book
### *"What's past is prologue"*

The essays in this collection are organized according to four major themes. The first theme, "Animating Characters, Revitalizing Lives," focuses on how theatre involvement expands the possibilities to consider new ways of being, augmenting what is possible. The second theme, "Outsider to Insider," explores the challenges many adolescents encounter in finding their place in the adolescent social milieu and how theatre provides a place to belong. The third theme, "Connecting to the Audience," examines how theatre offers a robust learning experience and the opportunity for intentional risk-taking, and the openness that enables performers to expand their emotional selves in ways that elevate their performance and enrich their personal lives. In "Coming Full Circle," the fourth and final theme, the contributors describe how involvement in the theatre can influence a young person's career path. These essays are testimony to the powerful effects their participation in drama had on the contributors—an experience so intense and meaningful that they want to pass on what they learned to other young people around the globe; in other words, to pay it forward.

### ANIMATING CHARACTERS, REVITALIZING LIVES

For over three decades, social and developmental psychologists have investigated how "possible selves"—future-oriented schemas of the self—matter to individuals' motivations and life outcomes. Possible selves are not fixed; in fact, their malleability has been shown to support youths' wellbeing and deter delinquency. The concept is a key driver of programs aimed at helping youth find a positive life trajectory (Halverson, 2005).

The essays that appear in this section unequivocally link participating in theatre productions to an expansion of "possible selves." As contributor Philip Palmer noted, the "openings [that ensued from taking on characters on the stage] spoke of possibilities within ourselves that we took for granted." Indeed, as the writers in this section observe, the hard work of bringing a character to life expanded what they felt was possible in their own lives. When Harun Hasanagic recognized his hesitance to act out Prospero's harshness toward Caliban, he became aware of his undesirable trait of being a people-pleaser. He writes, "I have discovered that I have an inclination to absolute order and orderly conduct in … the way we treat others. This worried me, especially when I found that I took a liking to characters that are truly benevolent but enforce their benevolence and fairness with an iron hand." Robert Silver found that bringing Hamlet's character to life, including his rage, allowed him to explore a "wider variety of emotions than … [he had] ever personally experienced." Reflecting on his role as Benvolio in *Romeo and Juliet,* Rwandan Clovis Shyaka says, "Every day I went home with a new insight about life." He adds that "being a part of *Romeo and Juliet* … triggered a series of events that … put me on the right track towards my dreams." Palmer writes that theatre provides a safe way to explore the "range of emotions and understanding that go uncalled on in [adolescents'] day-to-day lives," adding that, "through drama, many of us were able to taste emotions and sensations we had never known before." These four authors reveal how theatre enables adolescents to discover their possible selves.

The three other writers in this section help us understand the consequences of ignoring adolescents' possible selves. Heather Fisher recounts how bringing Rosalind's character to life shifted her self-concept from one defined by a self-conscious stutterer to someone "unafraid to speak":

I sensed that my own spirit was no longer completely hidden from view. Though I felt vulnerable, I also realized … an emotional connection with the audience. Perhaps this was why, despite a slight quavering … I was able to speak with increasing confidence and strength. I faced the audience unafraid. … Standing alone, I became aware of my own self-worth, my ability to draw upon emotions inside of me and ... affect the emotions of others.

Brent Bambury similarly recalls coming to the theatre with "something inside of me [that] needed to be heard." Committed to making his Orlando "as energetic and animated as possible," Bambury discovered a new voice in himself, "a voice with something to say." With piercing honesty, Gail Taylor describes her traumatized high school self, who was "determined to stay closed into myself, to need nobody and to disclose nothing," especially after her father died by suicide. Taylor internalized her roles by inhabiting them as a way to "temper my own extremes of hungering madly for either an impossibly exalted life or for transporting death." For Taylor, the theatre is indeed "a mystery and alchemy" that enabled her to act out her deep anger at the world that had been so tightly contained within her. Her experience demonstrates how a rich text can speak to what is at stake in a young person's life: "It was the language of the play that most delightfully irrupted my defenses. I now believe that language changed my life forever."

Psychologist Carol Gilligan (1982), who led a groundbreaking research project on women's psychology and girls' development, found that, as girls transition from childhood to adolescence, they are forced to prioritize inauthentic relationships with others and forgo the kinds of relationships in which they can openly express their thoughts and feelings. Niobe Way later described this phenomenon as a "crisis of connection" that also affects boys (Way, 2013; Way et al., 2018). These works synthesize evidence of the negative impact this crisis has on adolescents' wellbeing. The crux of this crisis is the loss of voice and the ability to remain in genuine relationships with others. This vantage point helps the reader appreciate what is at stake when adolescents become involved in theatre, which provides a platform where young actors can discover that they have a voice—and have something to say.

### OUTSIDER TO INSIDER

Perhaps every adolescent veteran will recognize the acute need for social acceptance that defines this developmental period. During adolescence, we are hypersensitive to social rejection from peers and yet simultaneously driven to contribute to others who matter to us (Andrews et al., 2021; Fuligni, 2019). Unfortunately, for many young people, peer exclusion and other forms of othering permeate and exacerbate their experience of schooling (and, arguably, youth programs too). Contemporary research doubles down on what earlier scholars found: that the most powerful learning environments for young people—inside and outside the classroom—are intentionally designed to foster a community of inquiry and encourage the development of skills for positive social interactions (Baldridge, 2019; Mehta and Fine, 2019).

The essays under the theme "Outsider to Insider" remind us that finding one's place in the social milieu is a central task of adolescence—one not easily done. As the writers in this section note, non-curricular activities, including theatre, can ease an adolescent's transition from being othered to belonging. For Lani Selick and Robert Brym, theatre provided a place to belong, even as their peers beyond the theatre targeted them for being different. Selick, an awkward, solitary teenager, and Brym, a stranger from "an Eastern European working-class Yiddish culture," were able to alter these negative identity markers by taking on theatre roles. This helped them find a sense of agency and voice and to craft less limiting social identities. Wilmer Joel's account describes how the stage functions as an arena where "the cast and audience forgot themselves. … The cast forgot that they were shy, quiet, and innocent students. The audience forgot we were good-for-nothing rascals in the community." Joel writes that participating in community theatre broke "these norms and unleashe[d] the youth's fullest potential to become someone who could contribute to the welfare of society. … They now saw us in a positive way."

Yet, as the other two writers in this category, Selina Leem and Mark Blagrave, caution, whatever their intellectual merits and however intentional, adolescents' educational milieux are imbued with seeds of exclusion and othering. Leem and Blagrave point out that, even in the theatre space, the dramaturg's decisions to hold public auditions or to double-cast expose adolescents to the risks of social comparison, if not social rejection, in precisely the space where they thought they could belong. The dramaturg's commitment to shaping the social and intellectual lifeworld of the production around solidarity, community, and bringing a production's narrative arc to life temper the social rejection's kill-switch. For Leem, "theatre became a space of expression, with freedom and without judgment, only critical feedback," and Blagrave found similarly that the theatre experience provided a shared, "genuine, unposed interest in things artistic and intellectual … [where] you could belong and remain yourself."

CONNECTING TO THE AUDIENCE

In a *New York Times* article on the influence of Peter Brook, the great British director, Tina Landau comments, "Theatre is a collaborative form and the greatest and ultimate collaboration is between the performers and the audience" (Collins-Hughes, 2022). Part of this collaboration, researcher Erica Halverson asserts in her recent book, *How the Arts Can Save Education* (2021), involves risk-taking, which is an essential aspect of a successful learning experience. Whereas it is commonplace for adults to view risk-taking among adolescents as deviant (as opposed to compliance with social rules), developmental psychologists Natasha Duell and Laurence Steinberg urge us to take seriously the positive aspects of adolescent risk-taking and its contribution to positive outcomes. Duell and Steinberg (2019) posit that, whether it is trying out for a new sport, actively seeking a new friend, or enrolling in a challenging course, positive risk-taking involves engaging in legal and socially acceptable behaviors that have variable and uncertain potential outcomes without compromising adolescents' safety and wellbeing. "Establishing one's identity and independence requires that youth be willing to try things they might not like or at which they may fail, which requires a tolerance for risk-taking," writes Duell (2019), adding that, given its "normative and adaptive" nature, "it is important that communities provide young people with opportunities to direct their propensity for risk-taking toward constructive activities."

As the writers in this section attest, participating in theatre affords an unusually powerful learning container for intentional risk-taking. For Julie Guravich, learning how to manage the adrenalin rush from performing so that it is not an obstacle but a catalyst for active engagement with the audience is a lifelong skill she first grasped during her high school theatre participation and now carries over into her artistry as a musician and performer. Wayne Best's and Erza Syla's essays pull the curtain back on the contours of risk-taking, from beginnings rife with tentativeness and self-doubt to a committed stance of faithfully portraying their characters despite feeling awkward about how strangely the characters' roles and personalities fit with their own. Whereas engaging an audience by showing a character as truthfully as possible was a virtue in these productions, Best and Syla point out that risk-taking—in a supportive container—is its own reward. Best writes, "I was making something happen; I had my fate in my own hands. … Although I was not pleased with my performance in that play, I was proud of myself. I had taken a risk." For Syla, acting Titania "was the perfect part to get me into acting, because it offered the ultimate challenge every actor faces, the one of not being yourself, and Titania was different from me in many ways." Yet her commitment to Titania's character, even when "Titania wakes up from her sleep and finds herself in the arms of a donkey-head [and] feels disgusted," was unwavering. When the audience burst out laughing at the scene and again at the end of the play, "when everybody was cheering for us," Syla writes, "we all felt immensely relieved for having done the best we could with our performances." In a society hellbent on disparaging adolescents for their impulsive and risky behavior, these writers' accounts are a counternarrative imploring communities to instead take seriously and celebrate adolescents' desire and attempts to take positive risks.

Yet, as Yolanie Jurelang reminds the reader, positive risk-taking is an undulating landscape involving lessons of commitment and letting go. Such risk-taking is a "rollercoaster" that may include "pleasure, sadness, and exhaustion." Jurelang describes how she "gave my all when I played [Hodel in *Fiddler on the Roof*]." She explains how she "had a difficult time separating myself from [Hodel]. … Even after the show, I had to take two weeks to process her journey and let go any sentiment or grief, sadness and regrets she might have had before and assure myself that everything was okay and that the love for her family was stronger than she ever knew."

Even so, it is essential to remember that the implications of positive risk-taking reverberate beyond the personal and encompass the social and political, as we see in the final three accounts in this section. For both Burns MacMillan and Muhamadi Nshimiyimana, risk-taking involves pushing back on uncritically accepted societal roles. "I was sucking up the rules of family, church, school, and community—institutions of authority that were to come under unprecedented attack by the time I'd reach my high school years," MacMillan writes. In SJHS theatre productions, he encountered his role modeling in risk-taking: "I remember being empowered to take risks as a result of Garrod's example, sleeves rolled up, tie loosened, on all fours with script in hand to model roaring and other lion-like behavior. I laughed until my sides ached." In Nshimiyimana's case, attuning to an "inner voice" is what propels him, albeit gently, towards positive risk-taking as he considers a potential disconnect between his culture "where most people are shy and not used to seeing actors participating in love scenes on the stage" and the unfamiliar territory of his character kissing another on stage.

These essays point out the need to more fully consider the role of culture and context in shaping whether and how youth approach risk-taking on the stage and to design enabling environments responsive to those contextual inhibitions or obstacles. In this regard, aspects of this enabling environment, such as warm-up games and other bonding activities during the rehearsal phase, are not to be taken for granted; where trauma makes us shrivel, creative expression holds the potential to help us unfold. In the present moment, where awareness of trauma-informed practices increasingly becomes part of youth's learning settings, it would be prudent that future opportunities for adolescent theatre consider the benefits and unintended consequences of leveraging expressive arts methodologies in mitigating or bypassing obstacles to risk-taking on the stage that may be rooted in cultural or generational trauma.

### COMING FULL CIRCLE

There is a literature on how extracurricular activities influence future career paths. In one longitudinal study that followed exceptional adolescents into their early adulthood, nearly 45 percent pursued an adult vocation closely tied to the focus of their out-of-school activities (Milgram and Hong, 2010). Some of the participants in my youth theatre productions were powerfully affected by their experiences with drama and realize today what a tremendous gift the experience gave them. In fact, a number of them have actively chosen to pass on what they learned to youth in their own communities.

One such case is Elizabeth Foster Chase, who writes that "my career led me in a full circle back to my beginnings." This sentiment is manifested in her direction of a new generation of student actors on her "old stomping grounds." Foster Chase applied some of her takeaways from her youth performances to her adult directing days. Among them are the difference between "onstage liaisons" and "offstage relationships," an understanding of the space that drama provides to delve into the full emotional range of human existence, as well as the "importance of praise" in directing. In empathizing with the feelings of confusion and vulnerability teenagers face in their day-to-day lives, Foster Chase notes that, "as an adult working with teenagers, the look of appreciation on their faces brings back some vivid memories of my own struggle to please and finding satisfaction in finally discovering an outlet where I could." It is this empathy that characterizes Foster Chase's directing approach to her students; she relates the experiences of her students to her own life, saying, "to find an adult willing to give you a chance, to challenge you, and who praises even the smallest accomplishments, can bring about a willingness and determination to demand nothing but the best from yourself."

In another case, Jobod Silk, a Marshall Islands native, describes the beneficial effects drama has had on his personal socialization and the Marshallese community writ large. In particular, he attributes the production of YBG plays to the increase in the incorporation of the arts into many social and communal activities, including "singing, painting, poetry, and weaving." In the context of the COVID-19 pandemic, he deplores the absence of theatre and expresses deep concern for the resulting deleterious effects on local youth. He saw himself in the kids who were left with "no means of exploring and showcasing their talents." However, this combination of COVID's impact on local children and the absence of YBG has pushed Jobod to take the initiative and opportunity to fill a gap in the arts himself. Starting off as an inexperienced cast member, Jobod has now come full circle and is "helping to produce and direct one [play] himself." Co-writing, co-producing, and co-directing plays about the stories of his people have become his reality, and he hopes to pass down this engagement in drama to empower youth.

The last two contributors in this section are Ilija Pujic, a Croat, and Mustafa Stupac, a Bosniak, both from Mostar. The two are good friends who met while performing in YBG Shakespearean productions. As a result of their experience with YBG and the intensive acting training they received at Shakespeare & Co. in Lenox, Massachusetts, both have committed themselves to a career in the arts.

Inspired by YBG's vital role in creating what Ilija calls a "magical atmosphere" for youth, he set out to emulate that magic by implementing the Shakespeare & Co. model with youth in Mostar: "My dream has been to create a theatre company in Mostar that will be a healthy place for youth to hang out and share their stories and dreams ... to gather people in a healthy community of theatre and to ... get them ... to strive to improve society and themselves." Ilija's vision is to involve those who participated in the YBG project to carry on that spirit of safety, friendship, and community. Having lived his childhood in a war-stricken region, his desire is to "bring theatre to children in post-war countries and to anyone who has somehow suppressed their emotions. Theatre should bring hope to our lives and teach us how to live them fully." This desire led him to found the Courageous Heart Theatre Company.

Mustafa has transformed his early theatre experiences into storytelling through theatre and film. These experiences "changed his perceptions of American youth, learning, and [himself] while granting him the courage to keep on doing what [he] loves." Mustafa long ago realized that he is a storyteller with "a lot of stories to tell about everyday life," and he believes that theatre and film are "the right place for me to do it." He has gathered a team and is preparing to film the projects Ilija directs for the next few years. For the two friends, this is all part of passing down knowledge to future generations, which has been a constant motif throughout their lives.

## References

Andrews, J. L., Ahmed, S. P., and Blakemore, S. J. (2021). Navigating the social environment in adolescence: The role of social brain development. *Biological Psychiatry, 89*(2), 109–118.

Baldridge, B. J. (2019). *Reclaiming Community: Race and the Uncertain Future of Youth Work*. Stanford University Press.

Boffone, T., and Gatta, C. D. (eds). (2021). *Shakespeare and Latinidad*. Edinburgh: Edinburgh University Press, 3.

Carrasco G. (2020) Possible Selves. In: Zeigler-Hill, V., and Shackelford,

T.K. (eds.), *Encyclopedia of Personality and Individual Differences*. Cham, Switzerland: Springer. https://doi.org/10.1007/978-3-319-24612-3_1965

Collins-Hughes, L. (2022, July 8). 'He Presented Another Path': Actors and Directors on Peter Brook. *New York Times*. https://www.nytimes.com/2022/07/08/theater/peter-brook-directors-influence.html

Duell, N. (2019, August 29). The positive side of risk-taking. BOLD. https://bold.expert/the-positive-side-of-risk-taking/

Duell, N., & Steinberg, L. (2019). Positive risk-taking in adolescence. *Child Development Perspectives, 13*(1), 48–52.

Fuligni, A. J. (2019). The need to contribute during adolescence. *Perspectives on Psychological Science, 14*(3), 331–343.

Halverson, E. (2005). Development Through a Performance-Based Youth Organization. *Identity, 5*, 67–90. https://doi.org/10.1207/s1532706xid0501_5

Halverson, E. R. (2021). *How the Arts Can Save Education: Transforming Teaching, Learning, and Instruction*. New York: Teachers College Press.

Loveday, P. M., Lovell, G. P., and Jones, C. M. (2018). The best possible selves intervention: A review of the literature to evaluate efficacy and guide future research. *Journal of Happiness Studies, 19*(2), 607–628.

Markus, H., & Nurius, P. (1986). Possible selves. *American Psychologist, 41*(9), 954–969. https://doi.org/10.1037/0003-066X.41.9.954

Mehta, J., and Fine, S. (2019). In Search of Deeper Learning: The Quest to Remake the American High School. Cambridge, MA: Harvard University Press.

Milgram, R. M., & Hong, E. (1999). Creative out-of-school activities in intellectually gifted adolescents as predictors of their life accomplishment in young adults: A longitudinal study. *Creativity Research Journal, 12*(2), 77–87.

Smith, K. (2015). Childhood and Youth Citizenship 25. *Handbook of Children and Youth Studies*, 357.

Way, N. (2013). *Deep Secrets: Boys' Friendships and the Crisis of Connection*. Cambridge, MA: Harvard University Press.

Way, N., Ali, A., Gilligan, C., and Noguera, P. (eds.). (2018). *The Crisis of Connection: Roots, Consequences, and Solutions.* NYU Press.

Zeldin, S., Larson, R., Camino, L., and O'Connor, C. (2005). Intergenerational relationships and partnerships in community programs: Purpose, practice, and directions for research. *Journal of Community Psychology, 33*(1), 1–10.

# PART ONE

# Animating Characters, Revitalizing Life

# Play Out the Play

Brent Bambury

CANADA

Play is the essence of childhood; it's what kids do. And the word *play* is probably one of the earliest in any child's vocabulary. We learn the word so readily because we love the activity. I remember my confusion when my parents said they were "going to the playhouse." I wanted to go, damn it! And anyway, play is for kids! What were they doing there? Why weren't they taking me? Eventually, of course, they did. It was during a family vacation when I was about seven; we all went to see *Anne of Green Gables* at the Charlottetown Festival. It was a musical, a simple story punched into life with flying sets and lighting cues and adults playing children and singing and dancing. The craft of it, the energy of it all made my heart race. But the real wonder was the vitality this plain story possessed. I remember crying at the appalling death of Matthew Cuthbert. I remember being astounded that everyone else was crying. And then there was the sincere and thunderous applause at the end when Matthew appeared for his curtain call, alive again. This trick of fantasy, this emotional heist to which we granted our approval to take each of us captive, was the inexplicable thing that made me fall in love with "plays." The ovation gave me a chance to show my emotion, to insist on taking my part in it, along with every other adult and child in the house. It would be years before I would come to realize that what makes theatre is that dynamic between the audience and the actors, but I know that from my very first experience in the crowd there was a bond like a high-tension wire going from my heart to the stage.

This newly intoxicated pre-teen was next taken to see a performance of a musical based on *Jane Eyre*. Before the curtain someone told me,

"This is a story of a man with a lunatic wife." A thrill went through me. It was someone else's imagination, so scary and alien, not a plot I would ever dream of. I had a ticket to enter this taboo and dangerous world. Wide-eyed and breathless, terrified at times, I must have been a great audience! But it was hard to convince others of my passion. I begged to be taken to the high school production of *Macbeth*, but was told I was too young, it would run too late into the night and, besides, I would never understand it. I doubted this. I knew the bare bones of the bloody story. Of course, I understood witches and blood, ghosts and murder! But it was not to be. My parents overruled me and I was left at home. Still, I begged. And I persevered. And then I started winning.

The year after I missed *Macbeth*, my older sister took me to see her boyfriend play a small role in the high school production of *Romeo & Juliet*. Now I was seeing someone I knew onstage, someone I looked up to as the love of my big sister's life. And I was watching a play about people their age, living through the enormity of love and adolescence. This was different for me. I did not live in that time and did not quite speak that language, nor was I yet an adolescent facing the same questions as my sister and her boyfriend. Nonetheless, I followed *Romeo & Juliet*'s teenage passion through the turns that led them to their tombs. And the teenage cast whooping and fighting, loving and raging seemed a direct challenge to me, a portent of my own oncoming high school career, of my own adolescence. It was near, within reach, on the stage in front of me and somewhere in my own little body. I wanted to play out my life the way these older kids were, to scream and cry and be alive. I wanted to have my voice heard. Maybe even do it in a beard. But high school (and a beard) were still a few years away. This will is what later became an enormous and burnished confidence, and it was buffed by what I was living through as an enthralled kid: *A Midsummer Night's Dream*, *West Side Story*, *My Fair Lady*, all amateur productions by the students of the school and all on the same vast auditorium stage where the professional company Theatre New Brunswick (TNB) plied their wares. My ambition was taking shape long before I would ever put a word to it.

I first got to play at acting when I was in ninth grade. I wrote a play with a Faustian theme about a London chimneysweep who sells his soul, falls in love, does battle with the devil and loses his life. Mercifully, it went unproduced. But something was happening to my curiosity. It was being replaced by something that more resembled drive. The shift was perhaps hormonally driven, or maybe it was the nascent intellect taking over. But the childish requirement of play was being consumed by the other thing that darkens the shadows of adolescence. Something inside of me needed to be heard, and it wasn't. The exhilaration of it being within me was equal to the horror of not being able to summon it up. There was a certainty that, as an individual, I had something to say and that simultaneously, if I failed to say it, I would die. The child could get by with diversion, but the adolescent demanded a voice. I wanted to shout out so loudly that I could never be ignored. I believed I could make people listen. A confidence was growing inside me as my body grew on the outside, but I didn't see it as confidence. Instead, I saw a place for myself in the make-believe world of play, a world that I could be serious about.

Starting your secondary education is always like being called up to the big leagues—elective options, career guidance, study halls, and a strong whiff of sex. For me, the big league really meant only one thing. The time for childish play was over. Now I would play with a greater seriousness. It was probably not the seriousness that my parents wanted to see in me. I know there wasn't the vague shape of a career inside me destined to sharpen into view a few short years in the future. I was becoming serious about how I would be seen, by my peers and by the world, how I would define Brent through the way I acted and the things I was passionate about. I did not know much about what I would do to define myself, or really even what these passions were. I only knew it was important and that theatre was going to play a part. Play would be the vehicle for my drive to survive, my need to be heard, for the demands of my voice, whatever that voice was.

At sixteen, I was not unathletic. I skied pretty well, I had been swimming since I was six, and a couple of years earlier I had a go at cross country running. I never liked team sports, so I was never in any sense a jock or part of the athletic sub-culture. But the fact that I was suddenly just under six feet and now the tallest person in my family robbed me of whatever grace I had mastered when I was a pre-pubescent gymnast. I was now quite awkward- lurching, gangly, and skinny. And here I was in a bare-chested donnybrook with one of the most athletic boys in the school, who promptly threw me to the floor. Next, he yanked on my bony arms while sticking his fat foot into my back and pushed. And at one point we rolled across the ground over and over with his tremendous weight crushing onto my slight chest. In the end, I somehow threw him over my back and landed him flat on the ground (I remember it as a bare floor, though there must have been a mat) where he remained spent and defeated. I had triumphed over this massive bully.

More accurately, young and tender Orlando had just beaten Charles-the wrestler. The first time we played this scene (I.ii.) from *As You Like It* before an adult audience they applauded. I felt like I was at the center of the universe. There was a great responsibility vested in me. I was proud and recklessly certain this Shakespearean romantic hero was within my abilities. Confidence and ambition were exploding within me. I considered it the lead male part in the play, although it is by no means the most memorable. Rosalind gets the best lines, Jacques the most famous speech and Touchstone is one of the few truly funny clowns in Shakespeare. But Orlando was a perfect part for me to play. He's young and impulsive; he falls in love with Rosalind in a nano-second and the only thing that sets Rosalind off on him is the way he looks in tights. It's well within the range of the experience of a sixteen-year-old hothead.

This hothead had been on the margins long enough. I was ready to take center stage, and no stage seemed larger than the one at Saint John High School (SJHS). I don't remember the audition, but I still remember the shock, mixed with obvious satisfaction, when Mr. Garrod, the director, announced that I was to be Orlando. It was a welcome shock, the way you feel when you first test the power of a new car. I was being given the opportunity, not to prove—because I had so few doubts— but to show off the equipment that was me. I had absolutely no doubt I could do it. I had been watching that stage for years, and what was being given to me was something I had desired and dreamed of and willed myself into. Of all the people who could have had this part, no one wanted it more than me.

We got started on the blocking right away. We took our texts up on stage with us and began working on the scenes. This really seemed like the acting process, but concurrent to it was a text analysis, which seemed more like school. It was held in a dreary classroom and it involved us reading our parts and trying to explain what the hell our character was saying. In hindsight it was necessary, and probably what made these productions work. None of us had had much experience with Shakespeare. I had seen a few productions and, by this point, studied perhaps two plays. Others were even more lost. I remember one of the Charles-the-wrestlers saying that his line "and never two ladies lov'd as they do" (I.i.) meant that Celia and Rosalind were lesbians. I'm pretty sure that was a joke.

What emerged from our text sessions was how earnest Orlando seems to be. The character is not complicated, he has no hidden agenda, and he's not the wittiest guy in the forest. I remember having a huge hassle with the opening speech, his complaint to his personal servant. They are the first lines in the play and they get to the business of setting. up the conflict right away. But they're plaintive and they can put the audience straight to sleep. That's not a good start. I decided that I had to make Orlando as energetic and animated as possible so his energy would compensate for his seeming lack of wit. That juice came in handy in the next scene when the long odds pay off as he throws Charles-the-wrestler. The real comic stuff for Orlando doesn't heat up until Act III, but by that point in any good production, Rosalind will already have stolen the show.

Orlando does get some good lines, particularly in his scenes with Rosalind. But the comedy of *As You Like It* may be played so broadly it's unlikely the male romantic lead will be anyone's favorite character. In our production, the shepherds Phoebe and Silvius were outrageous and the fop LeBeau massively over the top. Touchstone was subtly rendered, and the country hick William had an Appalachian charm. Sometimes in these productions a player would bring an unrehearsed bit onstage and surprise everyone. It's the kind of thing that could get an equity actor fired, but in high school I think it just showed how consumed we were by our art. I remember one night Audrey, the country wench, appeared to have three breasts on stage. She then extracted from her loose-fitting peasant shirt an apple, which she munched while alternately picking from between her toes. The audience went insane.

The rehearsal process took up a lot of time. After we finished the textual analysis, the blocking continued and rehearsals eventually moved onto the main stage, where our set would ultimately appear. The set for *As You Like It* was designed by George Fry and consisted of layered green drapery that, when lit, glowed an iridescent green. The stage was not banked or raised—all of the action was to take place on the flat stage floor. But the hanging forest greenery gave the forest a dreamy depth. It was to be my favorite set of all the productions I was in. We practiced as it appeared around us, still half-reading our lines from the text as familiarity with our roles grew. I remember some anxiety about learning my lines. I still dream about being onstage in a play and not knowing the first scene; it's one of the dreams people usually have about physics exams.

As opening night approached the rehearsals took up entire days, sometimes continuing on into the evenings. Everyday life receded from reality. We had undoubtedly been warned to keep up on our homework, but I don't remember doing any work during these periods. I don't know how I could've concentrated. I must have done something because my grades were always at least OK, but our final rehearsals took up the whole weekend, beginning early in the day, breaking for dinner and then returning for an evening run-through. The intensity and unreality forged some unusual alliances and friendships. I remember escaping in my mom's car for the dinner break with three or four others and drinking loads of tea in a bleary state of rehearsal overload. It all felt peculiarly adult, especially since I'd only been licensed to drive since the summer.

My dinner mates were sometimes quite different from the friends I usually associated with. One of the great strengths of the drama program at SJHS was that it drew its talent from the entire pool of student life. Andrew Garrod made real efforts to recruit and cast the jocks and athletes, the quiet kids and the class clowns, not simply people like me who would've turned up anyway. This led to an interest in the production that was shared by the entire school, not just the artsy kids in tights. I felt my status as a lead in the play gave me a kind of passport to cross all the social boundaries within this United Nations of students. I did become friendly, and in a few cases close, to kids I would probably never have otherwise spoken to. Romances bloomed between even more unlikely students. There was sex and intrigues and vendettas and jealousy, and I had some part in some of these. Through the lens of what was being created, these mundane and even tawdry events took on a kind of lustre. We were beginning to play at being adults. It was the best of both worlds.

*As You Like It* was a great success and so I think, was Orlando. It was a great first lead role for me, a performance which demanded neither nuance nor subtlety. But playing Orlando increased my confidence in every conceivable way. I was proud of what I had done and believed it gave me a kind of advanced status. It probably did. I had never been shy to speak out and contribute in class, but now I felt I had an extra authority, especially in the humanities courses. There *was* a voice in there, maybe even a voice with something to say. My marks in English were to remain my highest throughout high school, yanking my average to the high honours level by the time I graduated in spite of my ever-increasing interest in math and science. I didn't know then that theatre could be the root of the synthesis that you need to master the humanities. I didn't see my effort as offering up the key to the life of the mind, as I now believe it did. Behind Shakespeare's language, there was a voice, and that voice was mine. This boy bridged the gap between words and literature. That's the real triumph of my Orlando, which will forever trump the egotistical but admirable boy who wanted to be onstage to rev up his machine. I found something alive, even bursting off the page. And important things happened socially too. I think I demolished the social awkwardness that can be fatal in a less driven adolescent. The accomplishment I felt in the roles I played, beginning with Orlando, was a compensation for this awkwardness in a school that valued status, that posted everyone's grades, that was generally the playing field for the children of the community's rich and socially conscious.

One of my best friends in high school from my first day onward was Stephen Murphy. Steve had been a performer from very early in his life and was a quick wit and a gifted mimic. Aided by a stocky body and a firm chin, he had an incredible confidence on stage and an enviable ability to project a maturity far beyond his years. I think the friendly rivalry between us was a strong influence on my abilities. Steve was not shy about pulling out all the stops in a performance, and this kind of reach worked well on that huge auditorium stage. He loved politics and used his stage craft and parallel skill at public speaking to win the student council presidency. We were both obsessed with acting. We gossiped about it, and talked about plays we'd love to mount. We even planned to write a soap opera with a plotline parallel to what was going on in the real world of our lives onstage and off. I may have been "the male lead" more often than Steve, but he certainly got to play some of the best roles. Most of all, his singing voice was a shockingly powerful tenor. When it came time to do the musicals, Steve was a powerhouse.

We both had had bit roles in the musical that had been mounted in our junior year, and now we found ourselves jockeying for a part in *Guys and Dolls*. I didn't know the book or the score, but when I turned up to audition, I felt I'd earned the right to state that I wanted "one of the leads." This time, though, there was a singing audition to contend with. It was pretty simple, but awfully terrifying. Mr. Edwards, the musical director, probed our range and ear by hitting single notes on the piano and getting us to sing them back. I could find the notes but could not make them sound pretty. The previous year I learned the value of projection. I shouted out my scary note and hoped volume would make up for whatever it lacked in beauty. I got a good role. Not the romantic lead. Skye Masterson went to a real singer, Blair Hebert, a guy who sounded like Frank Sinatra. I was to be his sidekick, Nathan Detroit. Steve walked off with the character part of Nicely-Nicely Johnson, who gets to sing the showstopping, lung-splitting number "Sit Down You're Rocking the Boat."

*Guys and Dolls* is a musical about Broadway characters, gamblers, showgirls and the religious mission that tries to save their souls. My character has a longtime romance with a nightclub singer who wants to get married yesterday. Nathan Detroit, the smoothest of them all, falls for a mission gal who is ashamed of her obvious attraction to him. Once again the play ends with nuptials. Not being the lead was not at all bad. Nathan Detroit, like all the parts in *Guys and Dolls*, is a character role. Somehow (maybe it's an east coast thing) these Broadway types seemed familiar to us. Probably the archetypes have been so well-used by our culture we were able to slide into their skins well before our rented zoot suits arrived. While the Shakespeare plays carried the weight of some academic responsibility, the musicals were merely fun. It was easier to attract more diverse people to the cast, and *Guys and Dolls* had one of the most integrated casts I remember. A lot of jocks were in it, and the choreography was athletic and sexy. The friendships that emerged were once again of the hybrid variety. People who usually wouldn't have spoken to each other got to share this intense and ultimately hilarious experience.

*Guys and Dolls* is a play that begins with tremendous energy and just keeps getting wilder. By the final scene, when Nathan Detroit delivers his lost sheep to the prayer mission, our cast was having as good a time as the audience. There's a point where the gangsters distribute hymn books. We were asked not to throw the borrowed books at each other, but every night at least a dozen of them were in the air at once. It had a wild, improvised quality that culminated in Steve Murphy's rendition of "Sit Down, You're Rocking the Boat." He held the last note so long I thought he would explode. I don't think there was anyone else in the whole city who could've done it so well.

I hated closing nights. When the play ended, there was usually a party that I didn't like to attend. It was always a Saturday night and that meant the next day was the resumption of real life and a long hard assessment of what I'd been neglecting. I hated to see the sets come down and couldn't quite believe anyone would want to do it. When I graduated I found a quote for my yearbook entry about closing nights. It was unsentimental and brusque. It was a lie, of course. I was tremendously sentimental about closings and openings and everything else. I was exactly where I wanted to be—onstage with my friends, at the center of the universe, singing, yelling and rocking the boat.

Nathan Detroit cranked up my confidence yet again. It was not a difficult role; it carried no special demands. But I don't think I reflected on how little the part really demanded of me. Instead, it fed my certainty that I could do anything. I was just finishing grade 11 and we all talked about what the next year might bring. There was no question that if we mounted *Lear*, Steve would play the king. I'd have to play some dumb part like Edgar. But I entered my final year at SJHS eager to bite into any new challenge. The challenges that awaited were eager to bite back.

The summer before my final year at SJHS was not a happy time for me. I had a bizarre job seeking out and interviewing Indigenous people who had somehow slipped the bonds of our social services. I did not make a lot of money, but the people I was talking to were much poorer in every sense. Against this grim reality along the back roads of rural New Brunswick, my own future looked murky. The paradox of my life onstage was that I was becoming more discontented off stage. There was a profound bifurcation now between what I was dying to get back to doing, making plays and being onstage, and the demon called real life. This was a sore point to my parents, who noted the level of my obsession. I thought reality was thwarting me. In reality, I was thwarting me. But it did not matter. I had reached the stage where the need to play is equated with survival. I was desperate. I was as frustrated and difficult and discontented as any adolescent ever gets. But as the summer was ending something remarkable happened to me which probably kept me and everyone around me from losing our minds. Andrew Garrod had organized a group of high school students to visit Stratford, Ontario, to experience the Shakespeare Festival. Would I like to join?

Stratford was a revelation. It was the first time I had truly seen Shakespeare. It was also arguably the height of the festival's power. In its twenty-fifthth year and under the direction of Robin Phillips, the stage had attracted Maggie Smith and Margaret Tyzack and Brian Bedford and was mounting an impressive roster of plays. We grabbed tickets to *Much Ado*, *Winter's Tale*, *Romeo & Juliet*, *Richard III*, and *All's Well That Ends Well*. We slept on the steps of the festival stage to get rush seats for their sold-out *Macbeth* (finally!) and I was thrilled to see what Maggie Smith would do as Rosalind in their *As You Like It*. Looking back, I can't fathom the amount of energy (not to mention money) I was able to expend on theatre during what was a camping trip with some other boys and girls. But from the perspective of my adolescent angst, theatre and camaraderie were not mere diversions. They were saving my life.

It was not an official school trip, so the rules were relaxed when it came to food, drink, and socializing. But it was also strangely rigorous. We met in advance and read through the plays we didn't already know. We had spirited discussions post-play of the merit of the production, its cast and interpretation. The rich culture of the theatre began to assert itself; there was so much more than just plays and playing. As I reached for the mastery of the language and values of this culture, I was also playing a different role, trying on a new voice. There was a seriousness to complement my play acting and an intention toward the scholarly. But there was also the bright glamour of the professional world, of elderly bit players and English ham actors, of divas and leading men. It propelled me into a world that was grown up and professional and yet still tantalizingly make-believe. Could I belong in this world too? It was as though a part of me that had been missing was snapped into place. I felt more like an adult than ever, approaching the end of an apprenticeship of play. But I wanted more than ever to keep playing.

Throughout our involvement in the school's acting program Mr. Garrod was very careful to make clear one admonishment: How very foolish it would be for any of us to take on acting as a profession. At Stratford I began to nourish my secret desire to do just that. In a year I would be entering university. I would find a school that had a BFA in acting, get my degree, and become an actor. I was sure I could do it. I had seen *As You Like It* at Stratford and I believed that my performance of Orlando was better than that of the professional actor. Maybe he didn't like playing an adolescent. Anyway, I had no other career plans, no other ambitions … virtually no other interests. If I didn't tell anyone, no one could stop me. Of course, there were those who probably suspected. But I was negotiating my future pretty much alone. My parents were not leading me toward a profession. I knew they would not support me being an actor, so there was some tension there. And during that summer I experienced terrible loneliness. I had a strict curfew at home. I don't remember a single evening spent doing what other teenagers were probably doing. I wasn't at the beach; I wasn't taking illicit drinks at parties. There were no romantic prospects in my life. I was clueless, hopeless at getting anything to happen. My community now existed solely onstage, and maybe also in the books I was reading. I worked at my summer job, I devoured plays and I waited for summer to end so I could go back to school and get back up on stage. There was no clear picture of what would happen next in my life if theatre were not part of it.

But if I was failing to parlay my onstage confidence into the social sphere outside of school, I was succeeding beyond my expectations in another. My final year in high school began and for the very first time I had a course load that was tilted heavily toward the humanities. I was enrolled in two literature courses, a communications study group, and an enriched history class, and I was doing well. At Christmas I scored the school's highest mark on the enriched English exam. I was surprised by how easy it was to be number one. I had developed a life of the mind, a comfort with things literary, and I hadn't been aware of how advanced I really was. It was something that happened to me, not a goal I had set. It wasn't that I did not think I was smart. My goal had merely been to play, I did not think that the pay-off would come in this other highly competitive world of academic pursuits. A more purposeful sense of ambition and drive was still years away, but my single-minded affair with the stage had given me an unselfconscious comfort with things intellectual. This is definitely what carried me through my undergraduate years and into my graduate studies, notwithstanding how inadvertent it seems to have been.

One of the plays I saw at Stratford was *Much Ado About Nothing*. I had already read it in preparation, I think, for *As You Like It*. *Much Ado*, with its subplots of murderous jealousy, vengefulness, and courtly intrigue, was massively more complex than the bucolic Forest of Arden. *Much Ado* is about two couples, Beatrice and Benedick and Claudio and Hero. Claudio and Hero are young and in love and Beatrice and Benedick are older and comically antagonistic, but probably also in love. When Claudio is led to believe that Hero has betrayed him he disgraces her at the altar on what was to have been their wedding day. Hero appears to die and the play swoops toward tragedy. There is darkness in this play. Beatrice demands Benedick kill his friend Claudio to avenge her. Humiliation seems to cause the death of one innocent and pitches friend against friend. But *Much Ado* is still a comedy. Beatrice and Benedick are forced by the events out of their sophisticated merry war and into somber alliance. The romantic leads are real adults, not adolescents like Orlando and Rosalind. In *Much Ado* the characters adapt to near tragedy, they go through real changes with the shocking demand Beatrice makes of her soldier ("Kill Claudio!") and his equally surprising acceptance. It turned out that *Much Ado* was to be our school's Shakespearean production. I won the part of Benedick and, with great seriousness, set about bringing him to life.

Seriousness is one of the themes of the play, the loss of levity that love can extract as a toll on the lovers. And the text hands young actors the chance to play revenge, betrayal, denunciation and that most adolescent of conditions, uncertainty. But for me (at last!) I was playing an adult. Benedick is a grown man, the first character I played who truly seemed to have lived before the action of the play. He is a soldier who had probably loved before and has found something better with the prickly relationship he has with his Beatrice. Neither of them thinks they will marry—or do they? When he admits his love, Benedick also says he thinks it strange (IV.i.). Beatrice, on the other hand, holds out until the final scene and has still not owned up to loving Benedick when he "stops her mouth" by kissing her. It all seemed, well, grown-up. The levels of irony in Beatrice and Benedick's relationship, their skirmishes of wit, remove them from the more linear drives of adolescence. And I could feel myself reaching into that world where it is understood that what is said is a kind of code for what you mean.

The order of my life was restored with *Much Ado*. I was back where I belonged, back from the isolation of my sad summer, back on top in my mind. I was among friends and even admirers. So, Benedick's social facility came easy to me. Benedick is a man's man. He enjoys his comrades and thrives on their locker-room type routines. My friends Shane Ervin and Colin Smith played Claudio and Don Pedro and I drew from my own sense of well-being and comfort with my theatre buddies to give Benedick his good-fellow amiability. The trickiest part of Benedick, at least for a young actor, is the sarcasm and irony he uses when he talks to and about Beatrice. I just read aloud the speech (let's call it a rant) that begins "O, she misus'd me past the endurance of a block…"(II.i.) and can't believe that any seventeen-year-old boy would have as much fun with it as I just did. But I must have, because I remember the rolling energy of this scene onstage. It's a magnificent mix of hyperbole, cruel jokes, and bluntness. When I lived in Montreal, I was never happier with my French than when people were laughing at what I was saying and not how I was saying it. The telling of jokes is the sign of mastering a language, and when I was able to get laughs with Benedick's jokes, I knew the character was connecting with the audience because I was connecting with the language.

But it was finally the plot of *Much Ado* that brought our audience in, and it grabbed me too. When disaster presses down on the characters at the aborted wedding ("This looks not like a nuptial" is one of the greatest understatements I've ever found in Shakespeare, and I will think of it at every marriage I attend for the rest of my life), Beatrice and Benedick drop their masks in the face of a more serious conflict. Now, *this* is high drama. I loved it. In *our* production my friend and rival Stephen Murphy was Leonato, the father of Hero who, on the flimsiest of evidence, most cruelly turns on his disgraced daughter. "Why wast thou ever lovely in mine eyes?" (IV.i.) There is something Lear-like in his bitter selfishness and Steve found many opportunities to thunder in his speech. I remember a shattering silence in the house.

There was a time when I could recite all of Steve's speech from heart. In fact, I probably could have recited most of the play. My own speeches are nearly gone now, something I attribute to living recklessly as soon as I hit university. Lines from here and there remain, ruins really. My mind is like the Roman Forum in that respect.

Of all the roles I played at SJHS, Benedick is the one I would most like to play again. Today I see him as a man, more or less my own age of thirty-seven, who can't resolve the idea that he should probably settle down. He is fundamentally a comic character, and I think if there was one flaw in my performance it was how seriously I played him. But that is a review from the perspective of someone who's now been around almost as much as Benedick and fancies himself more worldly than he was at seventeen. Ultimately, there is room for sobriety in the interpretation of Benedick, as Don Pedro observes when he says, "What a pretty thing man is when he goes in his doublet and hose and leaves off his wit!" (V.i.) I thought my Benedick was just fine, but much more importantly, I loved playing him. I was very proud of our production, with its sunny, multi-level set of a Messina villa. My rented costume was red plush velvet with silver piping, originally rendered for a professional production of Verdi's *Falstaff*. During one of the performances mounted for students from other high schools when I made my first entrance with Don John, Don Pedro, and Claudio some of the girls in the audience screamed. It was too early in the action for screams of boredom, so they must've found at least one of us cute.

*Much Ado* had its closing night and with it came the now-familiar emptiness. The final stretch of my public-school days was upon me. I was applying to universities with little or no idea what I would do there. I don't remember which schools I applied to, but I intended to go to Dalhousie University in Halifax. They had a theatre program. I was still harboring my secret ambition to become an actor. Other symptoms of the impending deliverance included graduation photos, scholarship applications, exam distress. But there was also the announcement of the final production of the school year, the musical. It was to be *Fiddler on the Roof*.

This, I knew, was going to be Stephen Murphy's moment of glory: playing Tevye, the aging patriarch, the broad comedian, the big, tender voice of pathos. When the cast was announced there was no surprise for him—he was given the part as he should have been. I would have been happier for him if my own role had been a little more interesting. Instead, I was to play Perchick, a student suitor to one of Tevye's daughters. Now, to be fair, this play was the first in all the productions I was in at SJHS that had better, solid roles for women than it had for men. But the few men's roles that did exist outside of the lead offered a few possibilities. Alas, not even one of the character roles like the dim witted butcher Lazar Wolf was tossed my way. Instead, Perchick the student, a cog in the plotline, would be my swan song on the big stage. There would be nothing to look forward to that was equal to what I had already done. It was The Final Production in the spring of the last year. The most important thing in my life was already drying up.

Perchick didn't offer much to me and vice versa. I remember my first practices with the character as an utter failure. I could not shake off this incredible listlessness. Why I did not simply resign the part and go back to my books I do not know. I guess I was addicted. I think it would have been better for me if I had had a smaller part that would have allowed me to try something different, say, playing a very old man as my friend Brian Stephenson did when he was cast as the rabbi. Instead, as the wet-behind-the-ears suitor, I was once again the young dude. I was typecast. I believed I was underestimated. That hurt more than the size of the part. I had just played Benedick, a real adult, and I thought I understood him, got under his skin, lived his conflicts, wore his clothes and his beard. I didn't want to be seen onstage the next time as a mere adolescent. I tried to convince myself that having a voice was not the same thing as having to talk all the time. If my talent was an ability to be onstage and command attention, it did not have to be as a lead character. It was a matter of using skill and craft and imagination and discipline to command the merest instant of contact with the audience, to experience the hush, or the laughter, or any sign of engagement that makes theatre more than playing a part. I kept with it hoping to find the thing inside me that would make Perchick bigger than Brent. But it wasn't really working. How can you come back from playing Benedick and assume the role of a kid? I had already built a bridge into the adult world. Now I was being told not to cross it. Injustice howled around my ears.

I watched Stephen and tried to feel good for him. But he knew he was far ahead of me at this point in our rivalry. Stephen knew this was his moment and he assumed it with great dignity. He was restrained in rehearsals, though I knew when showtime arrived all jets would be firing. We were not as close as we once were. And I was jealous that his final performance in the spring of our graduating year was destined to be legendary. But there were other problems for him. He was our student body president and was involved in many activities both inside and outside the school. Like the rest of us, he had to think about the end of his school year and life after graduation. But most of all Stephen had started working over the past few months. He was putting in nearly full-time hours at his job as a newsreader on the radio. He was good at it. The electronic media seemed to be where he was heading career-wise all along. Many of us had part-time jobs while in school, but we were able to juggle our schedules to include the plays. For me it usually meant giving up a few work shifts around the last two weeks of production. But Steve seemed to be working 40-hour shifts while going to school and doing everything else. Within the first couple of weeks of rehearsals for *Fiddler* he came to loggerheads with Mr. Garrod. When he failed to report for a rehearsal one Sunday afternoon, he was fired, removed from the production, gone.

I can't tell you what effect this had on the rest of the cast. Steve was respected as a performer and as our student leader. The cast must have been devastated. But I can't tell you what it meant to them because I was so stunned by what it meant to me. I was given the part of Tevye.

I'm sure that there were people who had their doubts about my playing Tevye. Then, my ego was such that I wouldn't have entertained that idea as I assumed the mantle of the lead role. I thought I would have to work on my singing, and I would need to be bigger than life.

The comedy is broad and I didn't think it would be hard to get the laughs. But there were two legacies to contend with. The first was that of David McKenzie, a SJHS student with a bell ringing voice who'd played the part memorably in a school production six years before me. He had since died tragically in a plane crash and his Tevye was well remembered. The second legacy was the performance Steve Murphy never got to give.

One of the things that helped me enormously in my performance was the decision not to give Tevye a fake fat belly. I was lean with a lean face, and I knew I couldn't look like a fat guy just by stuffing a pillow in my shirt. In the end no one suggested I should. As I slogged away at the singing the role required (dancing was limited to shaking my hips during "If I was Rich Man"), the mannerisms of the old man came easily. The klezmer-influenced score was fun and invited movement. I was playing a character role, like Nathan Detroit. I felt comfortable in my own skin; I didn't need a fake one. There were lean old men, and my Tevye was one of them. The biggest turnaround for me was the first full dress rehearsal. In my false beard, which blended well into my own longish hair (this was 1978), I looked the way I thought Tevye should. Once again, I was overwhelmed by that confidence that now I can't believe I ever really had.

There were no defections from the cast. If they had their doubts about me, none of them expressed them to my face. A few made a point of giving me their verbal support and encouragement, for which I was massively grateful. I think a certain amount of humility came to me in this final production, not because I was not good, but because I knew the role had been for Stephen. The two of us were now, I believe, forever divided by what happened. I understood, though, that the play itself was not for him or for me, but for everyone who was in it—the chorus members, the assistant choreographers, the backstage crew, the make-up artists—all students, all proud of their work. In a small, improvised ceremony at the end of the final night, Ross Phinney, the head of the technical crew, gave me a sign from the production's railway station set that said (in Cyrillic script) Anatevka. I put it up on the wall of my bedroom in my parents' house and it hangs there to this day. I gave Tevye's milkman's hat to Mr. Garrod. It was the best gesture I could come up with to express the limitless gratitude I had for what had happened to me at SJHS. And what had happened was now over.

I graduated in the top dozen of my class. It was the highest academic standing I ever achieved in high school. I was accepted into Dalhousie University. God alone knows what I thought I was going to do there. Aside from knowing I wanted to act, I had no other expectations from university. I enrolled in a basic arts program and on the sly included a theatre course. There was an acting elective, but you had to audition to get into this small, selective class. I was accepted along with three other students. Our teacher was a dramatic looking New Yorker who had among her credits some soap opera experience. She was a fervent disciple of Stanislavsky, though not, as she passionately warned us, Stanislavsky as interpreted by Lee Strasberg. It was all a bit bewildering. If I was lost, I have no idea what the other three in the class were thinking. They seemed to have had far less experience of real theatre than I had and were not as intellectually ambitious. There was some valuable information. We did exhaustive textual analysis of a script and talked about things like subtext and memory recall, but not a lot of acting. The professor's level of unhappiness with her job and with Nova Scotia began to show in class. There were internecine department struggles, some students were sleeping with professors, the whole place seemed shady and undisciplined compared to the English department where my other studies were unfolding. I remember standing in the university bookstore in the English section and looking at the reading lists for various English courses and thinking to myself, "How wonderful to major in English. Look what you get to read."

English became my major. We didn't have to declare a minor, but mine was theatre. I acted in some of the department's productions. In one show I got a rave review in the local paper. Not the campus newspaper, but the real press. I think whoever reviewed us had never seen a play before. Incrementally the world of acting began to lose its appeal. It was disconcerting for me because I still had no idea what I wanted from life. One of the most valuable lessons I learned from my acting teacher was summed up by a phrase she used in one of her first lectures. She said: "If you continue to pursue acting in your life it will be for the sole reason that you cannot do anything else." I couldn't decide if this sounded noble or pathetic. But I knew if acting meant continuing in productions like these it was the latter. I felt that the level of productions in the theatre department were well below those I'd been in at SJHS. I rarely talked about my high school productions because I knew no-one could appreciate how good they were. Every school does some theatre. Most of it is just amateur fun. I couldn't express the level of quality and excellence that I knew bounded out of our shows.

My acting experience helped a lot in my English courses. Knowing a little bit about the method aided analysis of characters in Shakespeare. Theatre was not just another way of writing or reading prose but a real and living thing for me, just as I had made Orlando live when I was sixteen. I could synthesize, which I noted was difficult for even the cleverest students in my classes. I was not intimidated by Renaissance language. I could cross reference any number of Elizabethan plays. By my second or third year at Dalhousie I was no longer taking any theatre courses. In May of 1982 I graduated with an honours degree in English.

There was a lot of confusion in these years. The only real ambition in my life had been to act, and now I had abandoned it without ever even trying to make a professional debut. I did not think about what this meant in terms of my professional life. I was too busy trying to sort out my own identity. Who I was had been tied up in what I wanted since I was a kid and now the whole question of finding my voice was even murkier. I was ambivalent about university. My academic success was built on the fact that I could write and that seemed to come (in part) from what I learned by acting. So, I was not without resources. But I was also not willing to abandon the idea of play. My need to play was still overriding the tremendous career-oriented efforts I saw in those around me. But I didn't know how anymore. It was the beginning of the eighties and the time had come for everyone else to put away their childish things. Once again, I was isolated. I was a very lonely person.

In the summer of my freshman year at university I got an on-air job at a local radio station giving the sports scores. I actually didn't think I was very good at it, but I came away with a new respect for broadcasters, specifically public broadcasters and their programs. I continued to work for the CBC throughout my undergraduate years. When I graduated, I looked at some small radio stations for jobs, but no-one wanted to hire me. Maybe I still seemed like a kid, or maybe they knew I would soon tire of the small challenges daily regional radio can offer. I took off for Europe and spent a season bumming and then returned to Canada and, in the depth of the recession of 1982–83, ended up in Montreal, where rent was cheap. I was tired of doing nothing, so I applied to the McGill graduate program and went back to school to do an MA.

While at McGill, CBC Stereo launched the network's first youth-oriented national radio show. I knew some of the people working on it and I managed to get some part-time work helping out. But it was soon clear to everyone around me that I really wanted to go on-air. I had the instincts of a performer, and others saw that too. I also had the same kind of confidence I had when I first auditioned for Orlando. When the original host of *Brave New Waves* stepped down seventeen months after the programme's inauguration, I was there. It was my first full-time professional job. I was twenty-five years old.

I lasted almost ten years on *Waves*. It was a strange and eclectic mix of music and talk. I interviewed everyone from Quentin Tarantino to Margaret Atwood. The counterculture was given its say: conspiracy theorists, graffiti artists, minimalist poets, professional masochists. In the beginning, I was reticent and unsure of my abilities. But as my interviewing skills increased, I began to believe in myself the way I did when I was onstage at SJHS. That same confidence that pushed me when I was a kid still compensated for a natural shyness and awkwardness that had never really gone away. I was talking primarily to adolescents. They identified with me, or at least with the part of me they could hear. The voice. My voice. The most literal manifestation of my sense of self was now the way I made my living. It had indeed become the key to my survival. It was part performance. My public voice was not the same as my personal, intimate one. But it was much more than performance. I talked to people, and I learned how to make them talk back, to find their voice and to use it in a clear, concise, and imaginative way. In the end I think I was much older than most of my audience, but I was also kept young by them. It was an extended adolescence. I got to play for ten years. But it was play with a pay-off. Today people approach me to talk about these late-night radio broadcasts that spanned nearly a decade. They were listeners in the night, and these ephemeral shows were important to them. They feel they know me, that we shared time together. It was a national programme so we reached many isolated places. More importantly,

I reached many isolated people. I connected. Somewhere in there I grew up.

Three years ago I got a job in television. I am now the host of *Midday* on CBC. It's a national news and light information show—something like *Good Morning America* except it's on at noon and it's Canadian. The main part of my job is to do interviews, and I talk to politicians, actors, columnists, journalists, and writers, the significant and the obscure. The interviewing process is now the most important part of what I do. Of course, there's still a performance aspect to appearing before a camera and there are occasional moments when there is no other word to describe what I am doing but acting. However, interviewing a subject, finding out how to best give them the gift of articulation and guide them through their narrative, even preventing them from telling their story in a way that doesn't work, is the most satisfying part of what I do. It's not really acting; it's much more like directing. Some people would say it's not really working; it's much more like playing. And that's fine with me.

*Brent Bambury has been a professional broadcaster since he was a teenager. For a decade he was the voice of the cult radio show* Brave New Waves *heard nationally on the Canadian Broadcasting Corporation. He has developed many programs for the network including the broadcast* Day Six *on which he is heard across Canada and on public radio in the US. Brent lives in Toronto where he continues his lifelong love and support of the performing arts. This essay was written when Brent was thirty-seven years old.*

# The Journey Inward

Philip Palmer

CANADA

Thursday, November 21, 1963, was the eve of John F. Kennedy's assassination in Dallas. I was fourteen years old going on fifty—a ninth grade student attending my first live production of a Shakespeare play. It was love at first sight. The play, *Twelfth Night,* was performed by Saint John High School students under the direction of Andrew Garrod. At the time, I was already acting myself in a play at my junior high school—a small production with a cast of four. I was awestruck by the contrasting size and bustle of the Shakespearean production and the fun that I saw the actors were having. I knew from that moment that I wanted to be part of future High School productions.

I was the fourth and clumsiest of five children in a middle-class family. Had I been a graceful athlete, I doubt I would have been tempted by acting, but as it was, I had little or no athletic ability. My parents, who encouraged their children to take on challenges and assumed they would excel, were supportive of my participation in theatre— although, apart from my father's infamous performances in charades, there was no history of acting in the family.

In September 1964, I enrolled at Saint John High School. As much as I hated to admit it then, I hit some bumps in adjusting over the first few months. An introvert by nature, it took me time to make friends besides those I had known in junior high. I was intimidated by the older students: their apparent knowledge and *savoir faire* were something new to me. Feeling very much out of place, a friend and I would take our homemade sandwiches and eat them a few blocks away, near a horse trough donated in tribute to the tireless work of the R.S.P.C.A. Only winter's cold finally drove us to lunch with our new mates.

However rocky my beginnings at High School, I carried with me the image of the Shakespeare production I had seen the previous fall. When auditions were posted for a production of *King Lear,* I showed up, along with my best friend from junior high. We both won parts; I was given the role of "A Gentleman." My big moment consisted of a few lines describing to the Duke of Kent the awful state of madness Lear was in as he wandered about on the heath:

| **Kent:** | …Where is the King? |
|---|---|
| **Gent.:** | Contending with the fretful elements; |
| | Bids the wind blow the earth into the sea, |
| | Or swell the curled waters 'bove the main, |
| | That things might change or cease; tears his white hair, |
| | Which the impetuous blasts, with eyeless rage… |

And so on. My modest speech prepared the audience for the mad Lear they were to meet in the next scene.

I was more than happy with my minor part, which enabled me to experience stage fright without putting the production at risk. The Duke of Kent, who was played by my sister's boyfriend, had to save me more than once when I was in danger of forgetting my lines. Most importantly, *Lear* gave me a toehold in the much more grown-up world of high school, and introduced me to a circle of people, many of whom became true friends with whom I could share my interests and develop the insights that I would carry forward into my adult life.

Our theatre consisted of a double classroom, with seats banked on plywood risers. Our stage was composed of hollow plywood risers curtained off· in black velvet. The hollow stage echoed our hard-soled footsteps with a thump that easily drowned out our speeches. The few stage lights were constructed from tomato juice tins and other rudimentary components assembled in the school's science laboratory. Props were absolutely minimal, which meant we had to concentrate on our acting to add colour to the play. We did, however, rent period costumes and wear stage make-up, which helped us situate ourselves in our roles. There was always a tremendous wave of excitement when the costumes arrived and we got fitted for our parts.

Though my speaking part was modest, it seemed Shakespeare needed a gentleman or two in every act. So for weeks, after school, on week-ends, and on holidays, we beavered away under the critical eye of Andrew Garrod, who was both director and producer. I loved sitting in the back of our rehearsal room, watching the production being refined scene by scene. Andrew Garrod was not the first teacher to treat me and my peers as adults, but no one had ever given us so much adult attention in a form we could absorb: he explained the text and coaxed emotion out of shy teenagers, without the inhibitions that cause so many adults to appear condescending in their interest in the young. He was, for example, quite comfortable teaching a girl how to courtesy or make a flirtatious gesture. Garrod was a fine mimic, athletic and poised, who emitted a kinetic energy. He was good humoured and patient (but not limitlessly so), demanding, and gave rehearsals both energy and dignity. Garrod pushed himself as well as his actors. It was wonderful.

Garrod would sit near the front of our little theatre space, watching a scene unfold, occasionally interrupting to get a phrase right. Or he would leap up to demonstrate a point, hamming up a part a bit to make his suggestion obvious, and then return to his seat to observe the effects of his intervention. Actors sometimes had to repeat a line dozens of times until a gesture or an inflection was exactly right. Movement, voice, expression, gesture, and, of course, the lines themselves were all drilled over and over until they became natural to us.

We weren't students of theatre, however; we were putting on a play. Our productions were strictly extra-curricular, and we squeezed rehearsals in among our school work, domestic chores, or part-time jobs. Garrod didn't school us in acting techniques, such as breathing exercises or improvisations. What we did was perform the play as closely as possible to how Garrod saw it in his mind. We all took tremendous pride in coming close to realising his vision.

A Shakespeare play cannot come together without its traumas, and our production of *Lear* was no exception. A scene would work in one rehearsal, then fall apart in the next. Old errors were repeated, and new ones introduced. We just couldn't get it right, and, with a few days left before opening night, we were beginning to quietly despair. It was at that point that Garrod called the cast to a general rehearsal and proceeded to give us a tongue lashing that was a wonder to witness, not unlike the "hurricanoes" that Shakespeare unleashed on Lear.

The effect, as intended, was dramatic. The cast set to work with an intensity we didn't know we had, and ran through the dress rehearsal like there was no tomorrow. Our roles had, in a sense, become natural to us.

What both Shakespeare and Garrod knew was that, even in callow youth, there lies a range of emotions and understanding that go uncalled on in our day-to-day lives. Producing a successful performance called on us to shed our everyday skins, and to take on the emotional and moral logic of our assigned characters. And for the next four days of our performance, we were our characters. Anyone who saw us must have felt some genuine theatrical magic—the magic that is created when, for a short time, we become someone else. Through drama, many of us were able to taste emotions and sensations we had never known before, or that were socially unacceptable for people our age to explore.

Acting is a work of the imagination; thus, we can't act what we can't imagine. Many of us were able only to imitate the actions of our characters, as we lacked the emotional engagement that would enable us to internalize them. We needed to develop empathy with our characters, to live in their moral universe. Not many of us got there by any rational process. It took the fear of God and Andrew Garrod for us to realise what we had been learning in the rehearsal process, but we did in time become our characters in a theatrical sense.

Our production wasn't flawless, of course, but we tried to maintain a high level of performance. We had dug deep into ourselves and gotten a glimpse of what we could do, and, for the duration of that performance, we came somewhat close to living in the moral universe that Shakespeare had tried to convey—and that Andrew Garrod tried to recreate with his company of teenagers.

There was an excitement and a newness to the experience of acting in *Lear* that I have never been able to duplicate. The fact is that, like first love, there are things that can't ever be new again, no matter how intensely you work at them, and how important they are to you at the time. I can still remember lines from *King Lear,* even not my own, something that I can't do with the other plays I acted in.

I admired our leads and came to identify them with the roles they were playing, which made those roles become more a part of me. To this day, Paul Scofield's Lear takes second place to our Richard Green's, and no one can compete in filial ingratitude with our four actors who shared the parts of Goneril and Regan. *King Lear* is a very emotional play, which I suppose is partly what etched it indelibly in my mind.

For the next year's play, Andrew Garrod selected *Much Ado about Nothing*. By this time I was a seasoned veteran, and turned out for auditions as a matter of course. I was chosen to play Claudio, the young and vulnerable lieutenant of Don Pedro, Duke of Mantua. Claudio falls in love with the younger Hero, daughter of the household Don Pedro and his entourage are visiting.

I confess I have always dreaded knowing what Garrod saw in me to choose me for that role. Claudio is not a very developed character; Shakespeare apparently put his energy into other characters. So, while Shakespeare describes Claudio's heroic deeds in battle, there is little in Claudio's character that suggests he absorbed any emotional teachings from the death of comrades or the heat of battle, and he is distinctly lacking in wit and self-perception.

Nevertheless, I was pleased to get the larger role, and took it up with enthusiasm. It didn't hurt that my Heros were drop-dead beautiful; to this day, my memories stir the raw desire I felt so long ago. Acting is a highly social activity, and at our High School there was always a greater turnout of females. As a consequence, we few males had both the challenge and privilege of getting to know some of the most attractive and intelligent women in the school—a privilege of which I was wise enough to avail myself liberally.

*Much Ado* has two main elements: the bantering courtship between Beatrice and Benedict, a sort of Tracy-Hepburn battle of the sexes, which is set off by the teenage sappiness of Claudio and Hero. My hunch is that Garrod thought I was just right for the emotions that were called on to play Claudio, who has an awful quality of adolescent self-pity. That was an emotion that I could summon all too easily. I once read that self-pity was the essence of all bad poetry; I think it is the core of the teenage psyche, and I was a ready example of my theory.

By my junior year, I had acquired an active social life and a circle of friends. If *Lear* had helped me find a place in my high school, *Much Ado* led to a maturing of that place.

The rehearsals and performances of *Much Ado* flew by in a blur— almost as quickly as my infatuations and romances. They were leather-shod feet clumping over the hollow plywood-ox stage. The sweet-smelling make-up being removed by the foul-smelling cold cream. The misery of being told off by your latest girlfriend. Waking up when it's all over to find you have less than a month until exams, and a host of assignments overdue. Proof, should one have needed it, that all glory is fleeting.

The fall of my senior year, Andrew chose to present Arthur Miller's *The Crucible.* I was given the choice role of John Proctor, the accused adulterer whose life and family are destroyed by the hysteria that feeds on the puritan culture in which he ekes out his living as a farmer.

Proctor is a person of substance with some moral force in the community. The play revolves around the battle for Proctor's soul, as he seeks to redeem himself for the shame he has visited on his family by having an affair with his neighbor's niece, Abigail. Proctor eventually chooses to die rather than to sign a false confession of practicing witchcraft. He was thus a victim of the seventeenth-century witch-hunt that took place in Salem, Massachusetts—Miller's metaphor for the McCarthy-era persecution of suspected communists.

Proctor was a role that I could internalize, one that continues to have a certain resonance for me. Even as a teenager, I sensed within myself the difficulty of being a good man. I never considered myself a good person, and I was able to sympathise with Proctor, who was held in better regard by others than by himself. There was something in his plain speaking and in his difficulty in reaching his emotions that I shared with him, and that I hope I was able to bring out in the role. As a seventeen-year-old, I had already absorbed the workaholic ethos of my father and clung to rationality and logic over the heart. I was stilted in my relationships with girls, and not widely popular, and, like Proctor, I was full of emotions that lay unexpressed and unacknowledged.

Proctor, even when his wife has forgiven him, can't see the good in himself. He goes to his death not because he believes himself to be good, but because he cannot let others die while he buys his life with a lie.

I later saw a professional production of *The Crucible* in which Proctor was interpreted differently. I was somewhat embarrassed to see how other aspects of the character were brought out that I had no sense of, yet I still have a claim to Proctor, and who I made of him.

The rehearsals leading up to the performances of *The Crucible* sped by as my own life raced through time, full of activities and academics—the hectic schedule of a high school senior. As before, I sat in the back of our rehearsal room, watching the rehearsal of scenes I wasn't in. I took in everything I could about the play. It was a gift to be able to watch Andrew give shape to the play, bringing out the meaning of the scenes, and urging us to feel the emotional and moral currents that ran below the surface of the script. At moments I could sense how exhilarating and complex the job of director was.

I also saw new bits and pieces of individuality emerging from my friends. Andrew had to coax and cajole us to throw away our daily personas and replace them with characters guided by different moral and psychological imperatives. He had to use a mixture of techniques, ranging from explanation, to demonstration, to scaring the wits out of us, but he did succeed in getting us to imagine ourselves as our characters.

Remembering the experience of acting awakens long-dormant emotions, and permits a reevaluation of the process from a perspective of time and experience. More than thirty years have passed since I graduated from high school. I spent the subsequent ten years pursuing university studies, and have been a practising lawyer for more than twenty years. Acting represents two major influences in my life. First, my experience of acting was inextricably linked to my coming of age in the community in which I lived. It provided social interactions that were important to the maturing of my relations with my peers: it proved both a source of friends, and a source of knowledge of people. Acting was also a very personal challenge: I cannot discuss acting without reflecting on my personal motivations for taking acting roles, and considering what lasting impact acting has had on my adult life. Acting, as I said, was part of my corning of age in a particular place and time. Acting helped me and my co-actor friends step out of the traditional aspects of teenage culture, and forced us to relate to a select group of adults, giving us a closer view of their universe and its challenges.

We were lucky in our High School, specifically, with our teachers and a number of generous and supportive adults in the community who helped us reach out to the world. They gave us our first exposure to art, choral music, drama, debating, all of which provided opportunities for us to explore our world. There was a happy conspiracy between us and our teachers and adult friends.

Saint John, the city I grew up in, is an impoverished city, situated on bleak and windswept rock outcroppings on the edge of the sea. By the 1960's, it had been in decline for a century, but while I was in high school, post-war prosperity brought a period of renewal to Saint John. Though hardly a hot-bed of culture or intellect, the city was able to attract popular cultural figures of the time. I was able to see Allen Ginsberg give a reading of his work in a Presbyterian church hall, listen to Gordon Lightfoot at a coffee house set in a converted fire station, attend a concert by Simon and Garfunkel, and see the original film version of *All Quiet on the Western Front* at the local film society.

Strong liberal currents were in the air, and dress codes, hair length, and other cultural norms gradually gave way to the whims and tastes of the baby boomers. The Beatles, the Stones, folk music, folk rock all influenced my friends and me. Whether it was merely our age, or whether Saint John was in fact becoming more open to the outside world, my friends and I felt that we were connected to the broad river of cultural change that swept through North America. We felt connected to the freedom marchers in Selma, Alabama; we felt engaged in the struggle against *apartheid* in South Africa; we followed the Six Day War between Israel and its Arab neighbours; we debated nuclear disarmament, and were painfully conscious of the potential for nuclear annihilation. When we left Saint John, we felt fully equal to our big city cousins: we had flirted with existentialism, read the Communist Manifesto, and pledged ourselves to the NDP. In some ways we felt more connected to the big issues of our day than our city friends seemed to be.

Acting also gave me access to the Jewish community of Saint John. By my teen years I had had some experience of the Catholic and Protestant cultures of Saint John, which were sharply divided when I was a child. My encounter with the Jewish community was my first with a rich and somewhat exotic culture in which learning and artistic endeavour were strongly encouraged. I was welcomed into their homes and their social life, making connections that grew into friendships and even into love. With them I discovered classical music and jazz, attended theatre, danced, flirted, and shared their passion for life. Their finely tuned sense of irony and their detachment from the preoccupations of Christian culture were important in pointing me to the cultural alternatives that might otherwise have been denied me at that age.

An unexpected benefit of participating in acting was that it gave me access to others who shared or came to share my interests. From drama, to creative writing, to record club, to debating, a thread of common interests connected our young lives. Acting allowed us to explore our inner lives at the same time that we launched our search for external connections. This exploration, was, it turns out, a prelude to the interior voyages that were to follow.

It is difficult to imagine now the vitality we felt then. Saint John didn't, in the end, hold many of us. Few returned there after the university, as the industrial city offered few interesting professional opportunities. I did return to practice law for a time, but the adventure was not there, and I sought a different environment in which to realise myself.

Drama is a highly organised social activity. A production demands that a number of distinct activities be coordinated so that they all are "ripe" on opening night. It requires precise teamwork, between members of the cast and among the various supporting functions: sets, lighting, makeup, and so on. The success of a production relies on successful execution of on- and off-stage functions. Individual egos must be subordinated to the demands of the production: scenes must be shared so the meaning will emerge; the lighting must work to achieve the effects desired by the makeup. Each participant must consider and help others: there is no success that doesn't depend on the efforts of the many, no failure that isn't shared by all. A successful production shares the virtues associated with winning athletics: it is only the arena that differs.

The virtues associated with the playing field are, in fact, mirrored by many of life's other activities; for example, the aspect of theatre that demands taking on responsibilities parallels that required by sports. When I was in school, sports was very much king, and artistic, cultural, or intellectual endeavour was suspect, and practised openly by very few. I was more than once challenged by schoolmates to defend the legitimacy of the activities I pursued. I had to defend the notion that taking the lead role in a production might, within the pantheon of extracurricular activities, be equated with participation in varsity sports. I took particular pride in receiving a high school letter based on a portfolio from which any athletic endeavour was notably absent.

I didn't have many preconceptions of what acting would be like. I knew from my experience in junior high school that it was hard work and full of anxiety, but I never had a "star complex" and knew it was not a glamorous pursuit. The work was too hard and intense, the effort expected too demanding for anyone to pose and primp for long. I think, too, that Andrew Garrod, while closer to some students than others, scrupulously avoided creating a "star" system. Indeed, I think most of us found acting for Garrod to be a humbling experience; our pride in our personal accomplishments was commensurate to the effort we had made.

I cannot reconstruct my involvement in theatre without reflecting on the sexual dynamic at work among the cast and crew. Working together with beautiful and intelligent women was undeniably one of the rewards of pursuing acting, and there was real excitement in embracing or kissing onstage. More important, though, was the comradeship. We had to know and rely on each other in a way that was probably rare between the sexes at that time, when mixed activities were the exception. Most mixed activities corresponded with gender roles; thus intergender partnering in drama was a relative novelty to most of us.

The curious thing is that while I acted with a number of women I had crushes on, on-stage demands suppressed flirtation, if not desire, and created voluntary boundaries that were more effective than any that might have been imposed from without. There was an egalitarianism that seemed natural and unforced, which was as liberating for me as it must have been for my female friends. Acting was one of the few activities in which a young woman could gain recognition that wasn't solely dependent on looks. Women's sports were considered inferior, and cheerleading was not something every young woman aspired to. Working closely with so many intelligent and ambitious women was a real privilege, and I was lucky to have shared with them our coming of age.

Of course, equality and intense work are not desexualising: there are moments when the guard drops and something essential emerges from within a person, and there is no sexual rush like that when you suddenly see and experience something new and authentic in someone you know. To see your pretty classmate as a fire-spitting Goneril or a tormented Elizabeth Proctor is to meet a new and unique person beneath the shell of everyday life. Compared with a stage kiss or embrace, this was an aphrodisiac of unheralded potency: added to ordinary physical attraction was desire based on an imaginative understanding—heady stuff at any age. These openings spoke of possibilities within ourselves that we took for granted.

Acting was liberating in that it allowed us to share a rare collective intimacy, one that is enjoyed as a result of both group effort and a readiness for each to be individually vulnerable. I continue to find parallel situations in my professional life where, for at least brief moments, our everyday work and personal lives recede and genuine group effort is harnessed to achieve collective ends. The difference is that most of our adult energies expended in such collective endeavours must seem impenetrably mundane to all but those intimately involved.

Collective effort, vulnerability, sexual awakening, shared goals: the simple fact is that acting lent to our lives a quality of intensity that we didn't easily find in daily life—an intensity that I suspect few ever know. In general, teenage culture is cool, and the vulnerability that comes with showing excitement or engagement or enthusiasm is discouraged. As actors, we had to abandon self-consciousness, if ever so briefly, an experience that set us apart from our peers. For some of us, myself included, that experience set a standard against which to measure our subsequent life experiences. I still want to replicate that intensity of commitment, which is difficult in the context of family and daily routines that compete with the desire to excel and achieve.

*The Crucible* proved to be the apogee of my short career as an actor. I haven't acted since my high school days, nor have I felt the need to. But as a teen I had a need for expiation, and for trial, that acting uniquely fulfilled. Acting satisfied needs in me that had no other outlet and played a crucial role in shaping me as an adult. I have never expressed my feelings about this aspect of acting to anyone, even those closest to me.

What called me to acting in high school? What did I learn from it? What, as an adult, do I think was significant about it? I am not sure there are any easy answers to those questions, but I am curious about what drove me to act. If I try to situate myself in the times, I recall I found acting extremely difficult, verging on the painful. I think I was at least partly motivated by shame at the way my shyness and fear had governed me as a boy.

I had in fact been painfully shy, and as such was extremely sensitive to any public embarrassment. I therefore felt the need to overcome my self-imposed disability, which led me to student council positions, as well as to debating and public speaking. It might simply have been a part of the Protestant work ethic in which I was raised that drove me to test myself and to take risks. For me, to experience was to risk, and the highest risk was in acting. There, others depended uniquely on my performance. Any personal failure would have been very public, while any victory was very private. One had to dig deeper and harder in acting than in any other activity to be successful. I never shared this motivation with anyone, thus not even my closest friends knew what it meant to me to go through a performance. I now suppose that it was this risk factor that made acting so intense and intensely personal to me.

Acting requires not only teamwork, but also a lot of individual effort. I worked hard to memorise my lines, and lived in agony of botching a scene. I was extremely nervous before each performance, constantly on edge, which is perhaps why I remember so little of what happened on stage. For me, acting was a very introverted activity, one that forced me to go into myself to find something that added to the character. I didn't have the experience nor the emotional consciousness to draw on in playing such parts as John Proctor. I guess it must have been largely my imagination that got me through. What I mean is that in the midst of this very social activity there is this quiet process of self-discovery going on. It is not gentle, and I didn't find it easy. I don't think my friends and I were sufficiently conscious of this process to talk about it, and I thus found acting alienating at the same time that I was intensely involved with others.

I was, like many teenagers, introverted without being introspective. I had no vocabulary for my inner life, and little awareness of my own emotional processes. Like many other males of my generation, I was preparing for a life of surfaces, where unreason could reign, and emotion could be put to one side. In the mid-sixties, some of us were anything but liberated, and I certainly wasn't ready, filled as my life was with politics, social action, and other causes, to grapple with my basic emotions and needs. That would come only later, with failed marriages, career mis-starts, the desperate hopes of new beginnings, and the repeated damaging behaviour.

In acting, I did probe some of the depths I didn't reach in my everyday life. As a typical North American Protestant, I found the exploration heavy going. I always expected that if I explored my emotional depths, I would find a thoroughly weak and bad person. High school offered an external world in which I could lose myself and avoid questions of the soul. I reveled in that world, cocooned from self-examination and projecting myself into events that were beyond my understanding, and whose emotional core I could not reach. But John Proctor nibbled at the emotional bubble in which I tried to live. Though I scarcely recognised what was going on at the time, I think now that when I finished *The Crucible* it was with relief that I resumed routines that insulated me from my feelings.

As I look back, I can envision an emotional map of my life on which different colours represent the presence or absence of intense emotion. If everyday life is beige, periods of intense activity blue, and periods of personal emotion red, then the periods I was engaged in the dramatic productions would be among the very few where an intense shade of purple could be found—time in which life took on an intensity that was unmatched in earlier life, and scarcely repeated since.

What then do I draw on today from my experience of acting as a youth? How did it affect my life?

First and most obviously, it helped me overcome my personal reluctance to expose myself publicly. I now routinely speak before groups, make presentations, and enjoy reaching out to an audience of any size. Conquering my fear of an audience, having the confidence that I can muddle through, comes in large measure from having exposed myself to the risks inherent in acting.

Acting also helped me look more objectively at people and character. To take on a role, you have to divine the moral principles by which a character proceeds, and then try, in your portrayal, to make that evident. This requires a careful reading of the indicators provided by the author: What does the character actually do? What do we know about when it is done in relation to other key events? To whom or with whom is it done? These objective facts are keys to the more subjective and intuitive aspects of the character: Why does the character act that way? What do we know of the values of the character from what is exposed? What does that say about how he or she walks, talks, treats people, signals their emotions, or seeks advantage? The techniques of divining character is one that served me later when I studied history, and has served me in my career, both as a lawyer and as a manager. They have helped me evaluate the intentions of others through the clues provided by their conduct and choice of words, and this has permitted me to offer nuanced and holistic advice to my clients and colleagues. I think this was something I picked up as I watched Andrew Garrod tease from us an understanding of the characters we were portraying. The hours spent watching rehearsals from the back of our theatre space were not a waste of time for me.

Perhaps the most important thing I have carried with me is the extent to which life is about moral choices. In Shakespeare, as in Miller, the protagonists may have been given certain basic attributes, but it is from their choices, influenced by their values and their experiences, that ill or good arose. They chose their course of action, and thus the consequences that result from these actions. Acting provided a glimpse into the moral universe of our characters. We had to try to emulate them, an act that requires moral sympathy. However, that very moral sympathy awakened in me a keen awareness of other possibilities: Lear's destruction is the outcome of his vanity, which leads him to deny the truth that is present in the words of Cordelia and Kent. Lear chose his path to destruction, and that of his friends. John Proctor compromised his wife and family, not only in having an affair with Abigail, but also in not exercising his moral influence before the hysteria took hold.

Plays, of course, highlight moral clashes in a way that real life rarely does. In real life it is often unclear what consequences will flow from our actions. We often cannot see the moral aspects of our choices until we have already chosen, and realized that we have betrayed ourselves. Adult life is to some degree about living with the consequences of bad decisions made in ignorance. I think that in trying to live the moral choices of our characters, we were given an important insight into the world we were on the verge of entering. Acting was, in its very essence, a moral education. Shakespeare and Miller were our masters, Andrew Garrod our tutor who helped us see into the world of values that were painted by those masters.

The duty of moral sympathy is the basis of all informed legal, political, or business analysis of the objective world. Whether we consider the Bosnian Serbs or Mother Teresa, we must ask what is the moral universe in which they live and act. Our duty of judgement can, of course, require partaking in remote and political acts (do we ally with or check the excess of another nation?). However, most of our judgements, and those that are most important, are very personal and localised: do I overlook this conduct, or do I do business with this person? Acting played a vital role in creating my desire to understand the world, in my taking charge of how I conduct myself in it.

Part of the reason for Andrew Garrod's success with us was that he was one of the very first adults to treat us as complete moral beings. Most adults treat children, even teenagers, as lesser moral beings, and treat as exceptional the spheres of activity in which young people can make choices about themselves and their world. In our acting, Andrew never patronized us. We felt always that he assumed we were complete beings able to make and understand choices. In permitting us to test ourselves against the moral qualities of our characters, Andrew introduced us to choices that might have been far less evident in a reading of the same works. It was in the detail of piecing together our characters that we got to some of the truths that might otherwise have never come to us.

But Andrew could not have done that if he lacked the confidence that we could make our own choices: indeed, that only we could make those choices and those understandings for ourselves. In short, we were treated as adults in a remarkable and liberating way, for moral freedom depends on moral responsibility, and moral responsibility is the essence of adulthood.

Finally, acting was an exploration of myself. I can't pretend that the lessons of that exploration were immediately evident to me, or that I have some neat little collation of truths arising from my experiences. I did, however, learn a lot about how to work, both within myself and with others. I also conquered some important fears and reticences which would, over time, have limited my universe severely. But most important was to have explored, at least a bit, the possibilities that resided within me. The gentleman in *Lear* was a straight guy, an honest bit player who didn't fully share in the drama that was sweeping the central characters toward their destruction. If Claudio was un-attractive, it was because there were parts of me that were as naive and self pitying as was Claudio. John Proctor alerted me to the pos-sibility of exercising courage, even redemptive courage, where both innocence and virtue have been lost. In each case, the exploration of the character was, simultaneously, an exploration of myself. I can't say that acting made self-exploration second nature to me; I still don't find it easy or fun. But I think that acting alerted me to the power of self-exploration, and its necessity if I was ever to act consistently by my values.

Acting, more than anything else I did, set me on a journey of in-ward exploration, a process begun late and continued with interrup-tions and detours throughout my adult life. While I was a reluctant voyager at first, I have come to accept that only in self-knowledge can we be "good," and that lack of self awareness is fatal to moral be-haviour. This is not to say that I have achieved any great degree of inner knowledge. I can only say that the importance of it is a product of my experience of acting, and that my adult voyage was launched on a makeshift stage at Saint John High School, under the guidance of Andrew Garrod. It is no comment on my teachers and guides of those days that my life has been replete with errors and hazard; it is to them that I owe a debt of gratitude for having helped me gain an awareness of the nature of the adventure upon which I was embarking, and gave me some means to measure moral success or failure in the encounters I have had with life.

*After graduating from Saint John High School in 1967 and taking a gap year to hitchhike in Europe and England, Philip Palmer attended McGill University, where he studied modern European history. As a graduate student, he spent a year at the Free University of Berlin, and frequently entered East Berlin through Check Point Charlie. After much internal debate, he followed his father into law and was called to the New Bruns-wick bar in 1978. After three years in private practice, he joined the Ca-nadian Department of Justice in 1981. He occupied increasingly respon-sible positions within that department, and practiced in a variety of legal fields, including cultural law, communications law, Indigenous peoples' law, immigration law and competition law. Since his retirement in 2012,*

*Philip has been active in advocacy and policy work in support of an open and accessible Internet. He lives in Ottawa, Canada, and is enjoying the post-Covid resumption of live music and theatrical performance. Philip's essay was written in 1998.*

# Finding My Voice

Heather Chesley
CANADA

When I was eleven years old I developed a stutter. It was 1970, and I was entering grade six at Prince Charles School. My family lived near the center of town and school was only fifteen minutes away on foot, straight down Wentworth Street, past Hayward's funeral parlour, the United Church and the rows of red-brick rooming houses. For the past five years I had gone to Princess Anne Elementary School. Prince Charles was in the opposite direction from Princess Anne and the new route meant I no longer had to walk the first few blocks alone before meeting up with my girlfriend Cynthia.

Cynthia and I were inseparable; our mothers introduced us to each other on the first day of grade one and immediately we were kindred spirits. Every day to school in the morning, home for lunch and back to school again, we walked and talked and giggled, stopping at the corner store for bags of chips and ice-cream sandwiches for after-school treats.

Our house was on the corner of Princess and Wentworth Street and when I looked out of my second-story bedroom window I could just make out the fringe of the harbour. There was a widow's walk on top of the roof, and though you couldn't actually get up to it, I liked to imagine the waiting and watching for the first sign of the returning ship.

From our hilltop corner the streets ran steeply down in three directions and in winter when the sidewalks were covered with ice, we slid from one street sign post to the other on the way to school.

As Princess Anne Elementary only went up to grade five, and what with being the oldest child in my family, I had never really gotten to know many older children. Prince Charles, on the other hand, went up to grade nine, and even in my grade six class there were several kids who had been held back a grade or two. All the security that came from being in the highest grade had disappeared and I felt very young and unsure of where I fit in the social circle of these new peers. Those of us coming from Princess Anne were the outsiders and these new school-mates seemed very street smart and mature. Some of the girls were dating already, and I even heard whispers of someone getting pregnant.

Sometime during the year I started noticing that I was having prob-lems with speaking. I'd repeat a word, or mix them up if I tried to say too many words too quickly. Then I found that I couldn't say certain words easily, words that began with "m" or "p". The word would start but then something would happen and I'd get stuck and couldn't get the rest of the word out. The first word of a sentence was especially difficult regardless of what word it was and the harder I tried not to stutter, the worse it would become. I dreaded recess time. I tried to stay close to Cynthia, and hoped that someone wouldn't start teasing me about the stuttering or sing the song "K-K-Katie." If I did get teased, I'd pretend not to care; better not to let them get any satisfaction out of knowing that I felt ashamed of my problem.

I loved school in spite of everything. I liked my teachers, especially Mr. John DeLong, who taught English. As did all the male teachers, he wore a shirt and a tie to class, but his white shirt never seemed to get close to an iron, and was perpetually rumpled. This gave him a slight-ly endearing quality, like a great big teddy bear. He taught us a style of creative writing that was more of a game than anything else. Mr. DeLong would tell us to take a pen and just start writing down in the scribbler the first thing that came into our mind, no matter what it was. It didn't matter if the story made sense or was logical, we were free to make it as silly or as odd as we liked. Writing this way was a brand new experience and when combined with a voracious appetite for reading Ray Bradbury and Edgar Allan Poe, my imagination was fueled. No one other than Mr. DeLong saw what I wrote, and he encouraged my odd flights of fancy, with high marks and comments such as "good stuff," "interesting," and "amusing." When I wrote for him I could be-come whomever I wanted on paper and no stutter got in the way.

Gradually I did discover ways to avoid stuttering. I knew that there wasn't anything really wrong with my tongue or my lips because I could read a passage from a book out loud without any problem. It made sense to me that if only I could visualize the words in my mind, the stuttering would disappear. Around this time, a teacher wanted the school to put on a one-act play. Cynthia was eager to try out for a part and with a bit of arm twisting and double-daring I agreed to try too. We both got small parts and spent after school play-time at her house learning our lines together. I discovered that once I memorized the lines and knew ahead of time what I was going to say, the chance of stuttering became virtually non-existent. The play was set in Mexico and had something to do with a wedding and we got to wear white puffed-sleeve blouses and flouncy skirts with fringed shawls. The best part was getting to wear lots of makeup, bright red lips and rouged cheeks, colourful eyeshadow and for me, since I was playing an older woman, dark etched lines on my forehead. The stage was a makeshift raised platform set up at one end of the gymnasium. You had to be careful walking onto the stage not to touch the cardboard walls so as not to cause the whole set to shake. There were so many things to think about, when to enter, when to speak, what lines to say, where to move, that I didn't have a chance to worry about stuttering. The lines that I had repeated over and over to learn, so many times, came out easily. This, I figured, was a way to help my everyday speech. At home I practiced speaking slowly so that I could form the thoughts in my mind before I said the words aloud. Dad had built me a study corner in my bedroom and with my door closed I practiced in private. There was a mirror on the wall and by staring at my reflection I pretended imaginary conversations with my friends. Little by little the stutter disappeared and by the time I finished grade nine it was hardly noticeable at all.

In 1974 I entered grade ten at Saint John High School. Saint John High was housed in an imposing, big, old brick building that solidly represented years of educating the young people of Saint John. I walked down the hallways studded with decades of shoe marks and could see graduating class photographs dating back to the early 1900s. Both my father and my uncle John had graduated from this school and I loved to spot their clean-cut, youthful faces—proof positive they were once young. They had traveled these same halls and stairs and with enough searching, I felt I might find a desk or chair with their initials secretly carved into the wood. Dad had gone on to medical school and a successful career as a surgeon. It was very apparent to me that by entering

Saint John High I was taking the first important step in pursuing my own dreams.

Saint John High contained a large auditorium and stage that was at that time the main performing venue for theatrical and musical events in town. Both the Fredericton-based Theatre New Brunswick and the Atlantic Symphony from Halifax, Nova Scotia, regularly performed on this stage. The school was basically built around the hall and on occasion, while walking to or from class, a monitor standing in the hallway outside the heavy wooden doors leading into the auditorium would shush our too lively conversation. The stage provided the perfect opportunity for large-scale school productions and Andrew Garrod, an English teacher at Saint John High, embraced this opportunity. Each year, outside of the regular school curriculum, he organized and directed several student theatrical performances.

The first play I saw directed by Andrew Garrod was William Shakespeare's *Romeo and Juliet.* For two and a half hours I sat in the darkened auditorium, entranced, completely caught up in another world. I was stunned. This was a far cry from the one-act play I'd been part of at Prince Charles. The sets, the costumes—everything about the production was elaborate and detailed and looked very professional. This was no amateur student production to my eyes; this was the real thing. As I sat and watched, I gradually forgot that the players on the stage were student actors and I felt myself become a part of something much greater than ordinary life. I was familiar with this sensation when "lost" in a book-created world. Here, instead of the experience occurring in the intimacy of a cozy armchair, the story, created by actors not much older than I, unfolded on a stage for my eyes to see. The two students who played the roles of Romeo and Juliet were so beautiful and convincingly in love that it was easy to suspend belief and to forget that they were "acting". Juliet had fine, delicate features and long, thick, dark hair that fell below her slender waist while Romeo embodied tender yet masculine youth. I was drawn by their love for each other and the final death scene left me anguished and saddened long after the curtain fell. Later, seeing "Juliet" in the hallways of the school was disconcerting—I retained a lasting impression of her character on stage, a character imbued with qualities far removed from the daily routine of classes and schoolwork. In my mind she had not yet completely thrown off the cloak of Juliet, and I purposely avoided talking to her, and covertly watched her from a distance, not wanting to break the spell.

In the new year, Andrew Garrod held auditions for a spring production of *West Side Story,* a fitting companion to *Romeo and Juliet.* I was ablaze with hope that I could be a part of this magical world of make believe. The auditions were in three parts—dancing, speaking and singing. I had a fine singing voice—voice lessons with Mrs. Lund at her walk-up second storey apartment every Thursday after school and years of church choir had molded a clear and true soprano. Singing was just another way of making music and as such, held no special fear. Music was as natural for me as breathing; I couldn't remember not playing an instrument of some sort, whether it be piano, violin, recorder or clarinet. I wasn't nervous about the speaking audition either—by this time I'd had many chances to speak in front of others, and the fear of stuttering was a distant memory. However, a dancing audition was another thing altogether, a completely unknown factor. Aside from school "sock hops" and square dancing (girls only) in grade eight, I had never danced under the scrutiny of judging eyes. Most of my more adventurous dancing had taken place behind securely closed living room doors, to my parents' records played on the family record player—Nancy Sinatra, James Last. I had no idea what I would be asked to do at the dance audition and whether I'd be able to meet the test.

The other aspiring actors and actresses and I gathered together on a Saturday morning on the stage of the auditorium. Andrew Garrod introduced us to a woman who would be choreographing the dance scenes, and who would, together with Mr. Garrod, decide which of the students would become dancing members of the chorus. This woman wasn't a teacher at Saint John High—I think she was some sort of a dance professional from another city (probably New York) and was assisting our school as a favor to Mr. Garrod. I was quite impressed that a person from outside the school was helping us.

We warmed up with a series of stretching exercises, and it quickly became apparent that there were those among us for whom the exercises were familiar. A few could even manage the highly enviable feat of doing the "splits." I felt clumsy and stiffly inflexible, but as I looked around I noticed that I was not alone. In truth, the experienced dancers were in the minority. It was an odd mix of students, and I was surprised at how many "Jocks" had turned out in anticipation of getting a part in the musical. At Saint John High there was a clear delineation between the Jocks and the rest of the student body. The Jocks tended to be the largest, strongest and most physically adept students in the school and they would gather and commandeer the benches in the hallway near the entrance to the gymnasium. I used to hate passing by them on my way to the other wing of the school, feeling their scrutiny, feeling I always felt terribly insecure and afraid that they would make fun of me, whether it was how I moved or how I dressed. I had become very painfully self-conscious of my body and the thick glasses I wore to correct my near-sightedness and hoped that I was invisible. They epitomized to me what it was to be normal and acceptable and popular and it seemed they were always in a group, surrounded by friends, among them the prettiest girls in the school. They appeared very self-assured and nonchalant about their masculinity. I was surprised that these same students would be willing to participate in a theatre production, let alone to sing and dance on stage, exhibiting characteristics I associated with gentleness and femininity.

As the dance workout progressed, I soon had no time to worry about the other students or what they were thinking about me. Instead, I was anxiously trying to keep up with the fast pace as the dance instructor led us through the complicated routines. One after the other we ran and jumped and turned across the stage with barely time to catch a breath on the other side. There was no time to hesitate, no time to think "I can't do this"—I was swept up in the momentum of the constantly counted beat. I had to keep moving and following the person in front, avoiding the person on my heels. It was both exhilarating and nerve-racking at the same time and when the session was over, I hoped that I managed to pass muster with the expectations of the judges.

When Andrew Garrod posted the cast list on the bulletin board a few days later, my heart thrilled to see that I had made it into the chorus. I would get a chance to sing and to dance as one of the Puerto Rican girls. I loved the scene created around the song "I Want to Be in America" and I danced with all the energy I could muster to the fiery latin beat. Most impressive to look at was the spectacularly massive arrangement of metal scaffolding which created the set. For the final scene the chorus members had to drape themselves on this scaffolding and hold the pose in a freeze while at center stage Maria discovers the dead body of Tony. Though Garrod wanted the scene to look dramatic he also warned us to choose a pose carefully as we would have to hold still for a considerable time. It was vital that the chorus members be still so as not to draw the audience's attention away from the action at center stage. I found a position with arms outstretched on the scaffolding and felt comfortable and relaxed as the freeze began. However, as the long minutes ticked by, my arm muscles became increasingly tired and I started to worry that I wouldn't be able to hold the pose long enough. I knew if I moved, Garrod and everyone else in the audience would notice and I'd ruin the effect of the scene. I held on and willed my body to stay still even though my arms were aching. With relief the moment came when I was allowed to move again. I had made it through the scene without losing control and my heart started beating hard as I felt a rush of adrenalin. It was exciting to have taken this risk in front of so many and to meet the challenge. Even though my part was small, to me it had become a vital element that, together with everything else, combined to create the illusion on stage. From this moment on, I would always associate this particular thrill with the act of performing in front of an audience.

My appetite for the stage whetted, the next year I again auditioned and played a chorus member in the musical *Camelot*. In truth, what I really desired was a speaking part, but that biggest honour went to Philippa Mugglestone, whom George Fry chose to play the part of Lady Guinevere. Pippa lived down the street from me, barely a block away. Though she was a year younger than I, we had an easy friendship. She was of English background, spoke with an accent and seemed very witty and sophisticated. She would bring Monty Python recordings to my home and as we listened to them she roared in laughter at humor that I tried and failed to comprehend. Pippa had the most extraordinary blond hair that fell straight from her delicately boned head to her waist. I was slightly envious of Pippa's good looks and luck in getting such a big part in the play, but I don't remember any true animosity. Pippa loved to pretend to put on "airs" and act theatrically and this made her just quirky enough to not be perfect. There was a group of us at school in grade eleven who, rather than trying to fit in with the crowd, took an alternative approach and strived to make very oddness that kept us out of the mainstream a desirable characteristic. I had given up trying to look fashionable—girls idolized the Farrah Fawcett look, and I knew that I could never look even vaguely like her even if I had wanted to. Instead I found my image in my dad's closet where I dug out old sweaters and overalls, patched and moth-eaten. These I wore without any concern about looking beautiful. These clothes were a form of costume—they covered up insecurity and shyness about my looks and I felt that if I purposely dressed and acted strangely it would be this character who would be made fun of—the real person inside protected and hidden from view.

In the summer of 1976 my parents finally relented and allowed me to wear contact lenses to replace my hated glasses. I entered grade twelve starting to feel like a new person, no longer self-conscious about a pair of thick glasses on my face. Andrew Garrod announced that the school would present not one but two main stage productions— Shakespeare's *As You Like It* and the musical *Guys and Dolls*. I felt I had a better chance of getting a speaking part this year, but I was completely amazed when Garrod choose me to play the role of Rosalind in *As You Like It*. I felt honoured and excited to have such an opportunity, to play a lead part.

I started immediately to learn the many lines. At the public library I found a sound recording of the play with Vanessa Redgrave speaking the role of Rosalind and I listened carefully and critically to her inflection of the words, even though I felt slightly guilty about this imitation, as if I were somehow cheating. In rehearsal, Garrod helped me through the script and his sharp ear would catch any line I spoke that didn't make sense. It was frustrating to deal with so many unfamiliar expressions and words, especially since the script was full of literary puns, the sort of jokes that are not so much funny as witty and clever. Rosalind's character loved this play on words—barely could she utter a line without some sort of subtle secondary meaning hidden in jest. Yet often the phrases were incomprehensible to me, such as when she finds love verses addressed to her and says to her companion Celia: "I was seven of the nine days out of the wonder before you came; for look here what I found on a palm-tree: I was never so be-rimed since

Pythagoras' time, that I was an Irish rat, which I can hardly remember." The references were completely unfamiliar to me, yet somehow I had to make the lines sound natural and believable. Practicing the lines in front of my bedroom mirror reminded me of the practice I had done a few years earlier. What a long way I had come since then! Now, instead of worrying about a stutter I was worrying about which word to accentuate and whether to end the sentence with a rising or a falling inflection. Finding my way around the words was not unlike finding my way around a new melody—the sound I gave to each word contributed to the meaning of the line—and the changes in pitch helped me to accurately recall the words.

Andrew Garrod chose Brent Bambury to play the part of Orlando, the character Rosalind falls in love with in the play. I had been on stage with Brent before, in *Camelot*, where acting as members of King Arthur's court we stood and pretended to talk to one another during a scene. I liked Brent and I had liked it when he took my hand in his as we stood together. I also knew Brent through his friendship with Pippa—they spent a lot of time together even though not in the sense of boyfriend and girlfriend.

Brent had a gentle manner and an attractive appearance that was a charming mix of masculinity and youthfulness. In our scenes together his character was very believable, so much so that it stirred confusing emotions in me. He seemed so sincere in his love for Rosalind, I couldn't help thinking that part of the attraction was aimed at me. However, away from the stage, though I would search for some sign, he gave no indication of any interest in my company. He seemed much more comfortable with Pippa, and I felt like a tag-along when I was with both of them.

In Act III, Rosalind, while disguised as a boy, meets Orlando in the forest of Arden. She manages to convince Orlando that the only way to cure his unrequited love sickness for Rosalind, is to imagine me his love, his mistress. By pretending to be effeminate, changeable, proud, fantastical, apish, shallow, inconstant, full of tears, full of smiles Rosalind claims that this will wash him clean of love and he will suffer no more. Willing to take part in such a game, Orlando plays along. These were my favorite scenes to play as Rosalind—in the forest pretending to be a boy, in love with Orlando, yet only able to show my affection under disguise. I let Rosalind occasionally slip out of her disguise and expose to the audience her true love for Orlando, while keeping Orlando fooled. However, my "real-life" emotions toward Brent made the part more difficult, and I struggled with this extra dimension of confusion. Whereas Rosalind would finally reveal all in the play, I kept everything hidden.

At some point, after a futile search for some sign of attraction from Brent, I finally had to conclude and accept that any emotions I might be sensing from him on the stage, were only those in keeping with his role as Orlando. I still liked Brent, and now that I could think of him only as a friend, it was easier to play the role of Rosalind opposite him. It was a lesson in learning to separate my own personal feelings from those of Rosalind's and not to confuse relationships on stage with relationships between friends. I was glad I had not made a fool of myself by saying anything to Brent that would embarrass either of us. Now when Orlando replied, "I would kiss before I spoke" to Rosalind's "Come, woo me, woo me; for now I am in a holiday humor, and like enough to consent. What would you say to me now, an I were your very very Rosalind?" my mind only focused on the role of Rosalind and how I imagined this spirited and charming young woman would react.

I admired Rosalind's character; not only was she well-liked by all, quick to reply with a witty remark, kind and intelligent, but also able to make the best of whatever situation she found herself in. When banished by the Duke, she turns the banishment into an daring adventure, taking on the clothing and appearance of a man.

> We'll have a swashing and a martial outside,
> As many other mannish cowards have
> That do outface it with their semblances.

Of all the elements that made up Rosalind, this daring spirit I loved the most. She was willing to keep her fear hidden, to disguise herself and venture forth into unknown circumstances and possible danger. Through all she is triumphant, and in the end, when it is safe for her to remove her disguise, she and Orlando are finally together.

*As You Like It* ends with an epilogue given by Rosalind, where for the first and only time in the play, she speaks directly to the audience. Standing at the front of the stage and facing the audence alone, the fourth wall disappears and through Rosalind, I appealed to the audience:

> I charge you, O women! for the love you bear to men, to like as much of this play as please you: and I charge you, O men! for the love you bear to women,—as I perceive by your simpering none of you hate them,—that between you and the women, the play may please.

Though still in character, I was suddenly aware of my youth and aware that it was less Rosalind who addressed the audience, and more myself, the high school student, who so brazenly spoke to my elders: "O men … I would kiss as many of you as had beards that pleased me." The thin veil that hung between the play and the audience had all but disappeared and it was Heather who was daring and charming and witty—my guise as Rosalind had slipped away for a moment. During the previous scenes, I had taken on the words and actions of the character Rosalind, and I hadn't felt that I was exposing any of my own vulnerability behind the protection of the script. Like the moth-eaten sweaters I wore to school, Rosalind's character enveloped and protected my own insecurities. However, standing at the lip of the stage and directly speaking to the audience sitting in the darkened auditorium, even though the words continued to be provided by the script, I sensed that my own spirit was no longer completely hidden from view. Though I felt vulnerable, I also realized in that moment an emotional connection with the audience—an audience who, with silent attention and on equal footing, had taken part in the evening's creation. Perhaps this was why, despite the slight quavering I could hear in my voice, I was able to speak with increasing confidence and strength. I faced the audience unafraid and spoke the words of advice to my elders, reversing the usual relationship between parent/adult and child. Standing alone, I became aware of my own self-worth, my ability to draw upon emotions inside of me and, through the skills of communication, affect the emotions of others.

Away from the stage, I was preparing to leave home after the completion of grade twelve in order to gain further musical education. In a new city, far from my family and friends, I looked forward to an opportunity to start afresh, to leave my insecurities behind in Saint John and to become the kind of person I admired—daring, outgoing, confident.

Today I make my living as a musician, performing with the Victoria Symphony. The glimmer of an emotional connection with the audience that I sensed reciting the words of Rosalind's epilogue I still strive for today. In preparing for a performance I carefully practice the notes, plan the particular nuances and dynamics, work out the technical problems. When the music is finally performed before an audience I attempt to recreate accurately the particular phrasing and articulation that had been successful in rehearsal. However, no matter the amount of preparation beforehand, the moments I cherish the most are those when I feel most vulnerable, when I am able to touch upon an inner part of the music that had previously been hidden from me and reach out and communicate this feeling to the audience. The instrument in my hands disappears and the sounds become a direct embodiment of my inner expression. As my skill as a musician develops, my ability to respond to the demands of the music and to take greater risks with the music grows. By taking risks and not being content with a mere duplication of notes, the music becomes a living force and the act of creation results in emotions of exhilaration and satisfaction. Just as Rosalind bravely set off into the Forest of Arden, I too ignore my fears and willingly face the challenges ahead.

*Heather Chesley wrote this essay more than twenty years ago. Since then she made the decision to go to law school, obtain a law degree, go on to practice law and become a partner with a highly respected law firm in Victoria, British Columbia. Heather practices primarily estate litigation which takes her onto a new stage, the courtroom. As one would write a play, in the courtroom the trial is roughly scripted out with each participant playing a different role in real time. The decision makers are the audience. As an advocate for her clients, Heather recognizes her duty to perform well, and doing so involves much advance planning and preparation. Ultimately whether acting in a play, taking part in a musical performance (which she stills does) or being a lawyer in the courtroom, Heather understands it is all about effective communication.*

# My Characters

Harun Hasanagić
BOSNIA AND HERZEGOVINA

I'm a pretty standard example of a young Mostarian. When we have time on our hands, we sit for hours drinking coffee with the people we enjoy, often doing this multiple times a day. It sounds dull, but if you do it in Mostar, it's like a drug. You look forward to drinking coffee while you are drinking coffee. But one day I made a tough call and decided to break this habit by joining a crew of foreign people who were producing Shakespeare's *Much Ado About Nothing* in my hometown. My reason was simple: I was told that it would be more fun than drinking coffee and talking all day long (a hard sell, if you ask me). I did not know what I was getting myself into, nor did I have previous experience in theatre, and I had but slight curiosity about how everything was going to play out. I knew I had a gift when it came to words—I knew how to talk to people, I could sense how they felt while I was talking, and I always cherished my ability to, most of the time at least, maintain my sincerity. Sincerity is very important to me. I'll choose it over feeling good, even when getting to that point isn't pleasant. So, I thought it would be good to try out my acting skills in the controlled environment that was this play—a situation in which you cannot choose your words and you are at the behest of a character that lives in some playwright's words. So you see, my reason for getting into the play was pragmatic. But, I cannot stop my essay at this point because I still can't fully grasp why being a part of the play was, and still is, such an important part of my life and my development.

Acting was amazing. It was liberating and I felt free while doing it, and it helped me find a beautiful personal irony, which lay in the fact that my lines were determined by someone else.

Some would say that there's not much freedom in being controlled by a dead playwright. When you as an actor truly step into the shoes of a character, your life is written, your words are predetermined, and all you have to do is live that life, as best as you can, in front of an audience.

In *Much Ado About Nothing*, I lived my life as Leonato, a protective and caring father, an honorable man, a person who admits and rectifies his mistakes—all in all, a good example of what any man who lived in his times should strive to be. I liked this role because it felt good to become an old man with a sense of responsibility that stems from authority. There are many ways of portraying him, but I chose to play him as a man who truly wants what is best for his loved ones. Leonato's intentions, no matter how clandestine they seemed at times, were of more value to me than his actions that could be interpreted as erroneous. In my mind, his exaggerated reaction and immediate acceptance of the accusation that his daughter was promiscuous, and his wish for his own daughter's death—"Do not live, Hero. Do not ope thine eyes"—was always shadowed by my vision of him as an honorable man and the fact that his justified cunning is one reason the story has a happy ending. I believed that Leonato deeply wanted what was good for all, and that his actions were never the product of malevolence. I loved the play, and it provided a decent entry into acting. I also found that I didn't really understand Leonato and other characters from the play the way other people thought I did. It was difficult for me to put myself into the moral framework of the time in which *Much Ado* takes place. For example, I don't think I would react to someone accusing my daughter of being promiscuous with a burst of near-murderous rage.

After reading more than a few articles analyzing *Much Ado*, I learned that there is a plethora of opinions about Leonato. While one critic notes that he is a controlling father who is simultaneously wise and easily swayed, others view him as an honorable and generous character; this includes some theatre professionals. Some view him as being easily influenced by the people around him, such as believing the accusations; some see him as a man of trickery, as he is part of the plot to convince Beatrice and Benedick to fall in love; and some naturally consider him a just man. I could not see him as being influenced by others and as a trickster at the same time, so I decided that his compass gets disturbed when his honor is attacked, or that he trusts people who, like himself, hold high office. Being a young man who was born into and has lived a life gravely affected by uncountable national, religious, and political differences—you name it, Bosnia has had it—a mere difference of opinion was nothing out of the ordinary for me. Thus, it was crucial that I did not just accept that other people didn't see Leonato the way I did; I had to trust my view of him, trust that I was right to think that he is an important, experienced, and highly capable man of honor and strong morals, and play my role accordingly.

To play Leonato comfortably, I had to believe that he is not influenced by others because he is gullible but because he holds them in high regard, and that the mistakes he makes, especially with his daughter, are not a product of a flawed character. In my mind, they were due to his being extremely sensitive to issues of honor. Most importantly, I was comfortable knowing that the show would go on regardless of what anyone thinks about anything and that my assessment of Leonato was of no real importance. What mattered was that I could mold him to be closer to my ideal of a good man, as playing him as a gullible, easily influenced person did not feel right. Seeing that differences among people, especially differences of opinion, are something you can be comfortable with and forget about is an important thing I got out of acting.

In my youth, I studied in a high school in which Bosniaks and Croats attended different classes in the same facility. It would be fair to characterize it as a segregated school. Many foreign and local activists visited the school and held conversations with students (including me) about the war that had occurred in Bosnia and Herzegovina, including in Mostar, and about the ethnic tension that was apparent in our current surroundings. Somehow, every time we spoke to these activists, the conversation would stray into someone explaining to us how everyone loved each other in Tito's Yugoslavia and how our differences don't matter because it was "fine and dandy" in the past, and it could be like that in the future. I always had the feeling that these people were overly romantic about our unique experience; how could they hold our differences in high regard without being aware of how dangerous they could be? I think their view that the various peoples of Bosnia and Herzogovina loved each other before and can love each other in the future is pathetic romanticism. I would be lying if I said that I love and cherish differences, because I've witnessed how differences can lead to mass slaughter, concentration camps, and genocide. I always believed that tragedy is the endgame of differences.

We had a mixed cast of Bosniaks, Croats, and Serbs while working on *Much Ado*. This is where you mustn't get me wrong. At the beginning, I didn't like the fact that we had a mixed team. I thought it was going to be another one of those NGO things, where people who never experienced, let alone understood, war and hatred were going to come over to Mostar and tell us, the misguided youth of Bosnia, how we should love and care for each other. I was wrong. I'm glad I was wrong. The crew that worked with the cast weren't paying any more attention to these interethnic schisms then I was. A lot of foreigners who came to Bosnia spoke as if everything around us was somehow connected to the war, but this group did not. Being relieved of the burden of repeatedly saying I don't care much about our divisions felt really good.

When crossing the Old Bridge in Mostar, you would hear them say, "Ooh, look at the remains of the bridge by the river; it was destroyed during the WAR." When taking a stroll through the center of the city, someone would say, "This place used to be called the Boulevard of National Revolution, it was a symbol of unity before the WAR; now we just call it the Boulevard." Aggressive rivalry between the two football clubs in Mostar was always looked upon as something that came about after, you guessed it, the WAR. People, especially those from First World countries, have the nasty habit of categorizing locals in Bosnia into two groups—as if the ones we had before weren't enough! The first group are the enlightened locals who love, the second are the misguided locals who hate. I felt this habit was moronic and shallow, and I never experienced anything such thing while doing the play. We focused on Shakespeare more than we focused on each other, and this was splendid. Maybe the general acceptance of everyone who took part in the production is why I found acting to be liberating.

The same crew of people came to Mostar again. By this time they had become my friends and I wanted to spend some time with them. We could have done this by applying the Mostarian formula—drinking an unhealthy amount of coffee together—but, this time I had a motive that surpassed fun and comfort. I wanted to act!

I really wanted to play Shakespeare's Prospero in *The Tempest,* and sure enough, I was cast in that role. Most of the time I worked with Nina, a friend who was cast as Ariel, a cheerful, witty spirit imprisoned by Prospero and forced to serve him. We had a great dynamic, a warm wizard-servant kind of relationship, and it was hard for me to participate in the scenes where Prospero lashes out at Ariel. Nina is a positive and energetic person, and she was so cheerful and loving as Ariel that I, as Prospero, had no choice but to respond in kind. She made me, as Prospero, see Ariel as a family member rather than a servant. Being so interdependent in our roles made me feel more confident, because we could rely on each other while we were on the stage. I was happier playing Prospero than Leonato, because Prospero wielded his authority through a frequent use of his power.

I hated having to scold and threaten Caliban in *The Tempest.* I couldn't rid myself of my own character and I thought Prospero should follow suit. I had problems chastising Caliban as a "freckled whelp, hag-born, not honoured with a human shape," but alas, I had to make peace with the fact that sometimes you simply have to act it out. I kept telling myself that Prospero is saying these things out of necessity. I think I looked at Prospero as the person I thought he should be, instead of seeing him as what he is. Maybe instead of seeing him a benevolent wizard I should have seen him as a slave-owning, racist, pragmatic sorcerer who wields his power undisturbed by morals, but it would have been difficult for me to act out a person with such horrible flaws. That's a beautiful aspect of acting; it's not all about technique, and sometimes it's about personality and morality. I know this isn't important to someone who analyzes this play as an expert or critic, but it is something I came away with from performing in *The Tempest.*

A similar thing happened when I thought about Leonato. I could never think of him only as cunning or just as a politician; for me to play him, he also had to be benevolent. I do not wish to be misunderstood; I'm not particularly inclined toward benevolent figures when it comes to acting, but in Leonato and Prospero I sought to find some deep, all-encompassing benevolence. Looking back at the plays, I now see that my feelings came from the fact that both Leonato and Prospero had been hurt and they did not deserve it. I also realize that my assessment of these characters has been influenced by my own experience. In short, it could have something to do with what happened to good people in Bosnia and Herzegovina.

I was rectifying the injustice we experienced with what happened to Prospero and Leonato. In specific contexts, a person to whom an injustice is done is just. A person who has been hurt must be capable, strong, and smart so they can overcome the injustice, and they must also be benevolent so they can enjoy and strive for justice. Maybe that's what was guiding me as I played these characters.

My experiences doing the plays were not all positive. When they were done, I discovered that I had gained a habit of acting in my everyday life. I would let out a laugh when someone told a joke that wasn't all that funny, or pretend that a conversation was more interesting than it really was. These tiny everyday "plays" that I acted out with the unsuspecting people around me were not that troublesome, but they gave me a hint about a part of my character that I didn't like all that much. I found that I was prevailingly a people pleaser. Maybe I was like that before the plays and acting helped me see it, but in any case, I decided that it's more important to play a role well then it is to appease the audience. I think a lot of theatre actors want to be interrupted by applause and cheers of approval—this happened to me once in Mostar during Prospero's closing speech, and I won't lie, it felt good—but sometimes it's better to leave the audience in silent contemplation, to have them think about my character and actions before they applaud my performance.

I think the archaic language of Shakespeare's plays and some obviously far-fetched scenes help keep the actors' feet on the ground, but this brings me to another point. Although I love his plays, I feel that the language of the plays hides their true potential. I almost hated having to use pretty archaic English/Bosnian to convey the deep messages and emotions that live in Shakespeare's plays. Amateur actors will learn their lines well but will have difficulty understanding their characters through Shakespeare's English, which makes it hard to identify with the characters and to convey their emotions. Don't get me wrong—everyone will have fun, but some part of the audience will not feel Caliban's pain or understand Leonato's intentions or hope for justice for Prospero. In short, I took some issue with the language of the plays because I felt I couldn't fully express myself. I think that, in some instances, Shakespeare's plays would be better received if they were played in the local language or modern English.

The way I think about these characters has given me insight into my own character and my subconscious. I have discovered my inclination for orderly conduct in the way we treat others. This worried me, especially when I took a liking to characters who are truly benevolent but enforce their benevolence with an iron hand. Prospero was such a character. As I explored his relationship with Caliban, I could see how someone's concept of benevolence could lead to unhealthy results. I must admit, I still have an inclination toward the forceful enforcement of fairness and what is right, but the underlying tone of colonization that is recognized in contemporary analyses of Shakespeare's *The Tempest* has made me more careful in judging what is right and what is wrong.

Although I can't fully grasp why being part of these plays has been so important for me, as I conclude this essay I see that what I've written paints a pretty good picture. Facing the challenges of acting out Leonato and Prospero enabled me to explore parts of my own character that I didn't know were there. In a way, the experience made me pay more attention to myself and my ideals.

I still have many thoughts about *Much Ado About Nothing* and *The Tempest*, not as dramas or "life lesson" plays but as personal experiments in moral philosophy. An actor should not be a mannequin; he should bring a spark of himself to the characters, and not only identify with a character but look at it the other way around. It is liberating to carefully mold a piece of your character with your own views and your own experiences. I've done a lot of thinking about Leonato and Prospero, and it would be fair to say that this process has helped me grow. I don't know whether playing these characters substantially changed me or if I changed them, but in the end, there is no doubt about how much I have grown.

*Harun Hasanagić, MA, is a jurist who also works as a tourist guide in Mostar and operates his own workshop, where he specializes in traditional Bosnian woodcarving. He was born April 24, 1990, in Čapljina, Bosnia and Herzegovina. He fled Bosnia during the 1992–95 war and spent his early childhood in a refugee camp in Turkey. He later settled in Mostar, where he completed his studies and graduated from law school. While at law school, he took part in the production of two plays,* Much Ado About Nothing *and* The Tempest, *as an amateur actor.*

*After finishing law school in 2012, he earned a degree in international/maritime law from Ankara Uinversity. From 2016 to 2019 he worked as a project manager/event organizer for the Yunus Emre Institute in Mostar. He is fluent in Bosnian, English, and Turkish. This essay was written in 2022.*

# The Play's the Thing

Robert Silver

CANADA

It was a chilly, fog–laden afternoon. I could hear the deep muffled tones of a foghorn and the wailing cries of seagulls far off in the North Sea. The smell of the salt air was almost overwhelming. I began to shake intensely from the cold as the wind accelerated, creating a hollow whistling sound through the castle towers above me. Though surrounded by close friends and associates, I felt isolated, as though I was in a world of my own. Still, I could barely contain my excitement. Here I was in Elsinore, Denmark, at Kronberg, Hamlet's Castle with an opportunity to relive a pivotal memory from my past in the most vivid sense.

In 1972, as a senior high school student, I was honored with the title role in our high school's production of *Hamlet*. The role of Hamlet was different than any other part I had had. While in previous productions, my goal had been to effectively portray the characters I played, my objective as Hamlet was to *become* the character. I didn't want the audience to look onstage and see Rob Silver playing Hamlet; I had to make them believe that I *was* the "Prince of Denmark."

As I stood looking over the walls of Hamlet's castle into the North Sea, the experience of my dramatic efforts years earlier gripped me. The words of Hamlet's soliloquy at the end of the second act, an intense moment in which he weaves his plan to expose his Uncle Claudius' wrongdoing, came back to me easily, hardly affected by their years of dormancy in my memory.

—"Bloody bawdy villain! Remorseless, treacherous, lecherous, kindless villain!" Visiting the Kronberg castle was a moment of peak intensity for me, a vivid déjà vu of a significant experience in my life.

What better way to conjure up the past than to recite this powerful passage from the play in the very place where Shakespeare had created this story, set nearly a millennium ago? There I stood, peering over the walls of Hamlet's castle on a cold, damp Danish afternoon, surrounded by the North Sea.

At that moment I felt connected to my adolescence. When I think about what has determined who I am—how I have become the physician and teacher that I am—I am always drawn to the warm and vivid memories of my adolescent days in theatre. It was the fall of 1970 and I was a fifteen-year-old living in the small port city of Saint John, New Brunswick. It was politically and socially a tumultuous time—the days of the Beatles, acid rock, LSD, glue-sniffing, Vietnam, Apollo missions to the moon, and Woodstock.

When I entered Saint John High School, I was determined to be involved in the school's highly regarded drama productions. I had very limited experience in theatre, but I knew there was a distinct part of me that liked to perform. I had appeared in my share of music festivals and competitions and was familiar with the rush of adrenalin and the cathartic release of energy which accompanied the anxiety and panic of performing before a live audience.

The most enjoyable aspect of performing in live productions was the opportunity to interact with the audience on an intimate level. To me, communicating effectively with my audience was always the most important aspect of my performance. One of my primary goals in acting was to make sure that they enjoyed themselves. My sense of duty and obligation towards the viewers in the dark superceded even my own need for self-fulfillment. I was there primarily for their enjoyment and critical appraisal.

That being said, however, performing in theatre was indeed a very fulfilling activity. It was an opportunity to be self-critical and analytical and, as such, it gave me a clearer idea as to the potential of my abilities, both as an actor onstage and as a person in real life. Never was this truer than in my preparation for *Hamlet*. The intense process of self-scrutiny within the first month of rehearsal, prior to going onstage, allowed me to become the character I was portraying. I came to realize that I was actually capable of knowing and expressing a wider variety of emotions than I had ever personally experienced. I could truly comprehend Hamlet's rage, not just on an intellectual level, but also on individual, internal level, as though I myself had lost my father to a traitorous uncle and a deceitful mother. The process was physically and emotionally exhausting.

Which brings me back to Elsinore, Denmark. As I peered over the walls of Kronberg that afternoon, the words of Hamlet on my tongue, I knew that, although my time at Saint John High School and my involvement with the drama club might be a distant memory, it would never lose its vitality. The recitation of that soliloquy was a remarkable experience for me. It was as though I had been transported back to my teenage years: I could still see the same faces, hear the same voices, and feel the same spirit, undaunted by the passing of time. For a moment I longed to return to those seemingly simpler days of my youth. I took solace in the fact that what I accomplished during my time on stage at Saint John High School was part of what had created the essence of who I am today. My involvement in drama had given me the confidence and self-esteem to believe that any accomplishment was within my grasp. As I gazed out at the Danish horizon, I realized that this attitude of determination and strength had served me well throughout my life. As I spoke the last lines of Hamlet's soliloquy at Kronberg Castle—"The play's the thing wherein I'll catch the conscience of the King"—I smiled, feeling proud of and grateful for my time at Saint John and marvelling at how the words through which I had explored the role of Hamlet and my adolescent self were still with me.

*Robert Silver is a clinician educator at the Toronto Western Hospital division of the University Health Network and professor of medicine at the University of Toronto. His medical school alma mater is Dalhousie University. He completed his internal medicine residency at the University of Toronto and his endocrinology fellowship at Harvard University. An educator of great passion and energy, he provides an estimated 700 hours per year of formal and informal teaching in the settings of one-on-one teaching in the office, seminars, case-based learning, bedside, large group teaching and small group teaching within the specialty of endocrinology. He facilitates learning at all levels including undergraduate, postgraduate and continuing education. He has supervised an estimated 2500 students in his thirty-seven years of clinical practice. His favorite teaching activity continues to be a weekly interactive problem-based learning session with his endocrinology residents and students entitled "Coffee, Crumpets and Questions." He has a special interest in methods of evaluation and the creation of new and novel approaches to interactive learning. Throughout his career, he has served on more than twenty different medical education committees, at the hospital, university divisional and faculty-wide levels. His most notable administrative role was that of education coordinator for the University Health Network/Mount Sinai Hospital Division of Endocrinology for twenty-eight years. For his efforts in teaching and administration, he has been the recipient of thirty-six career teaching awards. His passion for theatre and music forms the basis of his creativity and innovation in medical education, he considers teaching as an in vivo "performance," requiring great focus, energy and enthusiasm, an emphasis on effective communication and a desire to be creative in the process of "entertaining" his students. He encourages a free exchange of ideas, while maintaining a sense of humor to make the learning more fun, but above all, he maintains a mutual respect for and a willingness to learn from his students, all the while in a highly energetic and interactive format. Rob, who is now sixty-eight years old, wrote this essay when he was forty-six.*

# Benvolio: The Peacemaker

Clovis Shyaka

RWANDA

One hot summer day, my friend Patrick told me there was to be a casting for a play production happening a few miles away from my university. "Casting?" I asked. I had never heard that word before, nor had I acted professionally. Patrick, on the other hand, had been in a few music videos and had a fair understanding of what happens during casting. My priority at that time was school—I thought that only through education would I have a chance of a better life. I was thrilled to hear him say, "There will be a team of Americans and Canadians training the cast for many weeks if we get selected." English is my favorite language, and I was ready to grab this opportunity to improve my language skills. The play to be performed was Shakespeare's *Romeo and Juliet,* so Patrick and I watched the movie *West Side Story*—which is a musical version of the play that takes place on the streets of New York—to have an idea about the plot, and we did some research on acting. This gave us an idea of what to expect.

Two young women were waiting at the door of the SOS, the Technical High School in Kigali, where the auditions were to be held. One was holding a camera with both hands, and the other was giving out a number to each person who came to the casting. I was quite nervous, for I had decided I *had* to get a part in the play, or my chance to boost my English skills would slip out of my grasp. It was a hot summer afternoon: we stood quietly outside for a short moment, waiting for the staff to tell us what to do next. An old man wearing khaki jeans and an old white hat came out of the school meeting hall, took off his hat, scratched his bald head, stopped for a few seconds, and continued walking toward the main gate. He looked both frustrated and nervous at the same time. It later became clear that his worries related to the fact that people didn't show up for the auditions until an hour later than the advertised time. An interesting twist happened when his worry changed from "We might not have enough showing up" to "How am I going to select a small number from such a big crowd?"

For the auditions, a scenario was described and we were asked to act it out. I was invited to run to a Catholic priest to tell him about the death of my girlfriend. I assumed the aim was to test my expressive powers. The auditioners were seated in a circle, and I felt all eyes were centered on me. I sensed an overwhelming pressure; my hands were shaking, my vision was blurry, and my armpits were sweaty. Suddenly, my nerves calmed, and I figured that I would just give it my all to see how well I could do. After the improvisations were complete and everyone had auditioned, we were asked to go home and wait for a text message later that day, should we be selected. I waited until I was almost sure I hadn't made it, but just as I put my phone away I heard a "ping!" and rushed to see what it was. It was a message from an unknown number, and it read, "You have been selected to be part of *Romeo and Juliet*." I was the happiest I ever had been at that moment and couldn't believe I had earned a part. I couldn't wait for that night to end so I could attend the orientation.

The traffic in Kigali is crazy in the morning. Buses take forever to get to their destination, and the smart move when one is in a rush is to use moto taxi. It's not the safest way but surely the fastest way during Kigali rush hours. These drivers will find a way to get between the crowded vehicles in the tiniest spaces. I needed to be on time for the orientation, so I used the fastest alternative, which got me there 40 minutes early. Andrew Garrod, the man I had seen at the audition coming out of the SOS meeting hall, was standing at the main gate of the school. This time, he was glowing! "Are you here for *Romeo and Juliet*?" he asked as he approached me. "Yes!" I replied excitedly. "Lovely," he said as he smiled at me. I thought to myself, what a nice man! Arriving early got me a little extra time to chat with staff members while waiting for the rest of the cast to show up. Kayley, a Canadian and probably the youngest of the team, seemed curious, while Charlotte had her hands full of production details. She was organizing the scripts, writing on her iPad, and performing acrobatic stretches every now and then. Tess, another Canadian, had already used her favorite word, "slama," meaning "all good." Ray, a well-built African American man, sat in the corner drawing things that would later become stage decorations. He was focused on his work and didn't talk much. He would later choreograph the fight scenes in *Romeo and Juliet*.

An hour later, everyone was there, and we gathered in the SOS meeting hall. Sitting in a circle on the floor, everyone introduced themself, starting with Andrew Garrod, who we found out was the director and the mind behind the whole project. He admitted that it was not an easy job to cast this play, for there were many good candidates for the roles but few slots to fill. We then did warm-up exercises and played all kinds of games, probably so we could become familiar with each other. My favorite was a staring contest. You had to stare at someone until they smiled at you, and when they did, they became "it." Abdoul, who played Mercutio in the play, was particularly good at this game. He had his fun way of making things naughty. Every time he stared at someone with his incredible smile, everyone burst into laughter.

The text of *Romeo and Juliet* is quite long. However, most of us having watched *West Side Story,* the readings went much faster than if we were hearing the story for the first time. We took the script to study at night, and in the next few days the group readings began. Of all the characters in the play, I found Benvolio particularly important. He didn't have a title, nor was he portrayed as a vital person in the story, but I found him to be the glue that held everyone together. He shielded Romeo from the ridiculous and dangerous advice of Mercutio and prevented fights from breaking out. He was a logical person who never let emotion get the best of him, and he did everything with humility. He seemed to me like someone who, instead of standing in the spotlight for the grand bow, goes in behind the curtain to ensure that the bow is truly grand. The character spoke deeply to my soul because it embodied the person I aspired to be—a peacemaker and a benevolent influence on society. I wanted to do something beneficial for the community, not for everyone else to see but for my own feeling of self-worth. Unfortunately, I did not know what I needed to do to feel that way.

Director Andrew Garrod, who already had earned our respect, welcomed us as we entered the rehearsal hall and read out the final character assignments. Benvolio, the part I was after, was still a major role in the play, and no matter how much I desired to get that part, it seemed a long shot. I thought the rest of the cast had more advantages than I did but, surprisingly, I got the part! "Benvolio: Clovis!" said Andrew. I couldn't believe it. At the end of rehearsal that day, I approached Andrew and asked him, "How and why me?" My memory of that conversation is a blur, but it seemed like he knew I was perfect for the part. I later observed that there was perhaps a correlation between the character of the individual actors and their roles in the play.

To understand this correlation and my reason for wanting so desperately to play the role of Benvolio, you have to understand a little of my own background and the recent violent background of my country, Rwanda. Now a scientist, my job is to understand why things happen in the hope of making something out of it. Despite my strong desire to make sense of what happened in my country, I will never understand the degree of cruelty that was unleashed in the genocide the Hutus carried out against the Tutsis in Rwanda more than 28 years ago. Traumatic testimonials of Tutsi survivors describe unspeakable tragedies that no one should ever have to go through. We have heard of children, now in their late twenties, who sat by their mother's dead body, thinking she would wake up and take them home to safety. Not having known death, they thought all they needed to do was to wait long enough for their mother to wake up, heal their wounds, or just shelter them from the cold, rainy April nights. We have read testimonials from people whose entire family was destroyed in front of their eyes, while they survived only by a miracle or by being taken for dead. No matter how I might try to paint the picture of this dark time in the history of humanity, it always comes out as an extreme understatement. There are no words that can express well enough the pain and suffering the Tutsi people endured in April 1994.

Over a million Tutsis were killed in only about a hundred days of persecution. It was not strangers who invaded the country and started butchering citizens—it was next-door neighbors, people once considered friends. In a number of cases, people murdered their spouses. Have these people always hated each other? No, it was not a situation where one greets a person with their right hand but holds a rock in the left. Rwanda's people lived together in perfect harmony. Tutsi married Hutu, they shared land and cattle, and the enemy of Rwanda was the enemy of all. But, the Hutus then turned against the Tutsis and set out to slaughter them with machetes—a slaughter that was meticulously planned by the wicked government which, with the help of colonialists, spread the genocidal ideology that later led to so many Tutsi perishing.

When the genocide was stopped by young people who were organized by the Rwanda Patriotic Front, the country was on the edge of collapse. "Everything was a priority," said President Kagame during a genocide commemoration. The infrastructure was demolished, hospitals and schools had been razed to the ground. Despite the urgent need to rebuild, mending the hearts of so many who had lost loved ones and ensuring that what happened never occurs again became the top priority.

The journey of reconciliation started right away, in an attempt to avoid the vengeance that could result in a never-ending circle of violence. Rwanda's new leadership created highly efficient post-genocide reconciliation programs, and some 28 years later, Rwanda is a country whose people see what binds them together rather than what separates them. The results are clear in the level and speed at which Rwanda has developed, due to the collective effort of Rwandans. We have come so far and we are never going back. However, against all reason, some people still embrace genocidal ideology and silently harbor hatred in their heart. This is one reason why it would be a mistake to forget the past and to take the reconciliation and peacemaking activities for granted. Constant education is needed if we are to eradicate hate in our community. Projects like *Romeo and Juliet,* which emphasize the folly of hatred and violence and promote love, are good examples of how to reach those who still appear beyond reach. *Romeo and Juliet* gave me an extraordinary opportunity to play the role of peacemaker in Shakespeare's great romantic tragedy and to prepare myself for the life role of peacemaker and to be an exponent of justice in a Rwanda still recovering from the trauma of genocide. I believe that my sense of the challenges that lie ahead for me brought a sense of urgency to my playing the role of Benvolio.

The rehearsals were intense but enjoyable. There was an immense amount to do in a short period of time. We had to memorize our lines, which were in three languages (Kinyarwandan, French, and Shakespeare's iambic pentameter), build chemistry among the players on the stage, and perform without constant prompts. Having some of my lines in languages other than English was not very hard, since Kinyarwanda is my mother tongue and I was already at an advanced level in French. The same was the case for most of the cast members, except for those who had little English. Rwanda had just switched from French to English as the language of education, and not many kids had enough interest to learn English by themselves, as I had.

In time, as everyone started to get comfortable with their part, we were able to relate to our characters while bringing out the appropriate reactions and emotions. This was mostly thanks to James, Andrew's friend and co-director from Dartmouth College. That man could make you do anything! He had his way of reaching into your soul, and everything he said in a particular moment would make sense. He was always surrounded by cast members, which made it difficult to talk to him unless he was offering suggestions on one's own character. I wanted desperately to have a conversation with James, but I wasn't sure it was a good idea to do so with other people standing nearby. What if I struggled to find words and embarrassed myself? What if my questions sounded stupid? All these doubts prevented me from speaking with him, so I instead took satisfaction in listening to him answer questions from everyone else. One of his comments that particularly stuck in my mind was his appreciation for theatre. He told us that theatre could take us to a different place where we won't be thinking about everyday routines and everyday struggles. In that state, he said, you are fully focused on the subject in the play and that is the best place from which to transmit a message. I couldn't agree more—a good play will remove you from your present place in time and transport you into an excited state, much like an atom in its highest stage of energy. Performing in a play will trigger your compassion and understanding, and make you challenge old ideas in ways you couldn't or wouldn't anywhere else.

A recent trip to Italy during a heat wave led me to remember my experience playing Benvolio, especially the last scene he is in before disappearing from the stage. Mercutio, Romeo, and Benvolio are wandering around the town after the party at the Capulet house. "I pray thee, good Mercutio, let's retire: The day is hot, the Capulets abroad, and, if we meet, we shall not scape a brawl," pleaded Benvolio. Benvolio was conscious of the dangerous situation they were in, due to the hatred between the Capulets and the Montagues, and he did everything to keep his companions out of trouble, including playing in front of the enemy's house. Mercutio, on the other hand, was all for fun, regardless of the dangers. Benvolio could have left the moment he realized it was not safe for them to stay and expose themselves to Capulet enemies, but he instead stayed with his friends. Even when Tybalt's gang showed up, as he predicted, he didn't run or play the "I told you so" card. He did all he could to prevent a fight from breaking out. Had Mercutio or Tybalt listened to him and cooled down a little bit, there might have been a chance to resolve the quarrels. But, of course, that didn't happen. Instead, a fight broke out and Mercutio was killed. Romeo, enraged by the death of his dear friend, went after Tybalt and killed him.

Immediately after the death of Tybalt, Benvolio shows his selfless character.

"Romeo, away, be gone . . . why dost thou stay?" Benvolio's words and actions were difficult for me to perform or to fully comprehend, as they did not reconcile with my personal character. My natural reaction in this case would probably be "Dude! We are so screwed!" and I would dash away before Lord Capulet could slice me into pieces. Benvolio, on the other hand, risked his life and stayed to explain to the prince what had happened in front of the Capulet mansion. This showed Benvolio's selfless nature and the lengths he would go to to ensure peace and justice. This to me was the most important thing Benvolio had to do. Although his friend Mercutio had just died in his arms and he was angry and scared, he had to be brave enough to explain the situation to the prince because Romeo's life depended on it. It was a tough spot for me as an actor, as the fight scene had drained all my energy. "How can I express all these parallel emotions at once?" I wondered. I decided to be on one knee to show respect to the prince, to speak forcefully to express my anger, and to tilt my head downward to show my sorrow. At the end of this scene, I was satisfied with my reactions and emotional expression, and I believe the audience was as well.

Spending so much time in rehearsals, we all grew closer and became like a family. We started opening up to each other as only people who are very close are able to. I found good friends among the cast members and directors, and I went home every day with a new insight about life. One day Andrew was conducting a survey, and he asked me if I would answer a few questions, on the record. We then had a conversation that completely changed my life. Among the many questions he asked was, "If you were to write a book about your life, what would be the biggest chapter in it?" This question shook me to the core. I had never considered what the biggest moments in my life were; up to that point, my life felt like something that had happened to me. I lived each day, and yesterday would pass when tomorrow came, and I moved on. I don't remember my answer to Andrew's question, but I remember the feeling it gave me. I said to myself, "I have to take control of my life and plan my future." So much has happened in my life since then, and as I now connect the dots, and I owe much of what has happened to the revelation I had after my conversation with Andrew. I also owe a great deal to Ben Proudfoot, the documentary moviemaker, who allowed me to tell my story in his movie of our production, *Rwanda and Juliet.* After the documentary, he remained a friend, a mentor, and he always showed up when I needed him.

When I participated in *Romeo and Juliet,* I was a college sophomore majoring in chemistry. I wanted to do more with my education before settling into corporate life. I had no fine car, or a house, favorite travel destination, or dream job. My financial situation and social exposure didn't allow me these luxuries. One dream I did have, more like a life goal, was to one day earn a Ph.D. I used to look at myself in the mirror and say, "Dr. Clovis Shyaka fits well, mister." These goals inspired me to stay focused and to maintain a position at the top of my classes. Despite my desire to pursue graduate school, I barely had any idea how or where to apply. I talked to Andrew about my grad school intentions shortly after completing my undergraduate degree, asking for him for guidance. "You need to work on your English and sit for the TOEFL test if you intend to apply for a Ph.D. scholarship in the US or Canada," he advised. I took his advice and passed the TOEFL test quite comfortably. I finished my master's degree in South Korea, published a few scientific articles in internationally recognized journals, and subsequently got a job as a medical research scientist in South Korea. Looking back, it seems clear to me that being a part of the *Romeo and Juliet* cast was one of the best things that ever happened to me. It triggered a series of events that eventually put me on track to fulfill my dreams.

It is almost a decade since our production, and I have stayed in touch with most of the cast members. Many of us have had a lot of success in our respective careers, and I can say with confidence that it has a great deal to do with our association with *Romeo and Juliet*. In my work as a medical research scientist, I am currently heading a project to develop an antimalarial drug. I strongly doubt that I would be doing this if I hadn't had the courage to audition for *Romeo and Juliet*.

*Clovis was born in the Democratic Republic of the Congo and grew up in Rwanda. He received his education up to the undergraduate level in Rwanda and continued post graduate education at the master's level in South Korea. He worked with EarthEnable in Rwanda as a research and development manager and at Sewon Biotech and A&J Science in South Korea as a research chemist. He currently works with new drug discoveries and development against urgent health threats. He is passionate about being a positive agent in his community and a role model to the younger generation. Clovis is at his happiest when he is playing with his siblings and imagining their unlimited potential should they be lucky enough to have all the tools they need to break through the barriers they will face. Clovis, ever since he was little, dreamed of being Dr. Shyaka Clovis. He wanted to earn a Ph.D. degree before he knew what that involved. Now that he knows, it is what keeps him awake at night. Clovis, a speaker of five languages [English, French, Korean, Kinyarwanda, Swahili] has published scientific articles in journals recognized worldwide and attended multiple international chemistry conferences. If Clovis had all the money in the world, he would start a world-class laboratory in Rwanda to help innovations and enable young scientists to succeed. He has a goal: "I would love to travel with my parents too! If you're dreaming, why not dream big!" This essay was written in 2022.*

# The Leave to Stop Posturing

Gail Taylor
CANADA

It was September 1962. Our newly abridged family was driving out of the sun-spotted prairie city of Edmonton where just ten days earlier we'd gone out for an A&W supper and left my father to his own devices in the heat-glazed PMQ on the Edmonton RCAF base, returning to a smell so ominous it is a neural fist jammed into my brainstem forever. The city of my ardent adolescent friendships and complicated sagas turned to memory in the way that living beings become ancestors in a nanosecond. My father's last and least ambivalent choice had rendered our family as strictly female and turned him into a chaotic and pervasive dream. My mother, the east light rekindled in her eye, parcelled us into the unreliable Austin with a few belongings hurriedly salvaged from the scene, and we drove away from five years of thick life on the prairie. As I regard the memory of our bearing east in early autumn, I see a cartoon image of female legs chuffing up clouds of prairie dust beneath the peeled-back tin can of our little car, my little sister's frail like twigs, my big sister's a curvaceous tracery of my mother's famous pair of gams, and mine sinewed like my father's had been, sturdy. Our heads are clamped onto the torsos of this upstart image like Tennessee Williams' no-neck monsters, expressions of forced anticipation over-top the bewilderment contorting our countenances. It was my mother who showed us, by example and admonition, to look ahead. Perhaps she thought that by banning the swivel of necks backwards we might escape the dreaded fate of Lot's wife, condemned to one point-of-view forever. Or maybe it was that if only we sped hard enough away from the scene of my father's despairing death, we could toggle free the ties to start anew 3,000 miles to the coast.

When we arrived in Saint John on the Bay of Fundy after what seemed like a mythic time on the road, we stayed with my father's sister and husband and six cousins, who must have been in a state of shock themselves but shared their home with us for several weeks while my mother found work and a place of our own. In all the years we'd been away on Air Force bases in Nova Scotia and Alberta, my mother and father had alluded to the experience of homecoming that would await our return to the familial birthplace of Saint John. But there was no frisson for me as I re-met the port city tarnished with fog, though I remembered it well enough from my first eight years of life when three of my grandparents were still alive. Whereas in dry, flat Edmonton the streets and avenues were right angled at predictable intervals, in Saint John they angled out like the tertiary branches of a light starved tree; I never knew quite where I was, except which way was west. There were spates of one way streets and the city's foundation of rock created a mythic conundrum out of simple things like storeys and exits. It was very hard to get oriented.

I was late for entrance to high school by the time we got there, which added to my immense reluctance. Somewhere in the span between Alberta and New Brunswick, just behind the clown mask I configured to keep my mother and my sisters laughing (my role of mimic was honed early), I grew a desolate brand of recalcitrance that forbade faith in the future. As far as that went, I had ceased abruptly to believe in God in the immediate aftermath of my father's suicide. Nor could I possibly have been ready to part so abruptly from the friends I'd navigated puberty and the portents of adulthood with. It was in that other life, now lost forever, that we laid down footsteps toward high school with a passion and fear I think of now as hope. My friends and I had planned to meet our cool and puissant grown-up selves ahead—together.

Now, as I regarded the hulking brick edifice from which my own parents had graduated in the 1930s, I began to understand that my high school life must be devoted to stratagems of captivity, for nothing else seemed possible. Determined to disclose nothing, I set off each day for a kind of internment in that brick mausoleum, head lowered against the ubiquity of fog and a ceaseless wind off the Bay of Fundy that I took personally.

My reaction to my father's violent desertion was to try and confabulate an identity from a place of special, secret vision. Schooled by him to regard suicide as a kind of enlightened choice, I thought I'd acquired this knowledge by contagion or legacy, a belief that manifested in a proud, painful solitude. The only way to survive school, I felt, was through camouflage—the punishing double vision of watching every move I made, which may be one of the elements that comes with the evolution of adolescence anyway, though I didn't see it that way at the time.

Into this precarious world, within short order, a new English teacher arrived from Britain. These were the days when school boards in New Brunswick were actively recruiting teachers from the Mother Country. Late for the opening of school as I had been, Andrew Garrod (Mr. Garrod for so many years, to me) was also a kind of exile, though voluntary in his case, which claimed my attention. Something about the brisk and energetic way he entered the cavern of my homeroom classroom—a corner of mildewed brick basement that repelled the harbour light—began at once to open up chinks in the cell of my school life. Within the field of his affable curiosity, cloistering became less desirable, and a sense of possibility occurred. As an adult, I'd call the quality he radiated one of rare, sustained, and equitable good will, but then I only knew that I'd been waiting without knowing what for, until his arrival. But this seems a treacherous thing to admit now, for the adults in my life had surely demonstrated interest, love, and concern—there were close relatives on both sides of the family whose warmth reached out to us, to say nothing of the large family of vitality and love we were part of, temporarily for shelter but pretty much forever via the ties that bind. Perhaps taking-for-granted is a common conundrum of youth, but I must admit that at the time, I held all my relations dimly responsible at some inadmissible level for whatever torments had driven my father to die, after which a dense silence amassed about his very being. For the most part, I kept this welter of unformed thoughts and feelings inside myself.

Andrew (Mr. Garrod in my memories of this time) bestowed the catalysis of keen attention on each of his students, a democratic distribution that acknowledged difference without any of the usual tacit rankings we all knew about. In his class, we were not treated as a monolithic group of teenagers, but rather as an assembly of disparate individuals who could learn, through the medium of literature and listening to one another while striving to articulate our inchoate impressions, to divest preconceptions; to "only connect" as E.M. Foster had exhorted. And while this new teacher did not appear to me (who was an expert in this regard) to be possessed of rage, he was not shy of expressing displeasure, and was never, so far as I knew, perceived as a pushover. Instructed by his model, I developed a more nuanced appreciation of my peers, learning by example to query stereotype and unfounded generalizations in ways that have been far-reaching for me as an activist, educator, and writer.

Had Andrew's interest in any one of us been preclusive, I for one would have found him suspect, for by then I'd grappled with issues of egalitarianism (the upside of my father's legacy) and bore a wariness of privilege per se. The other feature of his regard had to do with a friendly formalism that worked with courtesy to keep embarrassment at bay. I could assume a more relaxed reflectiveness in the stimulating class discussions and surrender some portion of the elaborate defences that exhausted my nerves.

As I listened to the responses of my peers to the largely colonial literature we read, my terrifying loneliness ebbed to realize that tendrils of our own experience could be legitimately brought to the interpretations of poetry and novels—and even to understanding Shakespeare! It was a capacious climate in which to try for greater precision and truthfulness, too. The discovery that even chaotic experience could be part of a critical arsenal was new to me; when bounded by structures of grammar and story and poetics, it was a fertile incubation for my imminent infatuation with drama.

Soon Andrew was collaborating with the music teacher to hold auditions for a production of Gilbert and Sullivan's *Pirates of Penzance*. The arts were valued in my family; my sisters and I were given lessons in music and ballet, my mother had a background in ballet and taught ballroom dancing during the war, and my paternal grandmother established a vigorous Little Theatre in the 1930s that her children also participated in, a local institution to be reckoned with. My maternal grandmother who died before I was born had trained for an opera career in Boston before marriage claimed her, and she sang in public for the rest of her life. And both my parents agreed that exposure to the arts was an undisputed post-war good.

I knew that trying out for the chorus would mitigate some of my mother's concern over my withdrawal, for I often felt powerless to alleviate the worries of her widowhood that certainly included me. And then, when I was accepted into the chorus of *The Pirates of Penzance*, I was surprised to discover how much I liked the vaulting acrobatics of sound made by our eager young voices. Even though I affected scorn for the lyrics that my mother referred to delightedly as *frothy*, I was exhilarated by the spiral of song and story that I entered as one would a new country. Sometimes I felt strangely paralyzed, as if a lurid spotlight could pick out my errant movement or missed lyric, but mostly I was immersed in the festoon of make-believe and extravagance of sets and costumes that took shape almost magically between rehearsals.

There were other perks, too. Rehearsals provided ample waiting time to indulge my appetite for watching. Transfixed, I followed the phosphorescent trail of the principals as they moved on and off stage to the rhythm of their own social dramas that counterpointed the libretto in swerves of temper and laughter, doldrums, tearful nerves, and a flirtatiousness I studied with special care. It was validating to see that even those with confidence and peer acceptance were prey to these assaults of mood and mishap. It seemed that drama made us all more permeable, springing leaks where ardour and anxiety gushed through even offstage. Simultaneously, I found myself more socially adept for the first time since coming to high school. Andrew had a rare knack for recruiting his cast across the normally inviolate borders that sorted students into cliques, and it was amidst this unusual hybrid of my peers, cast into unity as theatrical venturing must do, that I was able to make my first tentative forays into the social arena.

Even though I landed by luck in Andrew's English class again in Grade 11, and the adults in my life pronounced on my progress, I was prone to the indignities of depression (not openly acknowledged in those days) and peered into my middle year with that peculiarly leaden dread. My older sister, who stayed back from Teacher's College for a year to work and help my mother settle our family, had departed. All my life she'd been there just ahead of me, mitigative and kind and loyal; I could not imagine anything without her, even though she only went 100 kilometres away. We exchanged frequent letters, long distance phone calls being reserved for special occasions, and I fear she received some desolate epistles from me. But I did not begrudge her delight in her new life, noting that her roommate seemed to have taken my place and even looked a bit like me.

Into this vacuum, my hatred of school ballooned. My teachers grew impatient as I dallied over assignments and refused to engage with subjects I disdained. As I strayed from the main artery of school life, my anger seeped up like a virulent dye at inopportune moments, threatening the affection of anyone who came too close. I jigged school often, wandering toward the harbour that was just a gull's cry from the school. An older friend who also bore the marks of trauma and lived independently would wangle our way on board the ships that came from everywhere in the world to the deep port—places I wanted to be just because they were not Saint John. I drank ouzo with Greek sailors and tried to look cool, nodding and plotting escapes that even then I knew were pure fantasy. Sometimes, I'd go east to the freight yards by Courtenay Bay and watch the futile allure of other peoples' lives-in-motion, heads and torsos flickering by like old cinema as I edged up close enough to see how it would be to tip myself into those brief, blurred spaces between cars. In marginally brighter moods, I imagined riding the rails Depression-style in a ghost-like limbo; I wanted a nether region where choice was not required.

This was the way it was in the fall of 1963 when Andrew asked me to try out for a female lead in *Twelfth Night,* his inaugural Shakespearian production. Before I quite knew what I was doing, I had agreed. I've carried an abiding surprise over the recollection of my self-conscious sixteen-year-old self showing up to read the lavish lines of Viola. Yet, with hindsight, I can see that this Shakespearian theatre and the literature we studied in English class were not only contiguous but cross-pollinating and that drama was just a more animate form of what we did in class that relied on interpretive exploration to link us to one another and ourselves. The opportunity to add the element of the body in motion and in relationship made drama irresistible, a confluence that moved me from Enriched English class literally into the special space of sanctuary that drama provided, grounded in the wonders of language.

And then, I thought, for Andrew to have invited me to audition for a specific part must mean he could imagine something I could not, myself. So, it was my trust in him that made a bridge to the steeped-in-drama girl I would become for the duration of high school. And I did get the part, and thereby entered the intense life of the play that eclipsed all else for an entire term and made life possible again.

Shakespeare requires a form of absorption that seems akin to learning a new language and culture. The ponderous brick structure of the school was soon honeycombed with the bustle of reawakened Elizabethan England. In coveys of twos and threes, tucked into niches in the basement where we rehearsed, perched on the stairs made slippery by generations of footfall, we heard each other's frenziedly memorized lines; around every corner, actors mouthed soliloquies in a rapture of concentration. Ordinary, anxious adolescents in street clothes were made incandescent with wit and plot on the magical apron stage built specially for what was to become an illustrious tradition in that school. For me, collective make-believe tapped into the same heady collusion of play in my childhood, a fervent shared imagining with sisters and cousins that overrode the imponderable powers of adulthood. Now, I had to keep clamping down on my delirium, for this was surely too excessive to be allowed for long.

But it was the language of *Twelfth Night* that most irrupted my defences, the paradox of richly layered rhythm that carried revelation and information on which the elaborate plot is contingent, while still evoking the cadence of conversation. I was awakened by the strange, rough elegance of this poetic language. To hear it from the mouths of my peers made loops of connection among us that erased the harder lines of everyday affiliation. The play, perhaps paradoxically, granted us the leave to stop posturing.

In English class, I found relief in the labour of entering a Shakespearian text with all the complicated footnotes to unlock its subtlety and pun. Here in the theatrical enactment of text, we were also drawn into the spaces between the lines to take interpretive risks. It turned out that not even Shakespeare was immutable, and while Andrew strove always to help us understand the text, he also urged us to curve the parts kinaesthetically to ride the distance between character and player. And so, I have carried with me the notion that my Viola belongs to me (as well as to Shakespeare and to Andrew and the other *characters*); and that Orsino played so broodily by Jeffrey, Sheila's vivacious Maria, the sultry Olivia of Daphne—to name a few—are enduring. It was my first encounter with a spoken, moving Shakespeare, and I was won.

Many-faceted Viola was a character who gave me a chance to try out qualities I hadn't found within myself, as well as sharpen some I had, in fledgling form. Playing another character entails a flourishing of affirmation, for could I not understand Viola's dispossession, washed up on a foreign shore without her darling sibling? Buffeted by fate, however, she is not a victim but remains openhearted and resourceful, imbued with an Elizabethan sense of honour that was not entirely unfamiliar to me. Shipwrecked in Illyria and believing her beloved twin brother drowned, she makes the decision to disguise herself as a eunuch named Cesario to work in the court of Duke Orsino. Enlisting the aid of the doomed ship's captain, she supplicates: "Conceal me what I am, and be my aid/For such disguise as haply shall become/The form of my intent"—and since my own intent since entering the stranded world of Saint John had been concealment, it was a congenial ploy.

I worried about appearing in the doublet, tights, and feathered cap of Cesario until the imperious delight of illusion took over. It was never the audience that I wanted to fool; after all, Shakespearian audiences are privileged with much more information than most of the characters. But I as Viola wanted to make it credible to Orsino and Olivia that I might be a silver-tongued young man "semblative a woman's part." I played the entire part slouched over slightly to make me more convincingly concave.

What intrigued me most was Viola's steadfastness when everything about her world and persona was so fragile. I liked being a heroine who hid a fiercely focussed, desperate passion for Orsino behind a facade of sexless service yet was somehow personable enough to draw down the heart of the duke. Neither the audience nor the actors ever saw Viola in her "woman's weeds"; that she could be lovable anyway made me happy, for I thought myself sharp and strange to look at.

I do not recall the actual performances as vividly as I do the hours of practice inset with images that transfigured the basement corridor where my home room and English classes happened to be by day. From a functional, damp dimness, the hallway and classrooms were turned into a renaissance fair of make-up stalls, costume alterations, the litter of polymorphous props—along with the kindest volunteers, including teachers, who doted on the production and on us. But even as the long hours engrossed in the world of the play inured me from the jumpy world outside (and in), it was the very purpose of practice to provide feedback full of validation, surprise, and suggestion. Whereas performance was a one-shot deal, rehearsals provided opportunities to experiment—an incalculable boon in a world where grading and invidious comparison reigned supreme—and gave me hope in the power of change.

I remember the whirling figure of Andrew as he mulled over and coached our creations. Splayed text in one hand, he focussed closely on each role, walkons included, urging by example a regard for the play as a latticework of necessary pieces. When we teetered on the credulous brink between reality and illusion, he could restore the balance with a humour that was ironic but not malicious, a kind of mirror in which to see the muchness, and sometimes the madness, that theatre summons. As well as all of this, it was tremendous fun!

I was avid for attention, but through some origami of social and religious and moral provenance, believed that such desire was not appropriate for a girl. Theatre gave me a forum where I did not have to pretend that engaging the audience was something other than a bid for recognition. Although my family joked about my obsession (for I talked of little else), my mother and my aunt (sisters-in-law who were fortunately close friends) were especially relieved that I was involved, and in this case, it was something they valued as well. Although our social circles did not intersect, it was also a comfort to have my warm-hearted cousin play the part of Maria with the same spontaneous zest I both envied and appreciated in her personality.

In daily life, I tried to dissemble my hunger for attention, which seemed gratuitous while my mother was working feverishly to re-establish our lives and secure enough income from her work as an executive secretary to supplement a meagre military pension. I knew it was up to me to give her no trouble, for I could not miss the temperance and love that she and other relatives offered as they waited for the shock of my father's suicide to pass. I knew what was required, but did not want to give it, wavering like a bird on the wire between behaviour that befitted a girl of those times, and acts of stubborn sabotage; withdrawal was the default and a covering up of depression the best I could attempt.

My older sister had already made her sacrifice, and my mother said we must be prepared to "pitch in": my duty was to my younger sister, floundering at school and in need of attention herself. When I broke out of my fugue, I could see that I was not the only one reeling from the trauma of my father's death. Each one took our successive responsibilities to heart because families were meant to cope within the radius of community, which included the church I wanted none of. To me, this seemed to entail hiding your trouble and turning despair into a kind of dignified resignation. Although it seems very Victorian now, displays of raw emotion were considered unseemly for females and kept inside the private domain of the home or better yet, within the body itself. But seeing how hard my mother worked and yet maintained an air of cheer, it wasn't lost on me that while I might resent her "conventional ways", I and my sisters benefitted from the moderation she restored to our home. Certainly, she was emotionally reserved, but also warm and affectionate—and she did love to laugh. I carried a covert pride in her ability to rally and though I could not have acknowledged it at the time, her example taught me much about how to live.

Not surprisingly, when the play was over, I felt a cosmic letdown. Come back down to earth, the adults said—the very place I did not want to be. Gone was Illyria, though the basement corridor was redolent with ghost-speech from the play. A new musical in the second term provided temporary distraction but I understood now that nothing would touch the complexity of a Shakespearian female lead. I hardly dared hope for another chance in my senior year, by no means a given since Andrew and the school had yet to establish a program of Shakespeare and musicals to be offered over the cycles of the school calendar.

Post Viola, I was surprised when kids I knew from the production, and even some I did not, would hail me in the hallways. During the final stages of rehearsals for *Twelfth Night*, I began to smoke between scenes, which made me feel I belonged to a clandestine underground with a vague sense of protest that bound us together, though I could not have said precisely against what, except conformity. I began to think of myself as bohemian, a concept that prefigured the social revolution coming in the mid-1960s. Even though I might now cringe at this version of myself as an actress careless of infamy, it kept me going for a little.

It was this ambience that spawned an idea of a whole life in theatre. Because when it came right down to it (and I was close enough to see), stepping off a dock into the brackish margin between ship and pier was not much to expect—and perhaps I could spend my lifetime slipping in and out of dramatic guises to camouflage or even transform my jangled inner life.

Accordingly, I entered my final year of high school daring to believe that things could change. This time when Andrew announced auditions for a production of *King Lear* and suggested I read for the part of Goneril, the eldest and most awful of Lear's daughters, I knew without demurring that I wanted that part. By now, though still an infant tradition, the plays and musicals had attained a status that fanned a flame of excitement throughout the school. Playing a lead for two years in a row seemed to confer élan and caused me to try and reconcile a more self-possessed version of myself with the amorphous one within. It was this play that initiated a practice of alternate leads to extend the experience to more students; and so, there were two very disparate Gonerils though only one Lear played by Little Richard Green (there was another, taller one) with an emanant sadness that stilled us all.

It seemed I might form myself even transiently by looking out of the eyes of this character whose exacting nature caused her to make executive choices with no turning back. In her world, a woman who knew what she wanted could make a mark and satisfy her desire (even when it was wicked). Of course, in the end, Goneril does not prevail, but the point was that she acted as if her agency could matter. Where I was growing up, girls were not encouraged to achieve their ends in any pointed way, except perhaps through marriage, which did not interest me. These were of course tacit understandings that amplified my own ambivalence about what I wanted and what I might be able to have.

In the earlier days of my adolescence, confronting my father had given me a taste for a surge of adrenalin-soaked action I could still summon under duress, a rash energy I drew on to play a woman for whom excess was ordinary. Even now, to recollect the part is to feel that *thwock* of relief, like a long-held exhalation: I relished the acting out of Goneril's licentious behaviour and embellished my part with a sense of mayhem—a pleasure not to be forgotten.

Richard as Lear played his part with such an aching openness that my character's response as a conniving daughter was in jeopardy. Possessed by a dangerous pity that made me want to understand the other at any cost, my impulse was to offer myself even on a pyre if it could stop the other's pain. To witness the shifts of consciousness that Richard brought to Lear, from wounded vanity and querulousness through bewildered indignation and finally to grief and madness, was to suffer empathically inside the cage of character as destiny. Richard, too, seemed to act out of a certain woundedness and even when his fate was sealed as Lear, I felt the audience fastened to him by something like mercy.

Viola's open and affectionate nature could not have transported me quite like the disaffected Goneril's did. And perhaps acting Goneril made me edgier and more combative as she and I got involved in the way that best friends sometimes do, cross-influences moving in and out like a tide. Since character is formed through crucial relationship, why would this not be extended into the realm of literature and theatre? Even now, I think that the spirit of Goneril as conjured by countless occasions of theatrical intimacy by actresses down through time is afoot in a parallel lifeworld where she exerts a bearing on those of us who engaged her for a time.

Though I had limited critical skills with which to penetrate the whole play, I could see for instance that my character's ruthlessness depended heavily on actions going on offstage that would require intentional efforts to understand. I don't think I was very good at keeping this larger world in view, rehearsing the Goneril scenes obsessively and otherwise sort of switching off. But the scenes with Lear captivated me for I recognized that his gathering craziness was the occasion for disastrously missed communication, a dynamic that sowed the seedbed for treachery and fear. All sub-plots and characters seemed to gather like iron filings pointed in one inexorable direction toward Lear's madness. The tragedy satisfied something unnamed inside me.

Andrew coached us to act at angles to the ready temptations of stereotype or caricature—it was the way he taught literature, too, and this dismantling of assumption was highly formative for me. Looking at the play later on, I saw that Goneril and Regan were somewhat monolithic, reduced by their father's folly to a kind of two-headed mythic monster, corporately adulterous and "unnatural" in their actions in stark contrast to the goodness of Cordelia that does not, however, exactly save her. Where Lear in his plunge to madness is multidimensional, the elder sisters grow ever narrower, their final flatness ordained so that Lear and others can be elaborately configured.

What could I have made of this bad woman, cursed for her sex? A thankless, greedy daughter, sexual wanton, renegade with ambition? What did I think of her husband's curse?—"Proper deformity," he hurls at her, "shows not in the fiend/So horrid as in woman"? I subscribed simultaneously to the paradox of limitless choice on the one hand, and a fatalism imposed by circumstance and personality on the other, with nothing in between except unorthodoxy. I wanted to believe that women who defied the norms of their time could get away with it, although I knew in my bones it would be a rocky road. The complex Elizabethan view of nature and culture as interdependent was startling to me then, and I resisted the moral of *Lear*, disengaging as the play bore on, depriving Goneril of any chance at redemption.

As much as the gnarled plot and volatile language of the play, I remember how it felt to move, as Goneril. I wore a dark gown with a tunic overdress that gave me a sense of gravitas, cinched with a belt made from metal disks of which I was vain, a contrast that seemed to fit the nature of the character. I watched the inflections of voice and body made by the other actors and made minute adjustments that were never the same way twice, a somatic concentration that yielded surprise and occasionally a sense of my own limitations, along with Goneril's. In this regard, Andrew's blocking was supportive but unobtrusive, allowing us to trust our own inclinations—a gift that made me feel affective and supple and aware.

The ending of *King Lear* signalled the inevitable bathos of moving from performance to everyday life. But this time, in Grade 12, I grappled with the prospect of never again being part of this thronging together on an apron stage with adolescent peers, shepherded by our attentive director-teacher and culminating in audiences of friends, family, and community all primed for enchantment. In the new year, however, there was one more chance for me to hover in the time-free zone of drama when Andrew invited me to choreograph *The Gondoliers,* a gavotte and something exotic called a cachucha. My dance training was mainly in ballet with a little character dance, and research

at the local library turned up only the scantest descriptions, but Andrew seemed confident in me and full of enthusiasm. I let the musical
score wimple through me to leave a tracery of movements I then embellished from limited experience, a very few facts, and nerve.

It was heady to be entrusted with this adult charge. My mother, who
had done considerable choreography and dance in her life, contributed her excited interest while maintaining a circumspect distance: I
wanted to do this alone, but I was alert for her approval. She gave it
with tact, for I was soldered into that adolescent posture of resistance
to input from a parent and put on a show of mistrusting praise as much
as criticism. The success of the musical certainly included the dancers
who worked with gratifying ardour to learn the steps, an experience
of cooperation that surprised me because even those who were uncertain at the start emerged as irrepressible dancers and they all swept
the stage to make delighted filaments of connection with the audience.

At the time I think the choreography was an experience of spanning
the part of myself that faltered at the threshold of adulthood and a
Tinkerbell yearning to glitter above it all. Only much later could I see
that the drama and the dance together provided not just distraction,
but a kind of powerful psychic response to the haunting by my father.
What I could register at the time was more along the lines of the value
of play—something so life-giving that I wished then, as now, that it
could be availed at the turning points and passages that everyone must
navigate to grow up and then to grow old.

With just weeks to graduation, I had no plan, and it was in this state
of urgency that I decided to try out for the vaunted National Theatre
School in Montreal. It was both a bid for a life of creative plenitude;
and a need to stop time, to shelter in roles and stories that might, however, call on and create some of my own. I wanted to believe that theatre could disperse the Pandora's creatures that beset me without my
understanding or consent and set me free within the sanctuary of a
stage.

And at the level of perverse resistance, I also wanted to stymie my
well-meaning uncle's expectation that I would go to university, which
I peremptorily declared a classist option. Eventually and by labyrin-
thine routes, I did go, though there was no money, and it was perhaps
rash without support to do so. Like many of my generation of girls

and young women, I did not think of trying to fashion my life after my highly competent mother's, whose work included secret stenography for the navy during the war and many years of executive secretarial work in high-pressure and situations of harassment that did not then even have a name. I did not credit then her verve in establishing her own dance school when we were little, or performing manifold volunteer work throughout her life while raising three daughters by and large on her own; rather, her model of a woman's life came into view gradually over a period of years, like images emerging faintly and piecemeal in the chemical tray of a darkroom.

And so, I prepared my set piece for an audition (from *Streetcar Named Desire* of all things) with the National Theatre School, and took my first ever flight to Halifax, fighting incipient migraine and nerves. But long before they made it official, I think I knew I wasn't going to be accepted into that sanctum, for without the assembly of others on stage with me, to say nothing of the fostering presence of Andrew even in the wings, I was at sea. To send a precisely timed monologue extrapolated from a whole missing play into the glare from a lit-up proscenium stage to the shadowy adjudicators was, in an emotional, spiritual, and pragmatic sense beyond me. As for the improvisation, with which I had no experience, it rendered me stiff and strained, possibly strange. Even so, when I got my letter of rejection, my pride was shattered and the monolithic last-minute plan set aside. I felt as if the hard-won cache of confidence accrued by the high school drama experience was overdrawn.

For a few years following graduation from high school, disdaining the theoretical world of the university, I traced a path of random divagations across Canada, working wherever I landed and cobbling together an identity in the perilous ways of growing up via risk in jobs and relationships and the apprenticeship of hands-on learning. Though I was certainly foolhardy, I may also have been brave in the realm of sheer survival. Aspects of the parts I'd played—the shrewdness of Goneril and her strong will, Viola's open-hearted resourcefulness—and the creative inventions of choreography entered into the eclectic repertoire I was assembling to grow up and keep trying.

✶ ✶ ✶ ✶ ✶

To ask what I carry forward from the plays raises up the diasporic nature of childhood, that first charged settlement from which we must scatter but never quite cast off. Theatre allowed me access to a genus of emotional life that had been subordinated by my father's trauma, whatever that might have been—family, war, inherited susceptibilities. But mine was a kind of suppression fortified by the sociocultural context in which I was embedded, belonging to the ethos of postcolonial, post-war anglophone Canada. During my coming of age, the mantle of gender began to unravel, creating an experience of newlyminted possibility on the one hand, and evidence of indomitable barriers on the other. There was a maze of hazard that girls and women were called upon daily to negotiate, and the trick I learned early had to do with making this seem effortless and even fulfilling. As if, like the fabulous art of the ballet, girls must create the illusion that they do not sweat, and that skill, caring, and grace flood forth from the rivery mysteries of their hormones (the maddening etiology of their badness, too, as Shakespeare, too, had assumed), that the only fears they must endure are about childish things like mice and monsters. To look good even while suffering or extending oneself towards others with greater needs, and to mute, modify, mollify and smile—and then to discount that any of this required courage or merit, but was natural for the female sweet with selflessness, meant that if you didn't want to do it you were unfeminine and would not lead a proper life. It was not the kind of social environment in which to fetch up a very easy or interesting sense of self.

And if this was true then for a white, moderately middle-class, able-bodied, heterosexual girl, I came to understand in the life ahead of me something far more complex about the experience of marginalized people—women among others.

So, drama was a powerful countervailing catalyst that helped me project my voice and take up space as a complex character long before I could exercise an authoritative presence of my own. Furthermore, it required that I emote. I understood at a kind of fundamental, somatic level (and only later, conceptually), that to move others and be moved myself was a passage out of the cave of rectitude.

Closely related to such lasting impacts is the capacity of acting to canalize what socialization and various forms of civilization would tamp down, the very kind of exploration with which adolescence is concerned. Acting and dancing and singing—playing, mimesis!—can channel and sometimes even transfigure the chaos of change. And then, to be a character intimately, in a play, is a state like infatuation where the beloved is carried like a sublime refreshment from the tyranny of the inward gaze—and the efforts are all towards understanding, no matter how "bad" that character is construed to be. Perhaps we learn to be less judgemental, more forgiving and tolerant, by trying on an identity other than the one that besieges by being given.

In Shakespeare, too, I was intellectually and morally challenged by the notion of characters who sought to annul the very notion of inner impediment (let alone a fatal flaw). When first I read Regan's remark to Goneril that the King had "ever but slenderly known himself," I remember grappling with this idea of how self-delusion can ensnare others. I still reach for Shakespeare in times of muddle! The motif of theatre per se is imbricated in my perception and personal mythology, a trope for how to make sense of things. The poetry I write, and a lavish dreamlife, bear the repeated metaphors of theatre.

As one who contended with questions of death as well as chosen life in my youth, the porous camouflage of theatre gave me a protected space where I could nudge gingerly towards a more resourceful state of being. Perhaps I was saved from being just myself while simultaneously cultivating a self worth saving. Of course, this did not occur in a vacuum, but within the context of my mother's grit, the tenacious and even uproarious empathy I shared with my sisters, the example of certain relatives' wit and verve, and more freighted but true way, those times in my father's life when he dazzled by craning for the sun.

It is striking to me that I don't know an English word (but suspect that other languages, especially the Indigenous ones, might offer such locutions) for the fostering flame of Andrew who made things possible for so many of us. I think this unknown term must include the roles of teacher, mentor, director, community dramatic organizer, ethicist, and educator, among others—and embody a constellation of qualities that made him persist over many decades and as it turned out, across continents and smaller islands, with great zeal and energy and no doubt in the face of obstacles I know nothing about. And he possessed not only a talent for working with adolescents, but for attracting many generous others to the collaboration of theatrical production. So that is a candle I want to keep lit.

Hovering in a liminal between commitment and collapse is not as uncommon as I once believed and may even be endemic to the passage that is adolescence. And so, I want to make a passionate plea for theatre—along with the other arts—to be supported in the schools, which all manner of research has deemed developmentally beneficial, especially for mental health. The children who now have nearly unthinkable challenges before them will need more than the technocracy to furnish their ethical, imaginative, emotional, and spiritual hardiness—so investment in the arts is practical, as well as visionary. While the metrics of such outcomes may not be quantifiable, perhaps the pleasure and possibilities of engaging in theatre when young are in a deep, felt way—immeasurable.

*After high school, Gail Taylor worked at writing jobs in radio and TV and a nationally syndicated magazine, and as a student at York University had a play produced but graduated in Honours Philosophy. While raising her daughter as a sole parent in New Brunswick, she advocated vigorously for ameliorative strategies to combat racism in the public school system. Her work has been primarily concentrated in two streams: writing and memoir for marginalized groups including women, Indigenous communities, and those with barriers to health, as well as writing and editing for academic faculty and Ph.D. candidates; and empowerment-based programming in the face of poverty, violence, and discrimination. A contractor, she also worked in the public sector, education, and the non-profit world, and negotiated film properties for an independent feature film company. In mid-life, Gail earned an MEd and an interdisciplinary MA, both concerned with writing, literature, education, and identity. She has taught English to refugee students, high school English, and undergraduate and graduate courses. Her most fulfilling work was organizing residents of low-income neighbourhoods; and two terms of active service as a Board member for the New Brunswick Coalition for Pay Equity. Moving to Ottawa in later years to live near her beloved daughter and grandson, she achieved certification in the field of family mental health peer support. She continues to work as a developmental editor for scholarly publishing projects and was a co-editor for the collec-tion,* Sexual Violence in Canadian Universities. *A published poet and memoir writer, she is currently circulating a retrospective manuscript of poetry. This essay was written in 1998.*

PART TWO

# Connecting to the Audience

# Only Connect

Julie Guravich

CANADA

It's half-past-nine on a Saturday morning, and I'm backstage at the beautifully restored Rosalia de Castro Theatre in A Coruña, Spain. Peering out from a safe nook behind the curtains, I try to discern the audience's mood as my accompanist plays a tune to warm them up for this musical kick-off to a three-day teachers' conference.

Despite a simmering uneasiness within, I manage to smile as I recall my daughter Sabela's innocent question about the glorious Baroque angels that ornament most theatres here: "Mom, why is it they're always chubby and never black?" I ask myself, "Why do I feel somewhat awed in their silent presence?" Perhaps I'm concerned with how they will judge my performance. To me, even the elderly theatre attendant looks dubious as he opens the curtains to reveal the lustrous Steinway, adorned with beautiful Easter lily arrangements, at center stage. Sleepy teachers are still wandering into the theatre, clutching their conference folders. My challenge is to capture the imagination and interest of a group of some three hundred English language teachers, age twenty-three to sixty, on this early March morning. Most Spaniards don't consider themselves alive, let alone receptive, until after their first coffee break. How can we hope for a positive reaction to a jazz-blues duo at this uncivilized hour?

A keen shot of panic stirs my gut as I realize that, as usual, my pianist and I (incurable improvisers) have not yet settled on a specific repertoire. Added to this "unknown" is the novelty of total "unplugging": today there is no microphone to tease, rendering the familiar club strategies inoperable. This was a full stage, not a squeezed night club platform, and I hoped my voice would carry and convince the audience that we were worthy of this gorgeous backdrop.

Suddenly I am experiencing a *déjà vu* of heightened sensations: flushed cheeks, a momentary dizziness brought on by a heady mix of backstage aromas—heavy violet curtains, old floorboards, intense stage lights, a tightness in my belly. The last time I had felt this sharpening of the senses, the adrenalin rush, the self-doubts crowding in, was over twenty years ago, when I was waiting backstage at Saint John High School's theatre, preparing to open Scene II, Act III of *Romeo and Juliet*.

Why was it so difficult for me to face the empty stage alone in that scene, in which Juliet expresses a mixture of fearfulness and joyous expectation as she prepares to hurl herself into the magical, unknown world of sex? I wondered whether I would be able to hold the audience's interest during Juliet's breathless monologue without tripping over my costume or, for that matter, my lines. I felt a major responsibility to "fill" the stage for the short time before the nurse's entrance, which in the first performances of the play came as a welcome relief. It only became easier for me to express Juliet's nervous anticipation—"So tedious is this day as is the night before some festival to an impatient child"—when I learned to tap my own anxiety and convert it into usable energy.

Back in Spain, while the last stragglers take their seats to the tune of my pianist, I am literally missing. I have been pleasantly, though eerily, transported, and it is Juliet, not Julie, who picks nervously at her costume, wishing its deep folds had more substantive support. I even feel my toes cramp slightly, as they tended to with tension, within my feather light ballet shoes. I come to suddenly, and looking down at my short jumper and tall Nancy Sinatra boots, I check the angle of my cocky beret and I wonder if I will be able to jerk the teachers awake.

Will they even notice the strange choice of music, the odd couple of performers: myself, a Canadian singer with a Russian surname, and my sneakered accompanist? Using the backstage nerves to my advantage, and focusing my energy on communicating feelings, I try not to worry about how I will structure the monologue or the concert. I know that although rehearsals can locate the peaks in a certain speech or identify the heart of a particular song, feeling must be allowed to take the lead in true performing. This is where my two stage experiences, worlds apart on the surface, click together.

Just as the key had been to work up enough controlled energy to bubble, rather than boil, through Juliet's scene, I am now convinced that a degree of nervous tension is essential for a successful concert, especially at this God-awful hour of the morning. During the applause following the pianist's opening number, I swing boldly forward, headed for my haven—the crook of the Steinway at center stage. As a sweet hush falls, I am enveloped by the warm breath that the plush theatre seats seem to exude.

I discover happily that I am no longer intimidated by the sophisticated theatrical setting. Instead, I relax and feed on the sumptuous heat of the stage lights, taking time to introduce the songs in English, finding the concentration and freedom to explore the movements and gestures that are so much more restricted in clubs. Throughout the concert I am able to paint moods and dramatize the songs as never before. I leave the shelter of the piano almost immediately and it is so exhilarating that my pianist despairs of bringing me back to earth in order to consult which song will come next.

This anecdote, which led me through an emotional tango as I swirled in nervous anticipation back to my high school theatre experience, not only juxtaposes my performing past and my current singing career, but also highlights the most obvious connection between my past and present. The skills learned during my theatre experience in my teens have served me on countless occasions, adding "salsa" to facets of my professional life. Not only has my part time singing career benefited from my background in drama, but my full-time career—teaching English as a foreign language in Galicia in northwestern Spain—has also been enriched by my experience as an actress.

Developing these skills was not necessarily the result of hard work and discipline and dedication to the craft, though I did do a first year at Dalhousie University with a vague intention of majoring in theatre. However, I ended up travelling to Spain in the summer of 1976 with a scholarship from the Spanish department.

My objective was to learn as much as possible about life and ponder future directions, since I didn't feel confident enough to steam ahead with a theatre degree at that point. I also hoped to forget a disastrous relationship that had pulled my spirits down that spring, and also to pick up reasonable fluency in Spanish. Over that summer I was fortunate enough to achieve all three goals: I met a marvelous man who helped me expel hurtful memories, I became reasonably fluent in the language, and, by summer's end, I had decided that teaching English as a foreign language would allow me to continue living in Galicia, which had wholly captured my heart and imagination.

I could provide countless examples of how my involvement in theatre as a teen enhanced my self-esteem and helped me develop qualities essential to a club singer and E.F.L. teacher. The many valuable hours spent in intimate communion with the audience and the many more spent learning to work in close contact with fellow actors gave me amazing self-confidence for a teenager. They taught me to draw on imagination, life experience, and theatrical courage. For example, when memory fails and I must search within to improvise lyrics, or when I have to manage those stressful moments prior to a job interview, I can tap into the myriad resources developed during those adolescent years. My training in drama has enabled me countless times to win an audience or impress musicians or students. Correct body stance, ease of gesture, steady eye contact—the sheer delight in performing—have all come to me through my early experience in the theatre. Without these skills, I would never have managed to sing with such a variety of music groups, from Jazz Big Band to country-rock to blues.

To explain how I developed these abilities and what each adds to my professional life, I must refer to the very beginnings of my "stage experience" before high school, and to my three-year involvement with high school productions—from my first role, as Maria in *School for Scandal* in tenth grade, to my last performance, as Maria in *West Side Story* during my senior year at Saint John High School.

Were there any indications at an early age that I might find performing rewarding pastime? My mother tells me that, though I was a shy child who tended to hang onto her skirts whenever strangers appeared, I did enjoy dancing barefoot for dinner guests at the age of four or five. I had absolutely no sense of inhibition as I swung my limbs about in joyous free-form style. My parents eventually decided I should attend ballet classes, a logical step but unfortunately one that made me self-conscious about performing in formal settings. I suspect the discipline and control required for classical dance and the ballet teacher's critical eye led me to feel somewhat ashamed of my occasional clumsiness (I still knock into objects frequently, on and off stage) and basic inadequacy as a dancer.

My voice, however, is an instrument that I have always felt confident about. I became involved in the city's annual music festival at an early age, as part of the class choir. Eventually I moved into solo vocal classes. In grade four I had the opportunity to act in a school production of *Snow White:* my first leading role. The same stern but kind-hearted teacher who had punished me on one mortifying occasion must have recognized that I could project my voice well. She certainly knew that I loved language and would volunteer to read anything out loud. Whether it was that she recognized my delight in language or, as my classmates suggested, that I was the only girl with long, dark hair, I must thank Miss White for giving me that part.

I recall the excitement of dressing up in the puffy-sleeved peasant blouse with a black velvet bodice, the full skirt with its teal blue sash—how my confidence seemed to grow inside it! I found I could use my memory, my clear voice and tremendous energy. When I put away the costume (my mother has carefully kept it and both my daughters had their pictures taken in it), I felt it was an important treasure. I didn't perform on stage again for at least five years.

To help explain how I arrived at my first audition in the fall of my freshman year at Saint John High School, let me give an idea of my social and family background. I was attracted to, and somewhat awed by, Saint John's longstanding tradition of excellence in drama. My sister and one of our three brothers had attended S.J.H.S. years before me and had participated in musicals and Shakespearean plays. Their stories of wild cast parties dazzled me. Because I had been socially "adrift" during my junior high years, always depending on a group of overbearing female friends to determine my social posture, I was eager to find my "slot" in high school. Thus it was a major step for me when I *chose* to try out for *School for Scandal* soon after entering grade ten.

Two plays which we performed on the small, intimate Room Three Stage, *School for Scandal* and *She Stoops to Conquer*, provided me my first real training ground for club performances. It was on this stage, with its close proximity to the audience, that I grasped the value of subtle gesture, realized the importance of remaining in character, and learned to get over the fear of direct eye contact between actor and audience. I also learned to manage the initial difficulties that lack of experience brought on, such as avoiding unlit obstacles backstage and learning to take full advantage of a costume, rather than allowing it to intimidate me. Most important, however, was the way my confidence grew both on and off stage as my social circle expanded. I remember how I felt during that first try-out as I waited and listened to other already "developed" student actresses and actors. The words to a funky tune were running through my head—"Mr. Bigshot, who do you think you are?"—and I stood wondering who I really was and how I could stand a chance. With warm cheeks and dry throat, dizzy with expectation, I looked ahead on the page and found my thoughts ran far faster than the words in front of me. Though it was a competitive experience, I didn't sense I was being compared to others or judged in any direct way. I felt instead like I was participating in an extended classroom activity with a friendly learning atmosphere. This was probably the key to my staying power. In fact, I didn't run off after reading, but sat and enjoyed listening to others.

Once I was over the joyous shock of being chosen, I began to wonder what to expect and how much would be expected of me. Each step of the complicated rehearsal process came as a fresh challenge, a totally new experience—*Snow White,* after all, had been a recital of lines and choreographed movements all controlled by the teacher. This, however, was theatre, not a puppet show.

Perhaps the most important "direction" I recall from that first play, in which I played a minor role as demure Maria, the anti-gossip, anti-vice, and consequently anti-humor element in a sharply witty world, was to stay in character at all times, regardless of how small the role might be and no matter what was going on onstage. As I observe myself in a photograph taken of a scene in which I must sit for some time playing cards with Joseph, the hypocritical lecher, I feel once more the tension, the heat of the stage lights, and the eyes of a public that seemed terrifyingly near. It was all I could do to remember my lines without giving the impression of pasting together two people: Maria, the virtuous, mouse-like creature entirely unengaged in the witty exchanges around her, and Julie, the inexperienced fifteen-year-old hoping not to trip over her hoop skirt. I remember feeling annoyed with Maria's primness, her sense of moral superiority, qualities I could not identify with. Though perhaps somewhat shy at that time, I never felt morally bound. Maria's obsession with a flawless appearance, with maintaining the smooth surface no matter what worms might be wriggling beneath it, seemed odious and hypocritical to me.

My greatest fear was that I would bump some prop off a table or sit in an indecorous manner, exposing undergarments in a most un-Maria-like fashion. Costume jokes were the crew's entertainment backstage. I learned to return their gripes, and my initial embarrassment over the décolleté costume and the apparent interest these older boys expressed in me evolved into stimulating backstage conversation and, eventually, my first real date. I believe there was actually something magical in the way my costumes helped pull me out of my natural shyness and insecurity about my self-image. By the time I played Miss Neville a year later in *She Stoops to Conquer,* who, unlike Maria, was a dynamic and witty character, I thoroughly enjoyed teasing both with language and with cleavage. I was secretly overjoyed to wear a costume that lied a little, a sort of WonderBra principle in historical guise.

Looking back, I believe I drew in my roles on the adult irony, play on words, and lighthearted sarcasm that I was exposed to at home. My parents had the reputation, at least in the opinion of certain authorities at school, of being liberal, even permissive. By the time I reached high school, however, four years after my sister had graduated, the general atmosphere was not so tense, wildly experimental, or progressive. The sixties had passed, and my generation seemed both more frivolous, less concerned with political or social issues, and more personally ambitious, bent on forging an economically fruitful future for themselves. Perhaps in reaction to this, I found myself drawn to the stimulating circle of my brothers' and parents' friends, which included many artists and political activists, environmentalists, and generally unconventional people from all walks of life.

These people tended to treat me as a person whose ideas were worthy of respect, and would often include me in lively debates on such subjects as the legalization of drugs or abortion. Thus, the social criticism underlying eighteenth-century farce and the witty bantering were not entirely unfamiliar to me. Because my confidence in myself as an actress and as a young woman was growing, I was undoubtedly more comfortable on stage and off in my second play. I learned to laugh at myself when I stumbled backstage in the dark and did not feel ill at ease when "the boys" kidded me about costume or prop mishaps.

In these early plays, then, I got a taste of performing close to an audience, close enough to sense their body movements, their reaction to the tone of a scene, their chuckles or belly laughs, and I became hooked on the communicative aspect of theatre, on the electric shock of making contact through calculated gesture and pointed language.

An interesting comment from a club owner at a recent performance highlighted the importance of this part of my background: he told me he thought I was a very different person on stage than off. He noted I addressed the audience with an actress' skill, sensing when to pep them up with an old favorite, when to propose a toast or dedicate a tune. Winning an audience that ranges from seventeen-year-old grungers to smartly dressed yuppies, that includes drifters challenging me with "still hooked on heavy-metal" t-shirts and white-haired bank executives, takes a mixed bag of tricks. I call it "cabaret communication," the seeds of which I feel lie in those Stage Three productions. Now—as then—the costume is crucial. When I slip into an off-beat outfit of eye catching earrings, black stockings with horn players stamped in white curving down one leg, and my characteristic beret—presto. I'm in the mood.

When "everyday" Julie doesn't feel up to struggling with a crowd's initial indifference, when trying times at work have me in a less than buoyant mood, or when a hostile crowd leads me to the edge of despair, I slip into theatrical mode. In such circumstances it is an actress's job more than a singer's to win the crowd, which I do by coming on strong and using theatre gambits to grab the audience and hold their interest long enough for the music to take effect. Then I can let the singer in me do the rest. I'm sure it is the sense of confidence and my skills as an actress that I developed in Saint John High School's theatre that enable me to convincingly project an impression of ease, despite my dangling nerves.

In the twenty years I have spent teaching, I have had the opportunity to teach students with varying motivation and abilities. This has meant playing a clown, a director, a cool executive, or even becoming a one-woman-band in order to convert my lessons into entertaining after-school activities or relaxing moments of professional training.

It is immensely challenging to draw Spanish adults out of themselves, to permit doctors, engineers, and housewives to flounder comfortably together in a new language, and even to make fools of themselves without their pride and confidence suffering. I find it extremely useful to use tricks from teenage theatre workshops, in which we learned to trust one another to touch and be touched, to stretch our emotional range. Certain exercises can help students overcome the stress of feeling as clumsy and inadequate as adolescents when tackling a new language.

I vividly remember a drama workshop led by David Barnet, one of the *animateurs* from the 1974 Theatre Canada Festival who was an assistant professor of drama at the University of Alberta. He was an intense individual whom I couldn't help admiring and feeling quite attracted to. His drama techniques, which involved a great deal of improvisation and exercises in trust and cooperation, proved extremely useful during rehearsals for *A Midsummer Night's Dream,* which we performed the following year. I remember how he led us into situations with an explosive level of spontaneity, through which I learned to bring out the aggressively sexual aspect of Titania's conflict with Oberon as well as the tender, sensual aspect of her comical love scene with Bottom. These so-called "out-scenes," improvised situations that developed through a study of the scene sequence and text of the play, were especially helpful in grasping the emotional dynamics of relationships.

I distinctly remember getting over a barrier that existed between the boy playing Oberon and myself, a certain stand-offishness or insecurity in having to deal with adult conflicts and passions. As Barnet worked with us to approach the more challenging scenes from a contemporary angle more appropriate to our age-level, I found it easier to gain access to both Titania's humanity and my own emotions. In my own classrooms, my students have told me that they feel less inhibited after doing this style of improvisation, and they learn to listen to one another more carefully as well.

Barnet also deemphasized voice projection, working with us in a restricted space so that the subtleties of real communication could emerge. I find this type of exercise beneficial in my classroom. I even ask students to close their eyes and imagine where they are, and to speak in low voices for optimum relaxation. This helps them concentrate on intonation and emphasis, which improves their pronunciation.

My involvement in theatre caused no real conflicts at home or at school, since I managed to keep up my grades despite full involvement in drama. My parents understood that I needed to be pulled like toffee in all directions to stay spiritually, physically, and intellectually on keel. There was no question as to whether I was taking on too much, despite inevitable bouts of tears when exams on papers came due dangerously close to performance dates. I couldn't have had more tolerant and supportive parents.

The most mind-opening, comprehensive intellectual experience I had the pleasure to benefit from in high school was the process of learning about Shakespeare from a truly meaningful angle, that of interpretation on stage. Andrew Garrod guided us as both literature students and actors through gradual, challenging, yet entertaining steps, from initial background readings and discussions to the actual staging of the plays. In informal sessions in Mr. Garrod's living room, we discussed historical context, examined various interpretations of the play and its characters, and worked out the troublesome areas of language, character motivation, and timing. This provided my first taste of thought-provoking, participatory teaching of literature. He took our opinions into account, and together we identified the moments of maximum strength in a monologue, analyzed the play's structure, and grappled with the text—aspects of drama too often seen as an unreasonable challenge for teenagers. This kind of learning makes a structured classroom setting with its conventional format seem so inadequate, so inappropriate for eager young minds.

The transition between read-throughs and actual rehearsals was not, at first, a smooth one for me. It meant putting much more thought into when and why a character would move onstage, and I never felt completely comfortable with my gestures, or when I had to use my body to reach out of myself and express some element in my character. It was initially easier for me to understand on an intellectual level what was underlying the text, because I was more mature intellectually than emotionally or socially. My lack of emotional development made it difficult for me to bring feeling to my character's movements.

When I ask myself how independent and self-assured I was before participating in the plays, I have to answer, not much at all. Being in the plays not only helped me mature intellectually, but also taught me a great deal about working closely with both adults and other teenagers and allowed me to expand my budding social relationships. This helped me develop cooperative skills, self esteem, emotional and physical flexibility, and valuable personal qualities such as tolerance and adaptability. Along with the grueling process of rehearsals I experienced truly rewarding moments of communion with other actors and the audience. I also had satisfying opportunities to expand my social relationships during trips we took to Boston and Newfoundland with *Romeo and Juliet,* as well as numerous workshops and choreography sessions.

Traveling with fellow actors and crew members to Boston and St. John's gave rise to those first fleeting encounters with the opposite sex; in that close company, crushes finally declared themselves openly. However, I *distinctly* remember feeling quite unattractive on the trip to Boston. I had always felt rather insecure about my irregular features: thin, straggly hair, a prominent nose, deeply set eyes and far from sensuous lips topped off my poor self-image. Backstage, while I was applying my make-up for the Boston performance of *Romeo and Juliet,* one of the actors sidled up to where I was peering at myself in one of those incredibly truthful mirrors and commented bluntly that he had never noticed how conspicuous a moustache I had. Neither had I until that painful moment. Once in costume, however, I soon forgot about that dark shadow and, as Juliet, felt much more becoming.

On the return journey I was surprised to receive the attentions of a crew member whom I had always found very attractive in a sly fashion. Sly is the word, for he managed to maintain an "All's well, we're asleep" appearance when, in fact, a shared blanket and adjoining seats allowed for all kinds of hand acrobatics on that lengthy train trip. My self-image received quite a boost between the adrenalin high of a successful performance before a challenging audience and my feeling appreciated in a very personal way by someone I admired.

Another incident that stands out in my memory as a landmark in my emotional development occurred while in St. John's, Newfoundland, for the National Drama Festival in 1974. The visual impact of the journey across that province in chilly May, with its icy green rivers and barren, rocky terrain has stayed with me. I can still see from the cliffs of St. John's the jagged iceberg looming just beyond the harbor.

I also recall my freezing feet and numb nose as I stood chatting with one of the actors from a Manitoba troupe before retiring for the night, following our performance of *Romeo and Juliet* in the Dominion Drama Festival. Rough-hewn in aspect and charismatic, in a Gerard Depardieu way, this man in his early thirties chatted with me about my interpretation of the play and the difficulties I encountered. I confessed to this experienced actor how I felt I sometimes tended to exaggerate, using gestures larger than life, which, according to one critic, "anticipated the tragedy too early in the play." However, he was warmly encouraging and told me that "Romeo" and I had convinced him of the intensity of our love; in fact, he said, I had to be a special person to register such passion at an early age.

Looking back at this scene, I don't think he meant to impress me or to lead me on (though there was a brief suggestion that we could carry on the conversation in the warmth of his room). But whatever his intentions, his acceptance of my opinions and positive comments about my acting were marvelously flattering. In the end he kissed me in a tender, undemanding gesture of having delighted in my company, and I returned to my residence lodgings feeling I could truly identify with Juliet's longings: "hood my unman'd blood beating in my cheeks." I have to credit such sweet, broadening experiences with helping me grow to accept myself fully and to feel I was giving all I could give.

Learning to touch and be touched, to feel comfortable with my own body and those of the other actors and actresses did not cause me any serious problems. I did not feel self-conscious while rehearsing a love scene or when surrounded by semi-clad performers backstage; for most of us, it was a matter of-fact business to be dealt with, and possibly giggled over initially, that was readily assimilated as part of drama work.

In any case, if we had been at all shy about naked bodies, by the time we staged *A Midsummer Night's Dream* we were able to handle long body-painting sessions and being dressed scantily as fairies in burlap and macramé. In our interpretation of the play, the fairy world was a reflection of the 16th-century conception of the New World. Our costumes, designed by George Fry, were based on sketches of Indigenous North Ameticans brought back by explorers of that century. The makeup included painted on leaf patterns for the men and intricate flowers winding sinuously from head to toe on the women.

Solidarity and support grew out of working with large numbers of actors and crew members, both students and adults, on the major productions. One of the most surprising and delightful aspects of being involved in the plays was the sense of being part of something tremendously complex, an intricate puzzle of teenage emotions and egos, hard falls and adrenalin bounces, doses of sweet and sour humor that somehow charged ahead through snigs and snags towards an electrifying opening night.

Was I embarrassed the first time I had to kiss an actor on stage? I remember wondering how to approach Romeo and Juliet's first kiss in the masquerade. Since the rest of the players were frozen, this moment would stand out, and I hoped it would look convincing to both the audience and the rest of the actors on stage. We were directed quite carefully, as I recall, in terms of the distance to maintain between us, the position of our hands, and the angle of our faces at the moment of that delicate expression of youthful attraction. I believe both of us felt slightly stiff when we first staged the kiss, but by the time performances were underway there was a comfortable feel about it. I distinctly recall a sensation of relaxation, as if the bonding between the two young lovers transformed me as well and helped me beat any opening night jitters. I also experienced a most curious relationship between my character and myself. Juliet could give me joyous release and boost my self-image, allowing me to feel a much more appealing young woman, and I, in turn, could bring the pain of my father's fatal illness to her suffering. One run-through of a difficult, intensely dramatic scene of *Romeo and Juliet* caused more than a few problems in a memorable dress rehearsal, when tension was high and good humor lacking. It was the hour of exhaustion and giddiness, always a danger when performing tragedy, and on this occasion giggles were not to be avoided. The boys were wearing revealing tie-dye tights, and when Romeo stood up after having collapsed on top of my prone body, "dead," he had to bear a tide of barely suppressed guffaws, as there was no hiding his body's quite natural reaction to our intimate physical contact.

Musicals were colossal efforts involving clamorous rehearsals, exhausting but fulfilling choreography sessions, and what seemed too many diverse elements to possibly orchestrate in a limited amount of time. We were emotionally and physically tested to the limit. One of my greatest fears was that I would hold up dance rehearsals. What if I couldn't memorize the order of the steps? Left-right coordination has never been my strong point. Even now, I have frequent trouble maneuvering among the criss-crossed electric snakes and other sound equipment on stage and have learned to recover from flying mikes or sheet music; without my background in the theatre I could never "go on with the show" without showing embarrassment or discomfort. My expressiveness and energy communicate my enjoyment, which seems to have made up for the lack of precision and grace in my movements over the years.

Nevertheless, the musicals I performed in as a chorus member *(Annie Get Your Gun* and *My Fair Lady)* were a great deal of fun with a great deal less pressure on me. It was a pleasure to form part of the background bustle in a scene, moving as a unit with other chorus members, trying not to stand out on or offstage. The atmosphere was more relaxed than when I performed a lead: there were more kidding and giggles when zippers wouldn't zip or make-up took ages to apply. Nerves were less taut because the responsibility to entertain was shared. We learned a lot about tolerance, cooperation, respect, the same skills other students surely picked up through team sports. On stage, however, there was no competitive element and students from all types of backgrounds came together in explosive harmony.

One young man, whom I felt attracted to and admired for his unique spirit, wonderful rapport with fellow actors, and delightful sense of humor, left a strong impression on me during my teen years. While we rarely met during rehearsals for *A Midsummer Night's Dream,* we came together spontaneously after the final performance to share the inevitable let-down and emptiness of wrapping up. The two of us disappeared from the boisterous cast party and returned to the quiet beauty of the multi-level set. Lying in the dark on stage, each wrapped up in thoughts of painted flowers, brown makeup, courtly love, confusion, and delight, we shared the silence. Later, we walked home under a magic moon in snow deep enough to fall back and make angels. Saint John seemed so beautiful that night.

Although we did not initiate any dating relationship after that evening, the bond between us remained. I think of a scene from *West Side Story,* in which I played Maria opposite his Tony, and a rush of images and sensations floods my memory. Despite all the problems related to a complex musical score and dance sequences, despite the troubles of balancing schoolwork with drama, Tony was always thinking of others more than himself, always had time for a good-luck hug before difficult scenes and a smile and a friendly kiss to help forget the hard times.

I shall not forget how my feelings coincided with Maria's; whenever I sing, "There's a place somewhere," I remember with pain and fondness this first love in my life. I have never felt so close to anyone in moments of silence as to this person, and I mourned his recent tragic death deeply, since his life had touched mine in a special way. I believe drama allowed me to feel emotions intensely, to embrace moments of real communion with others without questioning motivation or consequences. Learning to focus my feelings to the limit for each moment of an emotionally packed scene and to use my intimate fears and illusions in different ways for each performance, each play, gave me an understanding of the notion "live life to the fullest." You learn to treasure the present and value communication even more intensely.

Between 1972 and 1975 my father was going through the last painful stages of a long battle with kidney disease, and my mother was performing full-time nursing duties. My brothers and sister were living away from home and I, the baby of my family, felt I should be helping my mother more with my father's care. I was torn between wanting to spend more time at home and being immediately tempted to participate in drama at school. Once I became fully involved in the plays, I had less and less time, but instead of suggesting I check my priorities, my parents gave only valuable encouragement. Often, after a late-night rehearsal, I'd go in to say goodnight. My father would ask how the play was progressing, feeling excited for me before performances and insisting that I live those years to the fullest. Sometimes I felt so helpless and insecure listening to my father's gentle queries, watching him wince as he rolled over in bed, seeing the pain in his eyes as he commented in the sweetest, most patient tone on different aspects of the play.

One of my most poignant memories is the time I visited him in hospital and sang "Somewhere" from *West Side Story*. In certain scenes from *Romeo and Juliet* the tears I shed were from thinking of his suffering, and the fears Juliet expressed were my own. Looking back at photographs from the play, I see my wrinkled brow, my tortured stare as I grasp the "poison" and express all the doubts of a child that has got in way too far. I understand that I identified more easily with the darker, more tragic side of Juliet then. She was frightened of death and all its trappings, "the horrible conceit of death and night." I was able to confess my own fears through Juliet's voice: "I have a faint cold fear thrills through my veins." For me the speech that Juliet delivers on the tomb was taxing, one I delivered in a somewhat hysterical tone, perhaps more than would be appropriate for such a young girl as Juliet. This may have been because I was expressing my very real terror of suffering, as I knew my father was approaching the end of his life and required medication to bear the pain. I did not wish to confront this fact, and, I am sure, the tension was apparent in my performances.

I learned to deal with constructive criticism, as *Romeo and Juliet* was adjudicated at two drama festivals. With burning cheeks and sinking morale, trying to cover my disappointment, I listened to and absorbed the critic's words. As a highly sensitive person I have had to develop strategies for handling criticism, and these were valuable opportunities to do so as a teenager. There were, of course, also moments of marvelous confidence boosting when members of the audience after the National Drama Festival spoke o the play's "vitality, life, freshness, and truth which produced gut reaction ."

Undoubtedly, performing was a kind of therapy that pulled me out of my real fears and anxieties and allowed me to vent these emotions. The nervous tension followed by a rush of adrenalin provided a much-needed release. Sensing that the audience had been moved by the tragedy, I finally was able to relax and let Juliet speak for me, concentrating on the beauty of the lines I had the privilege to struggle with.

I reached the conclusion that I would only give what was inside me to give. Yet our director, Andrew Garrod, managed to unearth a surprising wealth of emotional resources in me and in each actor/actress, encouraging us to use who we were to the fullest. Mr. Garrod treated us as young adults with whom he could, for example, discuss the sexual connotations of certain lines in a natural fashion, and we shared a relationship of trust and respect. It is clear to me that this opportunity to perform, to use all my emotional range and release the tension in my personal situation, was essential to my development. Andrew Garrod's method as a director of young minds was to formulate appropriate questions, providing prompts whenever we became insecure so that we, the players, could work out the answers. He always asked our opinion, considered it fully, then possibly suggested alternatives. Through his guidance, however, we were usually able to furnish the alternatives ourselves, a very rewarding experience.

Have I changed much since high school, I wonder? I believe that between the ages of fifteen and eighteen most of my raw material pulled together, and my "persona" emerged much as it is today. I learned to listen to my heart and to my mind, to take risks but only after careful consideration, to use my imagination and improvise, and, most importantly, that living intensely was a path I wished to follow for the rest of my life.

My present lifestyle does not easily compare with that of the average mother of two, in her forties, living in Cedeira, a fishing village on the northern coast of Galicia. I live with my husband and two daughters in an old stone house, in the never-ending process of renovation. My kids call me "lightning mama" because I move at full speed, in contrast to the steady, relaxed pace of this part of the world. Weather permitting, I get my errands done on roller skates, unheard of in these parts, even buzzing up and down the aisles of the only large supermarket. I don't worry much about people's comments on my eccentric ways because I'm quite comfortable with who I am and how I arrived here.

Life is a series of strange coincidences. When I consider my first exposure to Hispanic culture, *West Side Story,* in which I danced my first rumba and cha-cha-cha and tried to pick up a Spanish accent, it is curious to think how I've come full circle, living in Spain, dancing salsa, and feeling quite integrated into Spanish culture. Whether it is due to my basically non-critical nature or because of the high I experience whenever I reflect on my theatre adventures, I have never wished to go back in order to re-say, re-think, or re-order any of my life experiences. However, I must confess that reflecting on those three years in high school theatre has proven surprisingly vivid, an exercise in honesty that, at times, was emotionally trying. Reliving intense moments can leave one exhausted, but there is lots of pepper in the recipe to keep one motivated.

At that time I learned to juggle all kinds of activities, and I continue to do so, combining teaching, family life, and professional singing. So far the formula works, thanks to my family's marvelous support. I'm often referred to here among musicians, students, and colleagues as a born actress. This is not always meant as a positive comment, since they point out that I may show more interest than is warranted in a particular topic, heightening the tone of a conversation, for example. However, for me life is full of moments when one must inject a little enthusiasm and energy into a party that's fading, a concert that's "off," or a class that is lacking energy and motivation. Playing "animator" is a satisfying role that is as much a part of me as any other.

I would like to end by mentioning an opportunity that I recently had the pleasure of offering to my daughter, Sabela, and which I feel backs up my theory concerning the positive force of drama in the development of children and young adults. Last year I accompanied my younger daughter to her first audition at a TV studio in Galicia. Advertised in the newspaper as a children's program casting, we were attracted to this event along with hundreds of other families. When we arrived, children of all ages and descriptions were clustering, humming, and blocking the route to the door; the scene was just short of chaos. I wondered if Sabela would have time to feel nervous, but her name was called almost immediately and she headed in, with her head high and her eyes flashing with excitement.

She positively leaped down the stairs towards us twenty minutes later, dazzled by the experience of cameras and adult direction. She had been asked to improvise a humorous scene from *Little Red Riding Hood,* and the director had been impressed by her ease and expressiveness. We were soon notified that she was hired and Sabela spent two holiday months of intense recording activity away from home, in the company of three other children and the adult crew. The program turned out to be a delightful ten-minute slot aimed at educating young Galician children in the areas of social behavior, healthy habits, etc. It was a great success.

What most marked Sabela, I feel, what most contributed to her character development over those two long months of exhausting hours in very close contact with other children and the crew members was the entirely different context for learning that the experience provided. When she speaks of her television summer she uses the word "stretched," and eagerly looks forward to more such opportunities to push the limits of her energy, powers of concentration, and communicative skills. It has boosted her self-confidence, and I believe she learned more in those two months that are of value to her development as an individual than she would in a year of regular schooling.

To sum up, I believe that young lives can be enriched in countless ways through an experience in the theatre. I know that my own self-acceptance came about at a very difficult time of my life as a result of my experience with the Saint John High School dramatic productions. When I reflect on those experiences, I know they were among the most meaningful moments of my life, and thus an integral part of all I have done, of all I have since become.

*Envisioning herself snowshoeing and studying languages at Carleton University, quoting E.E. Cummings on the essence of teaching—was this typical yearbook fantasizing or sixth sense, asks Julie Guravich. After one year swallowed whole by the Dalhousie University theatre department, Julie's Spanish professor encouraged her to pursue a different direction, Cuba and full Spanish immersion. However, Spain had just re-embraced democracy and rolled four distinct languages and cultures into one nation. Thus, the summer of 1976 was spent hitchhiking over the Iberian Peninsula, falling in love with Galicia's Celtic tradition, allowing romance to strike full force. To remain in Spain, Julie tutored privately and taught conversation classes at the University of Santiago de Compostela. Between 1979 and 1984, she finally fulfilled her dream of experiencing Ottawa's winter wonderland, obtaining an honours degree in English literature and linguistics. Returning to Spain upon her first child's birth, there followed intense years of childrearing, teaching English at private academies, and singing with several bands, taking part in major jazz and blues festivals. Once her second daughter had flown the nest, she proceeded to obtain her Master's in Filología Inglesa at Coruña University, becoming a permanent English teacher at the Ferrol EOI in 2008. Julie's high-school stage experience has aided her in teaching foreign inmates, as well as handling any audience, from posh equestrian club members to rowdy rock festival crowds. Now sixty-five, Julie wrote this memoir when she was forty-one years old.*

# Conquering My Fear

Wayne Best
CANADA

When I was in grade four, I was in the health play and played Jimmy Germ. I got the part because I was more histrionic than the others; in other words, I died well. I did this hugely dramatic death. When the Germ was vanquished, I fell with such gusto that my legs shot up into the air and then crashed down onto the stage floor. It brought a roar of laughter from the audience, and I remember smiling to myself until my "corpse" was removed from the stage. I sometimes look back on that moment and think, "I heard that crowd's reaction and it did something to me."

Looking back, I am surprised that I was willing to take such a risk. I was shy and reticent (l still am, to a lesser degree), and I was frightened of any sort of public humiliation. I think that fear has a lot to do with my background. My father was a truck driver, a wonderful man but not educated. My mother never finished high school, and then she got married. They were not risk-takers. Fear of risks was a big thing with my mother, and I picked up on that. I was painfully aware of the fact that, if I made a strong statement or did something bold, there was a chance I might fail.

A big part of my adult life has been recognizing and overcoming this trait that was instilled in me as a child. I have taken an enormous number of physical risks in my career as a professional performer that I would never have taken when I was younger. I simply made a conscious decision to do it. I've done stunts, and fights, and I've jumped from the ceiling of the Stratford Festival Theatre face-first. Part of that is willing myself to go beyond what I think are the limits of my personality or the limits of the way I was raised.

Wanting to be recognized, to be applauded, was a great help in overcoming my fear. It was something that I discovered when playing Jimmy the Germ. That experience made an impression on me, showed me that I could elicit a reaction, a common reaction, from a large group of people. I felt I could control them, their psychology, to the point where I could will them to think one way.

Performing in an elementary school health play was, however, only a small victory over my fear. The true challenge lay in my decision to participate in the renowned drama program at Saint John High School. Here, the stage seemed infinitely bigger, the audiences more vast, the competition more fierce, and the degree of risk greater. Failure in a Saint John production meant large-scale public humiliation. It took my entire freshman year to simply work up the nerve to try out for a play.

I was not a natural actor; for me, the skills were something to be worked at and improved on. I spent some time with small roles and bit parts while developing my acting ability. My lack of natural ability was, in a way, fortuitous, for it allowed me to face my fears gradually. I was not forced to memorize hundreds of lines of dialogue as a lead in my first play; rather, I was introduced to the pressure of performing at Saint John in our performance of *She Stoops to Conquer*, in which I played a small role as a drunken singer. Although I was not pleased with my performance in that play, I was proud of myself. I had taken a risk.

Looking back at myself as a seventeen- or eighteen-year-old, I sometimes wonder whether any of the characters or any of the parts I played helped me discover a part of myself that I hadn't explored before. When I did the scene in *Lear* I never actually got to the emotional point that I thought that servant was at. I sort of sketched at it, but I knew my grief and outrage weren't truthful. But by knowing that I didn't get there, I also knew that I could. I knew in the moment that it was not quite believable, this emotion that I was playing at, but by knowing that it wasn't, I knew that I could do it, and I knew that I could be publicly emotional. That's something that I did learn about myself.

My acting skills improved and, consequently, the size of my roles increased. My high school theatre experience culminated with the musical *My Fair Lady*; I was cast as Doolittle, one of the leads. This was one of the greatest risks I have ever taken. Not only was I a lead, I was a lead in a musical. The role was a double chance of failure. I would have to both act *and* sing throughout the performances.

As nervous as I was about my singing ability, I remember particularly enjoying the two songs I had in the production: "Get Me to the Church on Time" and "With a Little Bit of Luck." When you're the lead in a scene or a play, you dictate the way things go. Mr. Edwards was conducting the music, but, as any musician would tell you, the orchestra follows the vocalist. And so every aspect of the song—the choreography, working with my buddies doing those numbers, having the orchestra up there—was under my control. I was making something happen; I had my fate in my own hands. I was just enjoying the demands it made upon me. Pulling all of the elements of the song and dance numbers together gave me a great sense of satisfaction. Our production of *My Fair Lady* was a success: I had taken a great risk, I had faced my fear, and I had been rewarded with applause and accolades. It was a turning point in my life.

I went on to play difficult roles in university, but I could never have done that before I did Doolittle. After that, I knew that I could take a chance. I could go right out there, put my ass on the line, and even if I made a mistake, the thing to do was just to keep going, to be in the moment. My victory over my fear helped me to answer the questions that all young adults ask themselves: "What am I? What do I decide to be? What is my relationship with the world? How do I grow up?" Being involved in theatre started to help me define not only what I thought I was good at, but what was important to me. I was no longer afraid of what other people thought of me. The opinions of my peers still mattered, but I had gained enough confidence and self-esteem to be comfortable with pleasing myself.

That was another part of the process—learning to be my own judge about the relative level of my success, trusting my own instincts whether or not I had been recognized for it. Having faith in myself. That's what my process was, and it was a significant part of my development as a person and as an actor.

Anything that gives you focus, anything that gives you purpose is hugely defining. And it was also being part of the community, starting to become an independent person, to have a life outside home and school. That was how I defined myself as a person. That community of people, we were part of the same community, and I found my place as a result of that.

Participating in drama affected my friendships, my academic achievement, as well as my relationships and self-esteem, but mostly I think it became part of how I defined myself. It helped take me through the process of learning things about myself, learning that I was watching myself and judging myself, learning that I was afraid to make these choices, but at the same time helping me to work past my fear and accept challenges head-on. And this is what's been a guiding principle, what has carried me through life.

*Wayne was born in Saint John, New Brunswick in the mid 1950s. He grew up in working class neighbourhoods and attended Saint John High School in the early '70s. After graduation, he attended the University of New Brunswick at Saint John for one year before moving on to the Ryerson Theatre School, which he attended for four years before graduating in 1979. Since leaving school Wayne has worked as a professional actor for parts of six decades. He has appeared in over forty television shows and over forty movies. He has performed in several radio dramas for the CBC and provided character voices for animated movies and TV shows. He has acted in theatres across Canada, most notably as Colonel Keller in* The Miracle Worker *at Theatre Calgary and Billy the Kid in* The Collected Works of Billy the Kid *at the Sadie Bronfman Centre in Montreal. In 2019 Wayne toured to Dartmouth College with Robert LePage's production of* Coriolanus. *For most of the past thirty years Wayne has been a member of the Stratford Festival acting company where he has appeared as Caliban in* The Tempest, *Astrov in* Uncle Vanya, *Leontes in* The Winter's Tale, *Mercutio in* Romeo and Juliet, *Edward IV in* Richard III *and as Lefew in* All's Well That Ends Well. *In 2012 Wayne received the William Needles award for his mentoring of young actors. Wayne resides with his wife Arlene in Stratford, where they very happily raised three children and now have their first grandchild. This essay was written in 1998.*

# Stay Committed to Your Dreams

Yolanie Jurelang

THE MARSHALL ISLANDS

"All of our dreams can come true, if we have the courage to pursue them," said Walt Disney. This essay concerns some of the dreams I have pursued while performing on stage. I've been active in Youth Bridge Global (YBG) productions for several years, seven of them so far, both Shakespeare plays and American musicals.

I met Professor Garrod back in 2011, when I was in tenth grade at Marshall Islands High School. The production for which they were holding auditions was Shakespeare's *The Tempest*. I was curious to see how things were done, as it was my first time attending an audition. I had always dreamt of fulfilling my desire to perform. I wanted to see for myself what makes a show interesting, how it is constructed, and why students who have been in plays feel they have been changed by the experience. I heard stories of how performing in a play can bring an actor to life, and that made me curious. I also wanted to work on my communication skills, as I stuttered as a child and was shy about speaking in public places. I got bullied for the way I spoke and that made me afraid of being around people. It was not until high school that I stopped being so afraid; if it weren't for my friends at that time, I wouldn't have the courage I have now. I became one of the helpers for *The Tempest* production.

I next went to watch the auditions for Shakespeare's romantic comedy *As You Like It*. I didn't think of participating in the play, I just came to watch what was going on. I vividly remember watching the student actors waiting for their names to be called so they could audition for the part they wanted. My classmate Ann was among them and I knew she'd land a juicy part. There were many excellent actors among the auditioners, and everyone gave their best. I was standing near the librarian's desk and thought no one would see me, but Professor Garrod did see me and he asked if I would like to participate. So, I auditioned with no thought of getting a particular role; I was okay with whatever part I might be given. I was fortunate to be cast as Celia, the second lead! I have continued to participate in the plays Professor Garrod has directed over the years.

I've usually played a married woman in the productions I've been in or someone about to get married. I wonder why I end up in these roles. Truthfully, it's never easy to play the role you have been given, but I love playing different kinds of characters, putting a different twist on each performance. I try to understand the person I play and to decipher their point of view. You have to try to bring the character to life, and how you do that is intimately connected to your own character and your own past experiences. I've played Hodel, for example, in *Fiddler on the Roof,* a role I hold dear to my heart. Hodel and I are similar; we both come from a religious background, we both respect tradition, and we both will do anything for love. When I was given the role of Hodel, I had to get to know her and work out how she was different from her four sisters. It wasn't easy at first, but as the weeks went by I was able to know her story from her point of view. Hodel was able to find love, but that love wasn't well received by her father. She was brave and strong-willed, for it is never easy to break tradition, but her love for Perchik was so passionate that Tevye, her father, eventually gave his blessing to both Hodel and Perchik. She went away with her new husband, even though it meant separating from her family.

Playing Hodel was quite a roller-coaster experience, with the ups and downs of pleasure, sadness, and exhaustion. I gave my all when I played Hodel, and I had a difficult time separating myself from her, for at that time she was me and I was her. I can't remember how many times I cried and couldn't stop crying until the end of the show. It took me two weeks after the performances ended to process and let go of her journey and to assure myself that her love for her family was stronger than she ever knew. Hodel was a dream role, a blessing, and a life lesson. I wouldn't trade it for anything.

While Hodel was a particularly challenging role for me, I would say all roles have been hard because of their unique traits. Another challenging role was Eulalie Mackecknie Shin in *The Music Man*. I never saw myself as a comic person or actor. When I auditioned for *The Music Man*, I tried out for the part of Mrs. Paroo, the mother of Marian, the lead female. But, Professor Garrod had a different plan for me, and he cast me in the role of Mrs. Shin, the eccentric wife of the mayor. I was worried because her character was funny, gossipy, snooty, and petty, and she was a member of every auxiliary organization you can think of. There was little in her character or behavior that I could personally identify with.

The challenge of this reminded me of what I had found difficult in my first lead role, Celia in *As You Like It*. In that role, I had to get inside a passive character, and I remember my instructor telling me the important thing was to portray my character fully to the audience. For *The Music Man*, she advised me to try to stand in Mrs. Shin's shoes and in her time in history, and to get the audience to see, listen, and understand what I did and how I reacted. I wanted to be perfect and not mess up for others, a feeling that has been with me constantly.

I've learned so much over the years from participating in both Shakespeare plays and musical productions. I've experienced the good side and the downside, and I know that all the hard work, the constant practice, and all the sweat and tears pay off. Particularly rewarding has been the feedback from the audience. I love working in an environment filled with great anticipation, challenges, and abundant fun! I always want the audience to enjoy the show, but I also hope they will give me the energy to perform. I suspect I speak not only for myself but for my fellow actors. Performing together bonds us into a family and connects us to the audience. Many YBG actors have continued the journey into making music and performing in local plays, which are often about climate change and even nuclear justice. One locally written play on the latter topic was performed as part of our annual celebration of Nuclear Victim's Day.

I have mentioned roles I found challenging, but my favorite role was Anita in the musical *West Side Story*. Something about her sassy and sarcastic character, a girl who likes to speak her mind, really attracted me. I also loved her great sense of pride in being Puerto Rican; she knew what she wanted and what was best for herself and those around her. Although her story was ultimately a sad one, there was a message in her reaction when Maria reminded her that, when you're in love, right or wrong doesn't matter.

I love the fact that the YBG musical productions are bilingual. All the dialogue is in Marshallese, while the song lyrics are in English. This is ideal for those who don't have good English-speaking ability, both cast members and the audience. When Professor Garrod messaged me that the winter production was to be *The Music Man,* he didn't know that I was back on the island after studying in Taiwan. I sent him my regards and my regrets about not joining the production, but on the day of the audition, my curiosity drove me to stop by. The cast members and Professor Garrod were surprised to see me! My appearance led to a hasty audition, which resulted in my playing Mrs. Shin. I was thrilled at the prospect of working with Carnie Reimers and Jobod Silk, who had been such a smash the year before in *Grease.* Working with them was a great pleasure, but being the oldest in the play, I also had to be a great role model for the younger generation.

My mind is filled with images from past productions, but one particular scene is imprinted on my mind. It is where I, playing Hodel in *Fiddler on the Roof,* say goodbye to my father and my family, not knowing when I will see them again. I could feel Hodel's emotion at that time and it really broke my heart. I was able to connect her feelings to my situation of saying goodbye to my family when I went to Taiwan. Separation is a given and it may come in a flash, so we must be ready when the time comes. It may hurt, but it is God's plan that we will reunite with our loved ones again.

It has taken a lot of hard work and dedication to navigate my path in life and to make my dreams come true. There are things that have held me back, such as responsibility to my family, or not wanting to commit to certain things. But, to be successful in life or work, we must stay grounded. Our elders want us to aim high and not be afraid to dream big—there are no limits to our dreams. My father quotes Thomas Edison to remind me of the power of failure: "Many of life's failures are people who did not realize how close they were to success when they gave up. ... I haven't failed, I just found 1000 ways that won't work." Despite finding many ways that didn't work, Edison kept moving forward until he succeeded.

Opportunity sometimes comes in unique ways. My curiosity got me interested in joining the YBG play productions, which helped me overcome my fear of speaking in public. By following my curiosity, I met wonderful people during my years participating in Shakespeare plays and American musicals. The plays have enabled me to speak my mind and at times to be silly. I will be forever grateful to Professor Garrod, the Dartmouth volunteer teachers, the choreographers I worked with, and the producer Bonny and her husband Ken. My favorite line from the *Carousel* song "You'll Never Walk Alone" is "Walk on, walk on, with hope in your hearts, and you'll never walk alone, you'll never walk alone." I know that my journey hasn't ended. I will face many challenges throughout my life, but I will be accompanied by my friends and family. I dream of being the first Marshallese actress to perform in New York in a hit Broadway show. Like the title of my memoir, there is no limit to what you can do if you work hard to achieve your dreams. A dream is like a blank piece of paper, and you are the pen. You can make your dreams become a reality if you commit to making them happen.

*Yolanie was born in Majuro, Marshall Islands, but was raised in the United States. She is the eldest of five children and grew up in Springdale, in northwest Arkansas. Yolanie eventually moved back to the Marshall Islands at the age of eight. She is a graduate of Marshall Islands High School and also has studied International Relations and Diplomacy and Chinese at the National Taiwan Normal University and Tamkang University. Yolanie's theatre experience is robust, having performed in* The Tempest, As You Like It, West Side Story, Fiddler on the Roof, Guys and Dolls, The Music Man, *and* Carousel, *all for Youth Bridge Global in Majuro. Currently, she is continuing her studies at the College of the Marshall Islands. Yolanie's major is Liberal Arts and she plans to continue her education abroad. She is a profound admirer of cultures, history, language and the environment. Yolanie also plans to explore her passions for theatre production and directing later in her career. This essay was written in 2022.*

# A True Midsummer Night's Dream

Erza Syla
KOSOVO

It is funny how life works out sometimes. I often find myself getting opportunities I didn't even know I was looking for, and those are the best kind. This was the case when I was part of Youth Bridge Global's production of *A Midsummer Night's Dream* in Pristina, Kosovo.

I had never seen myself as an actress and I didn't even know I had the guts to try out. Moreover, I applied to audition for a different reason. Being so ambitious at such a young age had its benefits. One of my biggest dreams was to study at a university abroad, as if that would fix everything wrong in the world. This was true of most people my age, who dreamed of leaving our country, which was torn by war long before we were even born.

Kosovo was under Yugoslavian occupation in 1998–1999, and the Serbs managed to spread terror and acts of violence that completely tore our country apart. Many of our soldiers died in this war while protecting Kosovo. The conflict was eventually resolved through the intervention of the North Atlantic Treaty Organization. When the war was over, the people of Kosovo had a lot of work ahead of them to rebuild the country. Many at that time thought the reality we live today would never be possible.

Kosovo has since grown as a country, but it still is lagging in the area of education. I tried to fill up my resume with extracurricular activities, since that seemed to be what foreign universities were looking for. I signed up to volunteer with TOKA, a nonprofit youth development organization in Pristina, which was the first step I took out of my comfort zone. I met every week with a group of people who shared ideas and had lots of fun, and I soon realized that taking risks wasn't so bad. After a few months, I saw a post on TOKA's Facebook page in which a theatre group was looking for applicants to audition for an upcoming production. I must admit, my first thought was "Hmm … a Shakespeare play. Lame!" Spoiler alert, I ended up changing my mind.

After some investigation, I found out that this was an American production directed by a renowned Dartmouth professor. I realized that having this on my resume would definitely add so much, but there was one problem: I had never acted before in my life. Aside from my imaginary world as a kid, the only experience I had performing publicly was hosting school activities. My one advantage was that I had always been good at English, so I thought I could maybe earn a secondary role in the play. Competitive though I am, on this occasion I only wanted to be a part of the production, no matter how small the role. After giving it some thought, I decided to leave my insecurities behind and go to the audition.

"What does one wear to an audition?" I kept thinking. Finally, I decided on a yellow T-shirt and a pair of not-so-skinny jeans. It was a typical June day in hot and humid Pristina, so on the way there I was sweating, partly from the heat and partly out of nervousness. I hadn't prepared anything. For some reason I decided to go "tabula-rasa" on my first audition ever, a decision I was regretting on the way there. When I arrived, people around my age were already there, waiting for the auditions to start. I signed my name on the list and took a seat. After a while, I heard some people speaking English and identified the Americans. The professor, Andrew Garrod, started out by introducing himself and the team and explaining the play. He told us it would be performed bilingually, in English using Shakespeare's language and in Albanian. I thought it was a good idea to honor our language.

As I saw their team become comfortable in the space with all of the applicants there, I started to realize that the audition would be open. This didn't help my nerves. Thankfully, they wanted the boys to audition first, since fewer of them applied. Our friend Art was the first one to try out, and he set the bar impossibly high for everyone that came after. You could see his talent in his eyes—his confidence in his own skin as he talked and moved. He would make a perfect Demetrius.

When it was finally my turn, Professor Garrod asked me which role I wanted to audition for, and for some reason Helena, the comic lead, spoke to me. I read her monologue with as much poise and confidence as I could; sight-reading in English was easy for me. When I finally finished the paragraph, I was proud of myself for those few minutes in which I had overcome my fears. I read one more scene later, and then went home. A few days later, Youth Bridge Global, the organization that was putting on the play, called each of us to tell us if we had gotten a role. I had been cast as Titania, the pugnacious and confident queen of the fairies—a lead role. I was to alternate the role with Agnesa Berisha, who would perform entirely in Albanian. I couldn't wait for rehearsals to start.

In preparation for playing Titania, I first watched the movie in which Michelle Pfeiffer plays that role and thought to myself, "I'm no Michelle Pfeiffer." However, after carefully reading her lines, I thought I could have fun with this role and give it my own spin. On the first few days, we went through the script, read the lines, and Professor Garrod explained the scenes to us, which I found very helpful. Titania doesn't come into the play until the second act, so I had time to prepare myself mentally. We were sitting in a circle, but when it was finally time for my scene, Professor Garrod decided to have the actors stand up and to perform the scene improvisationally, as much as we could.

The first scene in which Titania appears consists of a boisterous argument with her lover, Oberon, who in our production was played by Jusuf Tofaj—a large, handsome, experienced actor. I later found out he was a drama student at the University of Pristina. He had a loud, somewhat theatrical voice, and he didn't blink a lot when he talked. I, on the other hand, with zero experience, had no idea what I was doing. The only thing I was confident of was my grasp of English; Professor Garrod constantly complimented me on it, so at least I was pronouncing the words correctly. Even though I felt anxious before reading the lines, I didn't feel apprehensive while actually reading them. It was a bit frightening because everybody was watching me, but I didn't know anyone there, so it was all right. Getting through the other scenes then got easier. We always finished around 4 p.m., and in the beginning I went home immediately. I'm always quiet when I don't know people well, because it's hard for me to get comfortable with them. The first time I hung out with some of the cast was when they invited me to have lunch with them. It helped me get to know them better, and from then on we always hung out at lunch time. I think it also helped us to create chemistry as a group, which you could see when watching the play.

One time, Professor Garrod invited a small group of us to his apartment to practice our lines and movements. This was one of the most helpful rehearsals, especially for Jusuf, Agnesa, and me since we got to know each other and our characters more. Agnesa and I tried to help each other with the scenes we had difficulty with. Watching her helped me get ideas on how to tackle certain scenes, and I'm sure it was the same for her when watching me. However, it also was important for us to create good chemistry with our co-stars Jusuf (Oberon) and Arianit (Bottom). They were both very talented, so it was easy to go through the scenes we had together. Even though their love story was brief, Titania and Bottom were a hilarious duo that the audience liked. I found it a bit hard to act as if I was in love with a donkey-head. I remember Alex, our movement director, telling me, "I don't believe you are in love with him!" and I responded, "That's because I definitely am not." However, I managed to take Professor Garrod's advice and imagine him not as a donkey but as a handsome man. "Imagine he's Brad Pitt," he would say. Professor Garrod often made such comparisons; to help me play Titania more confidently, he suggested that I think of myself as Beyoncé when I walked onto the stage. Come to think of it, that did really help me.

Whereas Titania's relationship with Oberon was largely verbal, with Bottom it was more physical, which I got comfortable with as the days went by. I think you could see Titania and Oberon's relationship evolve throughout the play. They come together at the end, along with their fairies, and we performed the most beautiful and emotional dance that closed the show.

Titania was such a confident and complex character; she walked and talked with great power, was a strong leader to her fairies, and I would say a bit conceited. I guess that's understandable, what with being a queen and all. Professor Garrod used to say I was the opposite of her; however, I found myself wanting to be more like Titania, the positive attributes at least; her charm and self-esteem, her way of getting what she wanted. I learned a lot about myself by playing her. I learned I can pretend I'm asleep for a good fifteen minutes while other actors are acting out their funniest scenes. The mechanicals ran around the stage and spoke their always hilarious lines, all while I seemed to be in my deepest-ever sleep. This was quite challenging, and to this day I wonder how I got through it without even a smirk. I also found out that I have what I now call a "Titania voice." This voice enables me to stand up for what I believe in without fearing others. I think it was the perfect part to get me into acting, because it offered the ultimate challenge every actor faces, the one of not being yourself, and Titania was different from me in many ways.

Whereas I didn't find it hard to learn all the lines in English or Albanian, I did have difficulty interpreting one of Titania's longer speeches. It went something like, "These are the very forgeries of jealousy," and I had to express rage and resentment to Jusuf about an affair he had with another woman. This part really presents Titania as the defiant and combative leader she is. Even though it was difficult, it came to be my favorite part of the play. Alex Payne, our movement director, designed the choreography for the entrance of the different female and male fairy groups. The sudden surges of movement and angular actions captured the antagonism the warring fairy groups felt for each other. I liked this scene so much because I saw Titania as a very strong woman figure. I valued her standing up to a dominant male leader and wanted to portray her in the most convincing way possible.

Learning the lines was always somewhat easier for me than working out how to move. I found it hard at times to show what I was talking about without seeming awkward. Here again, Alex helped. We all loved Alex for his ideas and his humor. His warm-ups before rehearsals always put us in a good mood and made us ready to go. Also extremely helpful was a brief visit from Jessica Swale, the Olivier Award-winning director and writer from London, whose notes about our performances were penetrating and helpful. She once acted out the first scene in the play, when Hippolyta and Theseus first come in. Jessica demonstrated the body postures of both characters, and I remember being struck by how beautifully she moved. Her effortlessness was how I wanted to portray my character as well. I was so interested in hearing her notes after she saw my part. She said that Titania's long speech is usually very dull for her to watch, but when I performed it for her she found it much more captivating than she remembered. Hearing that from Jessica reassured me that I was on the right track.

Performance day was coming closer. The stage was starting to get built. The costumes had arrived. The play was becoming real! When I first tried on my costume, it felt magical. It had multiple pieces, all very colorful. At first it felt as if everything would fall apart once I got on stage, but our costume designer Alma made sure everything would stay in place and look beautiful. She even did my makeup on the nights we performed, and it's amazing how some eyeliner and a bit of face highlighter can make you feel like a true fairy! The costume helped me get into character even more, as did the scenography with its trees and a big moon, and of course the fairy music that accompanied our performances. The costume was the final touch to Titania and it completed her. While it was a bit hard at first to move like a fairy while wearing it, I quickly got used to it.

The first night we performed for the audience was memorable for all of us. I had constant butterflies before going on stage, and that's how I knew I was in the right place. My heart was beating so fast, and the music that led us onto the stage helped get us ready, as it was very upbeat and dramatic. But when the music stopped and I stepped foot on that stage and it was my turn to speak, everything froze. I didn't think about the people who were watching us. I was one hundred percent present in the woods of *A Midsummer Night's Dream,* and the words came naturally to me. Luckily, the lighting didn't allow us to see much of the audience, but we could always hear their reactions and I remember feeling happy whenever they laughed at the funny situations in the play. For instance, when Titania wakes up from her sleep and finds herself in the arms of a donkey-head, she feels disgusted. When I acted out that scene, the audience burst out laughing. Strangely enough, one of my favorite parts came to be the curtain call, when everybody was cheering for us. We all felt immensely relieved for having done the best we could with our performances.

Our performance in the second venue was even better. We performed in Kukaj, a magical village that was ideal for our play. It was the last performance for everyone, so the whole cast was feeling extra emotional. It also was more personal, since the audience was sitting on stone slabs and was intimately close to us. The stage was set outside, so you could really get the feeling of being in the woods. We put our heart and soul into those last few moments. When the play was over and our fairy team did the last dance, it was a bittersweet moment of relief and sadness, of knowing we would never do it again. Having been with each other every day for two months and now suddenly having to say goodbye—that was an emotional experience all its own.

What started off as a resume-building experience for me turned out to be so much more than that. I discovered a new talent, acting, which I still often have difficulty believing I am good at. Being an admirer of the arts, this came to be such a blessing. In his role as an American private school teacher in the movie *Dead Poets Society,* the late actor Robin Williams said, "Poetry, beauty, romance, love … these are what we stay alive for." I love this quote because it shows how much we need art in our lives, and I am thankful it is so prominent in mine.

During that first theatre experience, I made new friends from different backgrounds who helped me along the way. We helped each other with delivering our lines, with our movements, even just by watching one another perform. We did have many differences, from our ages to our different points of view, but we all came together when it came to making the play better, stronger.

I rarely see the other cast members now, but I will never forget them. Most importantly, I found that my favorite place to be is on stage. Instead of fearing the public, I have learned to embrace it and communicate with it through my words and actions. This helped me gain enough confidence to apply for a job as a TV journalist and presenter at ATV here in Pristina, where I am now seen every Sunday talking about movies, theatre, and culture in general. In my opinion, if I hadn't had that Shakespearean experience, I wouldn't have been brave enough to start the journey that eventually led me to be on TV.

All in all, my first acting experience laid the foundation that will enable me to achieve anything I want in the future. I remember my bus ride home after a little goodbye celebration we had the day the cast was last together. I put on my headphones and started to think about everything I had been through for the past two months. As a tear rolled down my face, I knew I would never forget this beautiful experience. My acting experience in the summer of 2019 will forever be my first summer romance, a love that was born between myself and the world of theatre. It now seems like a midsummer night's dream I had a long time ago.

*Now eighteen years old, Erza is writing about playing Titania in* A Midsummer's Night Dream *when she was sixteen. After the summer with YBG, Erza went on to continue the two years of high school she had left. She finished Don Bosko High School in Pristina with high honors. During her senior year, she was hired to work as a journalist at the then up-and-coming broadcast station ATV in Pristina. She initially worked as a journalist on the* Sunday Show, *with her thirty-minute segment called "SHARE." There Erza created stories about the latest social-media news. In September 2021, she was promoted to author of a new TV show, called* AFLIX, *focused in the latest news in cinematography. Erza has been working at ATV for a year and a half now. She continues to write and present* AFLIX *today, airing every Wednesday on ATV. Furthermore, while still in high school, Erza applied and got admitted to the Rochester University of Technology in Kosovo (American University of Kosovo). In 2021, she started her studies with a concentration on Computing and Information Technologies. She is to graduate in spring 2025. At RITK, Erza is part of the Media Club and has been named Executive Producer of the TEDxRITK event, which is hosted by RITK every year. Erza was eighteen years old when she wrote this essay.*

# A Rwandan Romeo

Muhamadi Nshimiyimana
RWANDA

It all started in 2010, when I became a student at the National University of Rwanda. I didn't have a specific plan to study theatre, dance, or any other arts activity while at the university. Like most students, my purpose was to get an education and do not much else. However, the university had well-known programs in the arts and drama, and through one of these programs I attended an international festival run by the University Center of Arts and Drama. I was riveted by the beautiful theatre and dance performances. In fact, I was so impressed that I sought to join a dance company that would enrich my university experience.

I finally became a member of the Inyamibwa cultural troupe, a traditional dance company, and the Inshoza Contemporary Dance Troupe. During my four years at the university, I performed at numerous festivals as a traditional and contemporary dancer and actor. I made a lot of friends during that time, one of whom was Abdoul Mujyambere, who became my best friend.

Using the networking skills and experience I was gaining, I organized a group that presented a theatre piece during the genocide commemoration week that was observed in Rwanda every April. The production had a different theme each year. Even though I had little training and was all too aware of my lack of skills, I both acted in and directed most of these productions. In fact, I considered pursuing a career in the theatre after completing my university studies, which led me to do a lot of research, training, and volunteering with various local theatre productions.

In spring of 2013, Abdoul told me he had read that the Ishyo Arts Center was casting in Rwanda for an upcoming production of Shakespeare's *Romeo and Juliet*. I was somewhat indifferent to Abdoul's enthusiasm, as I had worked with Ishyo on various projects and knew their general level of performance. I was also trying to finalize my thesis at the time, which put major constraints on my free time. Abdoul begged me at least to attend the casting, which I initially resisted, but when Abdoul returned from the first day of casting he was impressed by what he had seen. He said that the production was led by highly professional directors from the United States and Canada in partnership with Ishyo Arts Center, and he described the techniques they had used, such as individual and group improvisations and taking photographs of every participant. He insisted that participation in this play would boost my skills in theatre production. He also reminded me that many prominent Rwandan artists were attending the casting so I should be ready for a serious challenge. With all this exciting news, I felt both energized and scared, but I sensed that it would be worth attending the casting.

I remember taking a bus from Huye to Kigali and feeling the pressure of someone who is about to perform. When I reached Kagugu, the casting venue, I saw a lot of people, some of whom I knew and some who were strangers. I could tell that at least a few of them were apprehensive about the auditions, which made me feel that the project was serious. I began to feel really motivated, and a voice inside me told me that I not only could do the audition but that I could get selected.

I remember the director introducing his team and their Rwandan partners. He told us that the casting would be open and that the lead roles likely would be double cast. Everyone was nervous because the audition was so well organized—not at all what we were used to experiencing in our local productions. One memorable exercise we were put through was to take a slow, silent walk past a member of the opposite sex who catches your eye and holds it. You had to make the audience feel that you were highly attracted to each other and that the encounter could lead to a date! This was both tough and scary, since everything had to be conveyed by eye contact alone. I felt quite proud of my performance and remember thinking that the exercise was "tremendous and awesome." After another casting session, Andrew and James, the two directors, called out the names of the cast and the roles they would play. I couldn't believe I had been cast as Romeo.

As Romeo I had to participate in most of the rehearsals. The experience boosted my technical knowledge and theatre production skills, and helped me to present my dance festival successfully.

I was immediately impressed by the way the rehearsals were run, from the time we began in the morning through to the end of the day. We always started with some warm-up exercises that were intended to help us improve our voices. We would sing or scream out something, which was a lot of fun, and it also helped me and my colleagues strengthen our voices. It was important that we be able to project well and speak clearly, as we were not using microphones during the performances. During the warmup, we would also play some cool and entertaining theatre games that were related to dramatic performance.

We then would start reading the script, which was in English, French, and Kinyarwanda. The toughest job was to critically understand Shakespeare's English in the text of *Romeo and Juliet*. Fortunately, we had good directors who helped us overcome the challenges. At that time, my English was not very polished, but being in the cast of *Romeo and Juliet* enabled me to interact with people from various countries and my English steadily improved. As the main script was in English, it was important to me that I not only learn the vocabulary quickly but also that I improve my accent. To be honest, it was not easy to do this, as we had limited time. Sometimes I would get frustrated when trying to memorize words that I couldn't easily understand, but inside I heard a voice of reason that reminded me why I was cast in the lead role. That voice gave me strength to continue, and to work on memorizing the script while at home. I thank all the people who helped me overcome the English challenges—most importantly James, the co-director, and his wife Heidi, an assistant director. Today, I am fluent and comfortable speaking English, which is one of the biggest benefits I got from participating in *Romeo and Juliet* in Rwanda.

Once the cast members were more familiar with Shakespeare's text, we took on the challenge of blocking the scenes. We spent a great deal of time learning how to create our own blocking, based on the emotions our characters were feeling at that moment. The directors helped us do this, asking, "Where do you think you should move now?" and "Where do you think you should go in relation to other people on the stage, based on your reading of the text and your emotional state?" It took time to block out all the scenes and to feel comfortable with our decisions.

It is imperative for actors to make eye contact, and nowhere is this more evident than in the scene where Romeo first sees Juliet. When Romeo and his friends Mercutio and Benvolio crash the Capulet party, Romeo is immediately transfixed by the sight of a shy, beautiful girl who is standing with other ladies. When playing this scene as Romeo, I followed Juliet with my eyes while she danced. Juliet was stunning as she spoke these words: "Did my heart love till now? Forswear it, sight / For I ne'er saw true beauty till this night." I loved hearing her recite these emotional lines. We sustained eye contact, which showed how attracted we were to each other, and we gradually moved closer together.

I love the moment when Romeo and Juliet first touch hands, and the sonnet Romeo recites at this moment are my favorite lines in the play. I remember the exact blocking of the scene, and it was easy to memorize the lines, which were powerful, flowing, and natural: "If I profane with my unworthiest hand / This holy shrine, the gentle sin is this: / My lips, two blushing pilgrims, ready stand / To smooth that rough touch with a tender kiss." Our hands then touched and we had our first kiss.

This scene was the foundation of the relationship between me and Tete, who played Juliet. We struggled a bit to build our relationship, but as we practiced the scene became more natural and, therefore, more memorable. Exchanging a true kiss in the theatre was not something we were used to doing in our local productions in Kigali. In fact, no one in this city had ever played Juliet or Romeo, so it's understandable that we were shy at the beginning. I remember Andrew showing me how I could make my performance more heartfelt and convincing. To be honest, my adrenalin was high every time we rehearsed this scene, and it is still my favorite in the play.

The balcony scene is another I relished performing. The text is quite long, which made it difficult to memorize, but as it's the scene in which Romeo interacts the most with Juliet, it is an important one. I put my heart into this romantic scene and did my best to convey my love to Juliet:

But, soft! what light through yonder window breaks?
It is the east, and Juliet is the sun.
Arise, fair sun, and kill the envious moon,
Who is already sick and pale with grief,
That thou her maid art far more fair than she:
Be not her maid, since she is envious;
Her vestal livery is but sick and green
And none but fools do wear it; cast it off.
It is my lady, O, it is my love!
O, that she knew she were!

I often got comments from female students who had come to watch our rehearsals. One told me that I was "doing perfect" but that I seemed a bit nervous, which prevented my acting from being entirely natural. She said I should let things flow in a more relaxed way. I also remember Tete telling me that I needed to improve my body language so that we could deepen our emotional connection and make the scene more convincing. Frankly, this comment annoyed me a bit, as it felt rather mean. We were in the month of Ramadan and I was fasting, and around 3 p.m. I began to feel a little bit hungry. This really affected me, and it was tough to memorize all the lines and play naturally when I was hungry. I told some members of the cast and my directors that I knew I would do my best when we performed for an audience, as most of the performances would take place after I had broken my daily fast. I do thank them all for the support they gave me.

I cannot talk about *Romeo and Juliet* without talking about the memorable scene in which Romeo and Juliet make love for the first and only time. The scene was well designed and the blocking was amazing. We had a bed on the stage; Juliet was in her night dress and I was bare-chested. In our culture most people are shy, and the cast members wondered what the audience's reaction would be when they saw two people on a bed making love. But we just said, "Let's just do it, but we must be perfect and careful." Well, everything went successfully and the audience did appreciate the scene.

The end of this scene marked the separation of Romeo and Juliet. The final scene, in which Romeo and Juliet kill themselves, was not an easy one in terms of acting and emotional expression. It was imperative to be natural and, most importantly, to connect with the audience by conveying real emotions. We rehearsed this scene over and over again.

I had many pleasures while doing *Romeo and Juliet* in addition to the satisfaction I got from the rehearsals and the performances at different sites in Rwanda. One special pleasure was when we went to Kibuye on Lake Kivu to have fun as crew. We did indeed have fun, and this trip helped me to build relationships with my fellow cast members.

However, not everything was perfect. Most of the cast, including me, was frustrated by the fact that we weren't paid. From the beginning, everyone had the information that all cast members would be paid, but during one of the rehearsals we were informed that we would not be. This information was not well received by most of the cast. We had a meeting, and some of us were inclined to refuse to practice until we got paid. I shared this view with my colleagues, as I had made several sacrifices for the project. However, a voice inside me was saying that I should continue with the play, as the experience I was gaining was so important and future opportunities could come to me as a result of this project. It came clear to my mind that I should continue with *Romeo and Juliet* as an artist and be able to provide my contribution toward building our country in a world of no racism, social conflicts, and wars. I still believe we should have been informed from the beginning that we would not be paid, especially in consideration of the effort and time we put into the project. Eventually, most members decided to come back to finish what we had started.

I learned so many things through my participation in the performance of *Romeo and Juliet*. First was the chance to meet new people who became my friends, some of whom I still have a strong connection to today. I also was able to learn a lot of technical things from the project directors and other crew members. This has enabled me to be confident in myself and helped me participate in other successful projects. For example, after we finished the play there were casting calls for locally produced movies, and everyone who performed in *Romeo and Juliet* was considered a highly skilled actor. I attended two casting calls and was selected as an actor, but I eventually decided to follow another career.

The *Romeo and Juliet* project was an extraordinary journey that boosted my artistic career. Today, I work as a risk management professional in one of the insurance companies in Kigali. Even with my limited time, I still find time to attend theatre productions and organize theatre and dance festivals, which the industry recognizes as high-quality productions. I know I made the right choice in staying with the play.

I want to thank director Andrew Garrod and Carole Karemera, the producer and a distinguished Rwandan actress, for giving me a chance to be part of the *Romeo and Juliet* cast and crew. I also want to thank all my fellow cast and crew members for being such amazing people and for providing important inspiration as I follow my career path.

*After his 2013 performance in* Romeo and Juliet, *Muhamadi Nshimi-yimana served as a project coordinator at a statistics-based consultancy research company. In 2014, Muhamadi worked on several artistic projects, including performing as a mass display choreographer in the Kwi-buka 20 Exhibition—an annual event held in commemoration of the genocide against the Tutsi people in 1994. His involvement in the arts also includes his position as the founder and director of Inkera I Rwanda, a traditional dance festival co-founded with the Inyamibwa Cultural Troupe AERG/UR (Genocide Survivors Association at the University of Rwanda).*

*Outside of his work in the arts, Muhamadi holds a bachelor's degree in economics, and is currently pursuing a master's degree in Business Administration. He also holds different professional certifications in finance, insurance, and arts. He has been a risk manager in financial and non-financial services for the past seven years, and is currently serving as the Head of Risk and Compliance at Old Mutual Insurance Rwanda. Prior to this role, Muhamadi worked as an underwriter and treasury accountant at Old Mutual Rwanda, and served as a research facilitator at Partners in Health from May to October of 2014. This essay was written in 2021.*

# Blessings, Cursed Blessings

Burns MacMillan

CANADA

Spring, 1972; my senior year at Saint John High School coming to an end. The *Telegraph-Journal* (New Brunswick's unofficial provincial newspaper) has described me, in the words of unidentified teachers, as a "top all-round student—athlete, scholar, dramatist."

I am privately writing bleak, suicidal poetry:

May 22, 1972

*Crow's Nest in Cloud*
*Persistent attempts at perseverance*
*point probably nowhere at all.*
*By being and being and being—who gets the bargain*
*me … you … someone out there?*

*Success, glory, money, power, position—WOW!*
*Then again, why bother?*
*Seek out a tree, an empty garage, or a rusty razor blade;*
*peace without bother—much more than minutes,*

*P.S. Or hours…*

Later that spring, at the school's annual awards assembly, I am lauded for my achievements as captain of the Greyhounds' football and hockey teams, as president of the student government, as an academic honours student, as an alto saxophone player in the senior concert band, as a lead player in three drama productions, and as director of a multi-award-winning entry in the province-wide student drama festival.

I am embarrassed. Despite this evidence of accomplishment, I feel like a fraud. I am secretly exploring the possibility of running away to join the navy as an ordinary seaman, escaping the weighty chains of adult responsibility that I had so willingly and (apparently) so successfully borne during my high school career. I know myself in no other way than by the masks I've been wearing: *responsible, role model, achiever, good boy,* only (surprise, surprise), I don't know with any certainty that these are merely masks. I have an inkling there's something buried inside, but I cannot (or dare not) articulate for the world what is beneath my surface.

Today, as I reflect on memories that are now just shy of a quarter century old, I am reminded of the cliché, "Hindsight is 20/20." Perhaps more apropos is the title of the 1994 song by the rock singer Meatloaf who cautions, "Objects in the rearview mirror may appear closer than they are." No doubt the distortions of time and the selectivity of memory have conspired to create the "truths" displayed in this essay. Nonetheless, deep currents tie together these remembrances. No matter the degree of distortion in the rearview mirror, the vivid experiences of my high school years—both blessings and curses—certainly were crucial in forming the person that I am today. And, no part of my high school experience, neither inside nor outside the classroom, was more filled with blessings and curses than was my immersion in SJHS's drama program.

## Setting the Stage

When I entered high school as a 15-year-old in the fall of 1969—the same inner-city school that had been attended some twenty years earlier by my parents—the "Arts" flickered at the edge of my consciousness but did not occupy a central place in either my interests or in the identity I was fabricating for myself. Until the age of eleven, I had grown up on the streets of the lower North End, living in an oil-heated flat in a nondescript, three-story, wood-frame structure on Metcalf Street. Life was focused on Roy Rogers, the Lone Ranger, and other cowboy heroes who had infiltrated my imagination via the novelty of black-and-white TV. Johnny Bower, Bobby Baun and other hockey heroes from the glory days of the Leafs invaded my dreams via *Star Weekly* picture profiles, bubble gum cards, plastic trading coins, and

Saturday's *Hockey Night in Canada*. Life consisted of shinny at the old Forum in Indiantown or under strings of multi-colored lights on outdoor ice at the Shamrock Grounds; playing organized hockey for the PALS (Police Athletic League) and later the Shamrocks; attending Cub Scouts and Mission Band at competing Baptist churches located only a single block from one another; hurling rocks, knuckles, and lumps of asphalt-dried dog dirt at Guimonds and Keenans and other Catholic kids who retaliated with equal vehemence and ignorance and innocence against the Protestant urchins across the back alley.

I was sucking up the rules of family, church, school, and community—institutions of authority that were to come under unprecedented attack by the time I'd reach my high school years. On one hand were the warnings:

- *Don't argue with your elders; a child's place is to be seen and not heard.*
- *Don't forget to wash behind your ears; cleanliness is next to Godliness.*
- *If you don't have anything nice to say, don't say anything at all.*
- *Never discuss politics, religion, or money at the supper table.*
- *Don't stand around with your hands in your pockets; people will think you're lazy or that you're playing with yourself.*

On the other hand were the models of desirable behaviour. I still have tucked away in a yellowing scrapbook a certificate I was awarded for being the Robin Hood Oats MVP as a peewee hockey player in 1966. The certificate is anchored by "The Players' Creed," the words of which I reverently read before bed every night for almost three years:

*AS AN ATHLETE I will obey my coach's training rules and keep my body healthy by observing all the rules of good clean living.*
*AS A SPORTSMAN I will play the game according to the rules of the game, displaying at all times fair play and a respect for the abilities and rights of others.*
*AS A STUDENT I will carry out my academic assignments both in school and at home and obey my teachers and other instructors at all times.*
*AS A SON I will respect my parents and heed their advice at all times.*

*AS A JUNIOR CITIZEN, in training for adult contributions to my community and country, I will observe tenets of my religion at all times and associate with youth groups in my community to learn worthy social attitudes and to contribute to the community's social welfare.*

*AS A CANADIAN, whether native or by choice, I will bear in mind the proud heritage of my country and so conduct myself to add to it.*

I was a true-blue Believer.

Where in all of this were the "Arts"? Perhaps playing tambourine in a second-grade rhythm band. Maybe in recorder lessons at Alexandra School. Perhaps in the grandparent-applauded one-verse soprano solo as a seven-year-old at Portland United Church. Likely in family stories about my dad's performance as Tiny Tim in a school production of *A Christmas Carol.* Probably through the grooves of a well-worn recording of *A Child's Introduction to the Orchestra.* Unquestionably in my passion for books. Undoubtedly in the tears I pretended not to see as they welled up in my father's eyes while watching films like *Shane* and *Old Yeller,* parked in the dark at the Grand Bay Drive-In in our '52 Chevy.

At the age of eleven, my voice cracked and deepened, whiskers rampaged and demanded that I, bearing Wilkinson Sword blades, take arms against them. My parents discreetly left a copy of *The Stork Didn't Bring You* beside my bed. Pooling their resources, my parents and paternal grandparents purchased a hundred-year-old house, and my family moved to the outer fringes of the North End. To the east, our windows faced the public housing of Rockwood Court, representing values and lifestyles that resonated with what I knew as my own. To the west, we looked out on the exotic and tantalizing worlds of Seeley Street and Rocky Bluff Terrace, on the homes of doctors, architects, and industry magnates. Straddling the fault line between these diverging worlds, I entered adolescence and, unbeknownst to me, began my final preparation for high school, the whirlwind into which I would be swept a few short years later.

During my junior high school years, mainstream organized sports—hockey, football, baseball, swimming—continued to be my central preoccupation. But the interests and influences of the relatively powerful and upwardly mobile elements of my new social environment spurred me to take the bait of competitive academics, and opened doors to school-sponsored music lessons, participation in orchestras and bands, field trips to amateur productions of operettas and popular American musicals, as well as opportunities to perform in one-act plays as part of an intramural activity program. It was through the latter, while playing the minor supporting role of a sergeant in a forgettable play called *Wayside War*, that I made my first acquaintance with Andrew Garrod—the "drama expert" brought in from Saint John High School to adjudicate our mini-festival. The seriousness with which he discussed our efforts, his compliments on my small contribution, his selection of our MacDonald House play to proceed to the New Brunswick Competitive Drama Festival in Newcastle, and his direct invitation to me to consider auditioning for SJHS's school plays the next fall were instrumental, though by no means exclusively responsible, for setting me upon the blessed and cursed course to which I alluded in the introduction to this essay.

## Initiations

In the early spring of 1970, I was a member of a highly touted SJHS hockey team competing in a provincial championship in Chatham, a small town in economically depressed northeastern New Brunswick. It was Friday night on the Miramichi. The stands were overflowing with boisterous, green-and-gold clad supporters of the hometown St. Thomas Tommies. Midway through the second period the score was knotted at two, and I was skating backward in my customary position on left defence when a burly winger wheeled across centre ice and wound up for a slapshot. My spur-of -the-moment reckoning told me that unless I made some speedy adjustments on my skates, I was likely to be sporting a frozen chunk of black rubber right between my eyes. I lurched toward my opponent, hoping that somehow I would close the distance and catch his impending shot on my shins or some other suitably padded part of my body.

The next thing I knew, I was momentarily coming to, curled in a fetal position, having bitten through a plastic teeth guard, watching a dizzy sea of faces fade in and out of focus above me, feeling briefly aware of an unbearable crescendo of pain between my legs.

In the morning I awoke facing an agonized Christ nailed to a crucifix hanging on a wall in a spartan room at the Hotel Dieu Hospital. I was immediately aware, despite the effects of medication dripping into my veins, of the insistent throbbing of my right testicle; the size of a tennis ball, it strained the elastic limits of my scrotum which, like the insides of both my thighs, bore the deep purple stains of internal bleeding.

During that day, more embarrassed than I could ever remember, I put on a stoic face while my insides cringed and flinched beneath the probing fingers and eyes of nurses—all women, all nuns.

Before returning to our port city, my coach and teammates visited me. The boys brought disappointing news of our team's narrow defeat and offered a collection of "girlie" magazines, replete with pinups, designed to magically fix what ailed me. Unfortunately, while they were there, I learned I would remain alone on my back, in hospital, for another seven to ten days.

So many thoughts and feelings clamoured for my attention. *What does this mean for my manhood? Will I ever be able to father children? Will I ever be able to have sex? Will I be permanently disfigured?* On a more immediate level: *What will I say to my friends when I get back to school and they ask why I didn't return with the rest of the team? How will my steady girlfriend of six months react?* And I was deeply concerned and preoccupied by the impact my injury might have on my chances of participating in *Carousel*, the annual school musical— arguably the social event of the school year and unquestionably the SJHS activity boasting the highest profile both within the school and the community at large. In addition to performing as a humble chorus member, I had been selected as a dancer, pending my availability for a mandatory weekend of rigorous dance rehearsals which was now very much up in the air.

Thanks to ice packs, bed rest, and a contraption called a "scrotal support" I have since enjoyed sex, fathered children, survived the queries of my peers, and succeeded in meeting the timetable required to be a full-fledged *Carousel* participant—a rousing initiation and the first of a trio of memorable experiences I would have with musical theatre at SJHS. To say the least, the peculiar circumstances leading up to *Carousel* introduced a theme that would plague me throughout my high school years—my attempt to juggle the often-conflicting demands, both practical and emotional, of my various interests and commitments, and those I sought to please, most notably in the arenas of athletics and drama. Blessings and curses.

Before examining the *Carousel* experience in greater detail, it is necessary to turn back the calendar a few months and touch on my initial experience with drama at SJHS in a "little theatre" production of Shakespeare's *A Midsummer Night's Dream*.

## A First Taste

*Lion:* You, ladies, you, whose gentle hearts do fear
The smallest monstrous mouse that creeps on floor
May now perchance both quake and tremble here,
When lion rough in wildest rage doth roar.
              —*A Midsummer Night's Dream*, 5:2, 217–220

Those words, combined with a crude papier mâché head, a braided rough-hemp tail, wool mittens, and a simple placard ("Lion") that hung around my neck, essentially sum up my first role on stage at SJHS. It was the fall of 1969, my freshman year of high school had just begun, and when auditions for the "Room 3" production of *A Midsummer Night's Dream* were announced, I had never previously seen, heard, nor read anything written by William Shakespeare. Naively undaunted, I arrived at the appointed date and time, accepted a well-worn copy of a navy blue-covered Oxford University Press text and, while waiting for matters to commence, found myself mesmerized and awed by the photographic record of theatre history meticulously mounted on the converted classroom's east wall. It dawned on me that I was about to become involved in something larger than the present moment, something with roots and traditions, something that might well leave a legacy for the future.

The audition consisted of a simple reading exercise. As though part of some preconceived plan, I was asked to read only the role into which I was eventually cast. My initial reading was tentative and dry, dry, dry. My insides were turning backflips and my ribs were slick with sweat cascading from my well-deodorized armpits. After a few words of advice from the director about the relative "doltishness" of my character, I was offered a second opportunity. Drawing from Walt Disney's Goofy, I leaped into exaggerated stupidity. With imagination in gear, my nervousness left me, and to my pleasant surprise, my peers responded with laughter and genuine amusement to the thick-headed character I was presenting.

I remember little about the actual performance of the play. What I do recall is mainly from rehearsal: I remember the camaraderie shared by the small group of "rude mechanicals," among whom I played one "Snug the Joiner." I remember the careful attention to text, and the hours spent ensuring that each and every cast member understood what they were saying so they could deliver their lines naturally and fluently. I remember Andrew Garrod patiently attempting to get me to roar in the manner of the MGM lion. Relatively unworldly, I was not yet familiar with that cultural icon, but I pretended. I remember being empowered to take risks as a result of Garrod's example, sleeves rolled up, tie loosened, on all fours with script in hand to model roaring and other lion-like behaviour. I laughed until my sides ached. I remember Garrod's high expectations, both for performance standard and commitment to the project. For the first night of many, I listened to him, prior to curtain on opening night, remind the cast that our task was to create an illusion, to enable audience members to "suspend their disbelief" and enter into our imaginary world. Our goal was to perform in such a way that our audience would later say they had witnessed a first-rate performance, unqualified by any reference to the fact that we were "merely students."

Mine was a tiny part. But there was nothing tiny about the experience of *A Midsummer Night's Dream*. It laid an important foundation for what would come later.

In the middle of my tenth grade year, Andrew Garrod and SJHS decided to mount a serious play on the school's mainstage in the 1,000-seat auditorium, a venue that up until then had been reserved for the popular spring productions of musical theatre. The first offering was ambitious—Peter Shaffer's *The Royal Hunt of the Sun*. While I was intrigued, I declined an invitation to audition, honouring a pact I'd made to limit myself to two productions a year and save myself time for academics, hockey, swimming, band, and a relationship with a steady girlfriend. This pact remained intact during eleventh grade but crumbled from without and within during my senior year.

### Through the Eyes of a Fifteen-Year-Old

In preparing to write this retrospective, I spent some time thumbing through the yearbooks I've saved from my SJHS years. One of the gems turned up was an essay I'd written to describe the first-time experience of performing in a school musical, namely, the 1970 production of *Carousel*. While my status in the show was merely that of a humble dancing chorus member, I relished entry to that highly esteemed facet of school/community culture. At the age of fifteen, I wrote:

*On auditions:* The hardest part was the beginning, especially the trying out. Singing a few notes in front of a bunch of snickering guys and giggling girls made me feel like digging a hole and crawling into it, but I survived, as is customary, and managed to stumble out of the music room, greatly humbled and very, very red with embarrassment at the mangled bunch of notes I had just emitted. A few hours later, my ego had begun to return and after thinking it over I came to the conclusion that my squawks were as good as anyone else's—at least any male's.

*On dancing:* Judy Scott, our American choreographer, appeared late Friday night, but it was well on into the morning when we were permitted to lay down our tired bodies for a night's rest. That first audition for dancing once again produced a great swarm of my colourfully-winged friends and this time I wasn't as lucky as previously. I couldn't remember the steps, I couldn't remember their order, and when things became slightly organized in my mind, my feet wouldn't always do what I wanted them to do. The looks I got let me know that something had to be done. Next morning from eight to nine I practiced by myself and by the start of the next session at nine I had mastered the initial steps. Saturday and Sunday were long days but at their end everybody had a warm feeling of self-satisfaction and accomplishment. To me dancing was undoubtedly the most enjoyable and rewarding part of the show.

*On performance:* One day's rest, then opening performance! By this time the butterflies had died or taken a holiday, and the nerves were non-existent. Words, emotions, everything came simply, as if by second nature. Only, for the first time a feeling of naturalness was present, and the essence of the play seemed to invade me. I wasn't me. I was a fisherman. Everything was just right.

### Divine Providence or a Crap Shoot?

My hidden preoccupations with metaphysical questions took a decidedly serious turn in eleventhth grade. Externally, I was still putting together pieces of the "All-Canadian Kid" persona. Internally, I was a seething cauldron of unanswered questions—questions of the ponderous "What is the meaning of life?" variety. The SJHS yearbook, *Red & Gray 71*, contains a poem that illustrates my preoccupations and provides a window on my unusually jaded outlook on the human condition. To read the poem today, is to see the ominous connections to the overtly suicidal "Crow's Nest in Cloud."

Spring, 1971

**An Answer**

Desire to live—Life's Constant.
But as Life proceeds how constant is this Constant?
On the bed of death and as the tide begins to ebb
Does it—this precious Life—exist and really have
        the great importance once attached?
I wonder if—when Life from you begins to flow—
You will strive to preserve what little scrap you can
        of what there used to be;
Or will you passively admit that life for you is through?
If told that you had one more day,
That life had run its course,
Would you preserve—would you accept—or would you just deny?
I wonder

It amazes me now that the unintentional signals in the poem did not alarm my teachers, friends, or family members. I wonder now why nobody checked in with me. My masks of self-assured competence must have contained powerful magic.

Fueling my intellectual/emotional search were my Grade Eleven enriched English course and my participation in the SJHS drama program—both led by Andrew Garrod. In his classroom, desks arranged in a circle (unorthodox in those days) to facilitate discussion, we were introduced to Thomas Hardy's bleak fatalism in *The Return of the Native* and D.H. Lawrence's exploration of sexuality and the dynamics of relationships in *Sons and Lovers* and *Women in Love*. While studying the then-current and controversial rock opera, *Jesus Christ Superstar,* I struggled with Christ's divinity and Judas's culpability, declared myself agnostic, and challenged the "born again" members of the class to provide me with concrete proofs. And the world and works of Shakespeare continued to provoke me, demanding that I assess the merits of sixteenth-century notions of Divine Providence against twentieth-century investment in Human Self-Determination. This was a heavy and heady mix.

Many of these themes were reinforced in the drama program. In mid-winter the school staged a highly successful production of *Macbeth* that drew a remarkable audience of some 3,500. The set for this show featured prominent phallic symbolism and reinforced the primitivism underlying the director's interpretation. These elements were also evident in the costuming—rough grey kilts held in place by rugged leather belts, fur leggings, coarse woolen cloaks, crude jewelry, and much brazenly-exposed male skin. In this atmosphere of primitive power and sexuality, my body looked and felt virile.

Playing "the worthy Thane of Ross," I performed a relatively small role, and my function in the play was primarily to convey information essential to the advancement of the plot. I remember the genuine inner conflict I felt as the "bearer of bad tidings" to people I loved and to whom I had pledged allegiance. I remember the softness I felt towards Lady Macduff and her children, the tears that filled my eyes as I told her that out of loyalty to country, her husband, my cousin, had abandoned his family and temporarily left it vulnerable to Macbeth's sinister machinations. I remember the intimate, brotherly affection I felt toward Macduff and the gut-wrenching turmoil in telling him later of the slaughter of his wife and children during his untimely absence.

I ached in concert with the anguish expressed by Ross near the end of
Act IV when he says:

> But I have words
> That would be howl'd out in the desert air,
> Where hearing should not latch them.
> —*Macbeth*, 4:3, 221–223

Ross got beneath my skin (or I got beneath his). Like more substantial roles I was to take on in my senior year, Ross gave me license
to explore a broad expanse of emotional terrain that would not have
felt possible nor safe in other social contexts. The split between Ross's
public persona (Thane, Nobleman, Warrior) and the sensitive private
self I attributed to him, somehow reinforced my sense of contradiction
between the person I was and the person I was *being*. Blessings and
curses.

On a personal level, my involvement in serious plays, particularly
the Shakespearean productions, was much more meaningful than the
experience of participating in high school musicals. Nonetheless, the
musicals were tremendous fun, high-energy, upbeat social events that
focused the attention of the school community and engendered a powerful sense of teamwork and school spirit.

In 1971, the annual school musical was *Guys and Dolls*. I was initially disappointed to have been cast in the non-singing role of "Big Jule,"
a tough, uneducated gangster and high-stakes gambler from Chicago.
As I was only five-foot-five, this casting was hardly a piece of subtle
humour, but this joke didn't make me feel self-conscious or uncomfortable in anyway. No matter what other insecurities I harboured, I
was confident and comfortable in my physical self. In some ways, my
role in *Guys and Dolls* was an opportunity to try on a criminal, "tough
guy" role, very distant from the "good boy" image I was cultivating,
and safely buffered by the frivolity of music and comedy. While I sang
lustily in the chorus and danced as part of the male ensemble, I privately aspired to have a solo singing part, and vowed I would in my
senior year.

My "tough guy" stance, of course, brought me into direct opposition
to the romantic lead, Sky Masterson. In one performance, Sky, being

played by David Mackenzie, let loose a right hook that got away from him in the heat of the moment and knocked me stone cold. I remember coming to with the play raging on about me, while my sidekick, Harry the Horse, was frantically slapping my face and shaking me back into consciousness. For a few tense moments, the lines between fantasy and reality were certainly blurred.

While *Guys and Dolls* had none of the seriousness of *Macbeth*, it managed in its own way to reintroduce the tentacles of sexuality and religion that were woven through my eleventh-grade year. On the one hand, the show was erotically charged by the revealing costumes and grinding dance numbers of the Hot Box girls, and the raw Cuban dance number which erupted into a full-scale brawl. On the other hand, Lady Luck was being invoked as a goddess by gamblers who staked fortunes, reputations, and relationships on the whims of chance, while nearby, the Salvation Army Band was exhorting the sinners on the street to leave their self-absorbed and self-gratifying ways, to get in step with the "truth," become believers, and "Follow, follow the fold." The play offered many interesting windows into which a declared agnostic could peer.

Near the end of eleventh grade three events set the stage for the whirlwind and whirlpool that was to be my senior year at SJHS. First, my role as co-captain of the school's fledgling football program was confirmed for a second year. This meant summer-long conditioning, a commitment to pre-season training camp in August, and a willingness to play an active leadership role in a program that was still getting its feet under it and was bound to suffer some setbacks. Second, I succumbed—against my better judgment—to pressure from peers and teachers, agreeing to take on the role of president of the student government. No doubt echoes of "The Player's Creed" were ringing in my ears when my twisted sense of community duty kicked in! And third, I was cast in the demanding lead role of "Bitos/Robespierre" in an intellectual Jean Anouilh play titled *Poor Bitos* that was slated for performance on the Room 3 stage in early autumn. To say that internal or external expectations of me for my senior year were high, or to say that my plate was full, would at best be understating the case.

## The Show Must Go On

My senior year in the SJHS drama program was passionately and shockingly launched during a September matinee of *Poor Bitos*. My character's flashback-filled eyes riveted on an intense female face in the second row of the darkened Room 3 Theatre and my lips spit a venomous accusation: "Whores!" Then, for a split second, I realized the coincidental target of my/Bitos' violent condemnation was a stern, middle-aged, Roman Catholic nun accompanying a group of girls from nearby St. Vincent's High School. Time slowed, breathing ceased, I couldn't avert my eyes. In the stunned silence I could hear hairs rising on the back of my neck. A line had been crossed; a taboo violated.

The moment passed.

Later that night, I found myself trembling beneath the sloped ceiling of my attic bedroom, shaken by my character's verbal, but nonetheless sexually assaultive, encounter with Adult-Woman-Celibate-Catholic-Teacher. Somehow, I felt both ashamed and profoundly challenged to make sense of the powerful impact this incident had had on me. I breathed a word about it to no one.

Three days later, filling in for the injured punter of the SJHS Greyhounds football team, I fractured my right ankle. For the next few hours, my greatest concern was how I would be able to meet the strenuous demands of my leading role in the Saturday night finale of *Poor Bitos*. Never "if" I would be able, only "how" it could be accomplished. The show must go on, and Burns MacMillan must never disappoint anyone who is depending on him. Amen.

An oversized shoe was found to accommodate my swollen and carefully wrapped foot and ankle. And, assisted by a cane, I was able to "heroically" hobble my way—in considerable pain—through what was, I believe, my finest performance in the role of Bitos. Blood was spilt; tears were shed. The shifting lines between fantasy and reality once again blurred.

Of the seven parts I played while in high school, the role(s) of Bitos and Robespierre (the former's historical alter ego from the French Revolution) came closest to the hidden core I now understand to have lived within me during adolescence. Behind a brittle mask of competence and superiority lay a deep pool of pain, insecurity, and raw vulnerability fed by creeks flowing from the murkiness of childhood.

By twelfth grade, as implied by the overtly suicidal poetry which introduced this essay, I was expending substantial psychic energy in seeking ways to relieve that pain, once and for all. Re-reading *Poor Bitos* some twenty-five years later, I am struck by the way in which Robespierre, in Act 2, describes death as an agent of comfort:

> I shan't speak. They'll never hear my voice again.… They'll never know what I was thinking, from the moment that young ruffian fired his pistol full in my face. I looked at him as he pulled the trigger.… I let the pain open in me, suddenly, like a great red flower. All the noise, the fury and the agitation, the hatred and the hurts—gone with a pistol shot. As my blood oozed away through the hole in my jaw, I felt one by one, all my other wounds close up inside me. Just a little more life still left, and then I would be cured, at last. It all falls into place. But it took a long time to learn.

Taking on this persona, trying on these feelings, speaking these words—I wonder how, if at all, I was affected? Did I make connections to my self? Was I enticed by this vision of relief? I don't recall. But it would be hard to enter into a dramatic experience as openly and completely as I know I did, and not be marked by my relationship with the character I assumed and the characters with whom he interacted.

### Whiskers and Other Rank Offenses

While the role of Bitos/Robespierre resonated most strongly with my emotional life-experience, the part of Claudius in SJHS's mainstage winter production of *Hamlet* provided the greatest intellectual stimulation and required by far the toughest personal stretch. One might well question how credibly a seventeen-year-old youth could portray an adulterous, murdering, middle-aged monarch, but I attained some measure of success. How I succeeded is not particularly clear to me. However, it is likely that at work was some combination of Garrod's emphasis on the informative power of text, a breadth of vicarious experience fed by a voracious appetite for reading, and an active imagination capable of synthesizing the foregoing into the creation of a character.

A less self-interested view of this accomplishment was reflected in comments by a theatre critic for the *Evening Times–Globe*:

> Three other performances that would be good from any amateur company were exceptional from young actors. The emotional range and subtlety of characterization required from the Queen, the King, and Polonius are very difficult to achieve.... Burns MacMillan gave the King incisive power. He handled situations swiftly with imperious gestures and firm voice. We had to admire his physical courage and respect the sincerity of his pricking conscience.

My physical maturity may have been a factor in helping me carry off this role. In preparation for this production, I grew my first beard—surprisingly thick and full; predictably, the envy of many of my peers. Interestingly, the influence of that beard played out in other ways. Having spent my childhood and early adolescence in the 1950s and '60s, I had been required by my father to wear a closely trimmed crew cut or brush cut until the age of fourteen, and the hygienic and social virtues of a clean-shaven face were not infrequently extolled. Needless to say, growing facial hair in the name of "Art" did not go over well on the home front. In the school setting, my beard did not gain universal admiration either. I still have vivid memories of the resentment I felt when, as student council president, I was introduced by the school principal to present the routine list of activity announcements at the weekly assembly of the student body. In that introduction he sneeringly stated that I would provide the assembly with an explanation of the "dirt" that had appeared on my face. In the ice hockey arena, the whiskers also produced an unanticipated result. Unwittingly, I had taken on another mask, a mask that presented me as older and more serious. Combined with my aggressive, physical style of play, my new image earned me an undeserved reputation among opposition, fans, and players as a mean-spirited villain.

But, back to *Hamlet*. Shakespeare's tragedy raised provocative questions for me, ranging, for example, from Hamlet's ponderings about filial duty, to the relation of courage, cowardice, and comfort to the act of suicide, to the existence and nature of an afterlife, to the implications of illicit sexuality in the relationship between Claudius and Gertrude, to the nature of villainy. However, there are two personal moments in the play that are particularly marked in my memory. The first occurred in Act 3, Scene 3:

> *Claudius:* O, my office is rank, it smells to heaven,
> It hath the primal eldest curse upon't,
> A brother's murder! Pray can I not,
> Though inclination be as sharp as will.
> My stronger guilt defeats my strong intent,
> And like a man to double business bound,
> I stand in pause where I shall first begin,
> And both neglect. What if this cursed hand
> Were thicker than itself with brother's blood,
> Is there not rain enough in the sweet heavens
> To wash it white as snow? Whereto serves mercy
> But to confront the visage of offense?
> And what's in prayer but this two-fold force,
> To be forestalled, ere we come to fall,
> Or pardon'd, being down? Then, I'll look up;
> My fault is past. But, O! what form of prayer
> Can serve my turn?…
> —*Hamlet*, 3:3, 37–72

Playing downstage centre, my hands desperately clutching a wooden crucifix hung around my neck, I remember the anguish I felt as I struggled with my guilt, yearned for forgiveness, and was unable to enter into prayerful communication with the God who might somehow provide me with relief. During that speech, as strange as it might seem, I knew something about the essential goodness of humanity, something about the difference between evil acts and evil nature, something about the complexity of human nature that defies the simplistic labeling of good and bad to which we are so easily drawn. I know that, as with Bitos (and with myself), Claudius was not a simple, two-dimensional villain. Delivering this soliloquy, I was aware of the power I held as an actor, the power to make people listen, to make people squirm, the power to demand attention, to create relationships with strangers on the basis of emotional affinity.

The second memory comes from the final scene of the play, just after Hamlet has finally taken his revenge on Claudius by running him through with a poison-tipped rapier and forcing him to drain the dregs of a poison-laced goblet of wine. During one performance, the "pearl" that had been used to poison the wine became lodged in my throat. Lying "dead" on the stage floor, my face only partly averted from the audience in the right-hand side of the house, I was literally choking to death. Finally in one last—though clearly belated—spasm, I coughed up the pearl which, sounding to my ears like thunder, rolled across the stage before dropping into the orchestra pit. I held my breath waiting for the others on stage to break into gales of laughter, destroying the illusion we had worked so hard to create, ruining this crucial moment of high tension in the play. It didn't happen. How the remaining players managed to maintain their concentration and composure is a mystery, but some credit must go to the vision we shared of the importance of the venture to which we had committed ourselves. This was not to be taken lightly.

## Wonder of Wonders, Miracle of Miracles

The final musical theatre experience of my high school years was *Fiddler on the Roof*, the first performance of the Broadway smash to be staged anywhere in the Maritime provinces. Though it lacked the emotional intensity and intellectual challenge of Bitos or *Hamlet*, it provided considerably more to chew on than had *Carousel* or *Guys and Dolls*. Having invested some seven months in weekly classical voice training, I finally achieved my goal of obtaining a solo singing role—Motel the Tailor, a meek, mild, and somewhat comical young man (quite a contrast to Claudius and Bitos!). He falls in love with and marries Tzeitel, the eldest daughter of the play's lead characters, Golde and Tevye, Jewish peasant farmers scratching out a subsistence living in the days leading up to the Russian Revolution.

In my one opportunity as a solo tenor, singing the catchy and light-hearted *Wonder of Wonders, Miracle of Miracles*, my singing was clearly underwhelming. However, when combined with the skills and experience I had gathered over three years as an actor and dancer, the overall product was certainly acceptable.

The performance, though, is not my primary recollection of *Fiddler on the Roof*. Rather, what remains are connections the play made for me—connections to my ongoing explorations of religion and personal spirituality, fed by exposure to Jewish belief, history, and culture, as well as by the contribution made to our production by the excitement and direct involvement of the local Jewish community; connections to one of the most profound academic experiences of my high school years, the writing of a 100-plus-page essay examining the Russian Revolution as it had been presented in the Saint John newspapers of the day; connections to my preoccupation with the impending complications of adult relationships and responsibilities, underlined by the festive and sobering ritual of being wed under the traditional Jewish canopy, full of hope but facing the prospects of a most uncertain future.

## Synthesis

A time-honoured yardstick of learning is the ability to make practical applications of what has been learned. A practical opportunity to demonstrate what I had learned about the theatre after three years under Andrew Garrod's influence came my way in the final months of my senior year at SJHS. At that time, the last segment of the twelfth-grade English curriculum was a unit of independent study. And, coincidentally, the scheduling of the unit coincided with the province's annual school drama festival.

Earlier in the year, while attending an evening session of a Garrod-inspired extracurricular program known as Peripatetics, I had listened to a recording of Shakespeare's *A Winter's Tale*. I had immediately been taken with the potential for student performance of the portion of the play set in the relaxed, rustic kingdom of Bohemia. This idea quickly returned to me when it came time to plan my independent English assignment.

While I don't remember feeling particularly intimidated by the prospect of directing my peers in a Shakespearean play, today it seems like quite an undertaking for a seventeen-year-old. The success that was achieved seems no less remarkable. The cliché, *Imitation is the sincerest form of flattery*, seems to have been borne out in both the process and the product. In fact, in the aftermath of *A Winter's Tale's* presentation at the New Brunswick Drama Festival in Campbellton, adjudi-cator Ted Daigle was quoted as saying "Burns has previously worked under the direction of Andrew Garrod, and it shows." At the com-petitive drama festival, up against fifteen other entries, most of which were adult-directed, *A Winter's Tale* received awards for best actor, best supporting actor, best student director, and best production.

Like the Russian Revolution paper, *A Winter's Tale* was experiential learning in action—a profound demonstration and confirmation of much that I had learned during my three years at SJHS about Shake-speare, about plays, about leadership, about organization, about my own abilities.

However, despite all this success and affirmation, I am reminded that the timing of *A Winter's Tale* corresponded fairly closely with the writing of the poem "Crow's Nest in Cloud" that opened this essay. "*Success, glory, ... power, position.*" I had obvious experience of these external referents, but there was something hollow in it all, something I couldn't understand until I was scalded by a serious personal crisis years later.

### Threads, Connections, and Closure

*So it is more useful to watch a man in times of peril, and in ad-versity to discern what kind of man he is; for then at last words of truth are drawn from the depths of his heart, and the mask is torn off, reality remains.*
——Lucretius, *On the Nature of Things*

Last June, my seventeen-year-old daughter, Megan, graduated from Saint John High School and in September headed off to Acadia Uni-versity in Wolfville, Nova Scotia, to study outdoor recreation. At the age of forty-two, it neither surprises nor perplexes me that my daugh-ter is on the verge of adulthood, but there is something unsettling in the fact that she is at a place in her life which, in the vividness of my memories, seems like such a recent occurrence in my own life. How can it be that those days seem so poignantly fresh despite the irrefut-able evidence in my external world that those days are long since past? What is my point? Merely to suggest that in the face of memories that remain so alive, memories that have fueled the sights and sounds, the smiles and tears, the anecdotes and reflections that make up this essay, it would be ludicrous to state anything other than that my high school years in general, and my involvement in the SJHS drama program in particular, have had a profound influence on the ways my adult life has unfolded and continues to unfold. Mind you, unraveling specific points of influence is a considerably more challenging enterprise—the task to which I set my mind as I draw to a close.

When I departed the Prince William Street hallways of SJHS in 1972, I dutifully trundled off to Dalhousie University in order to fulfill the expectations set for an All-Canadian kid—to enter a pre-med program, achieve a medical degree, and ultimately assume a respected, leadership position doing good in the world in an acceptable, conventional manner. By October of my freshman year, while watching a physical chemistry class on a hallway monitor with other medical school wannabes who hadn't gotten a seat in the lecture hall, the penny dropped. A few days later, I had taken the steps to transfer into an Arts program and earn a double major in English and Theatre. Rebellion. No obvious career path. Taking a step toward claiming and honouring the parts of me that were creative and reflective. And, while these moves did generate tremors and aftershocks, the sky did not fall.

Years later, I was able to obtain an education degree and spend a few years teaching English and directing plays at the secondary level. In both enterprises, seeds planted in the SJHS drama program could be seen to bear fruit. My classes and my plays bore witness to my love of the language, power and dramatic potential of poetry, to my belief in the often undervalued and untapped potential of young people, to my high expectations of student performance, to my encouragement of a pursuit of excellence, and to my commitment to a process of experiential learning—a process that doesn't restrict itself to a classroom setting, a process that acknowledges the transformative power of demanding, real-life, first-hand experiences.

Other than in the direction of student plays, the theatre has retained a place of personal importance in my adult life. I have been house manager with a professional theatre. I have reviewed plays as a newspaper journalist. I have acted, sung and danced in community theatre productions. I have continued to attend professional and amateur theatre on a fairly regular basis. And, from time to time, my passion for literature leads me to read a play.

Connections between my adult involvement in and approaches toward education and theatre, and the SJHS drama program are not too difficult to uncover and itemize. However, those connections do not reflect the deepest places I believe I was touched by my three-year encounter with the program. I have already suggested that high school drama was for me a blessing and a curse, a double-edged sword. And, I have insinuated that the wearing of metaphoric masks was a primary agent in allowing me to taste blood drawn by both edges of that sword.

The SJHS drama program was the place where, protected by the conventions of theatre and the masks afforded by assumed characters, I was freed—I was given license to take risks in exploring and experiencing the limits of who I was, experimenting with life in ways I was otherwise too afraid to touch. The SJHS drama program was also the place where, hidden by the conventions of theatre, I was able to dissemble, I was able to practice and hone my ability to wear masks without detection, to act convincingly, to increase the separation between external presentation and internal reality.

It is no great surprise to me now, that when in my early thirties—deeply depressed, full of shame and self-loathing—I checked myself into a psychiatric hospital, there was no one, not even those closest to me, who had suspected the existence, let alone the depth, of my despair. Until the last possible moment, my masks had borne up under the scrutiny of my world. And, when the first masks fell and shattered at my feet on that brittle November morning, it is also no great surprise to me now, it took some time and considerable healing before I was either able or willing to reveal my nakedness, move out from the place of asylum I had sought, and exist genuinely in the world. That, however, did happen, and often in the course of subsequent therapy and recovery, the metaphor of theatrical masks, the notion of life as theatre, has served as a useful vehicle in peeling away layers and getting at the core of my being, a core that is at once both strong and vulnerable. Today, as I continue to open and grow in my life, I am no longer hiding behind my masks, neither am I driven to perpetually reveal my naked self to the world. What matters is to be able to differentiate between the masks and the authentic, to be conscious of when masks are in place, and why.

So, this essay comes full circle. There is little question my SJHS drama experiences were rich in experience, triumphant in achievement, excruciating in emotional intensity, and profound in their impact on the person—flawed, realized, fulfilled, and becoming—that I am today. Twenty-five years later, I am able to join songwriter Bob Dylan in claiming "I was so much older then, I'm younger than that now."

*Burns MacMillan lives in Saint John, N.B., with his wife, Judith, an English teacher at Saint John High School, and their dog, Maya. Burns has been engaged as a journalist and copywriter, parole office and case manager, high school teacher and a corporate trainer. While "officially" retired, he continues to take on supply teaching assignments at SJHS, where he also volunteers as offensive line coach for the school's football team. Burns enjoys sharing time with his children and grandchildren, exploring trails and waterways, following the exploits of the Boston-based professional sports teams, and feeding his active curiosity, love of a good story, and commitment to lifelong learning through books and other media. This essay was written in 1996.*

PART THREE

# Outsider to Insider

# Magnificent Obsession

Lani Selick

CANADA

"Who's *that?*"

A colleague of mine, passing by my desk at work, stopped in front of a large, dramatic, black-and-white photograph mounted on my bulletin board.

"That's my thirteen-year-old daughter," I replied, somewhat hesitantly. I wasn't sure whether to be proud or embarrassed. "She's crazy about acting and very driven. She gave us no peace until we took her to the professional agencies ... and one of them has taken her on. That's her 'talent photo.'"

My colleague clapped her hands enthusiastically. "Wonderful! I have a whole theory about getting through the teenage years. You've got to have a 'magnificent obsession.'"

A "magnificent obsession." What exactly does it mean? To me, it suggests a very special kind of pursuit—something more intense than a hobby, but less ideological than a cause or crusade. The idea speaks to a kind of passion that is inherently romantic—a love for love's sake. You engage in your chosen pursuit because it embodies worthy ideals and values and because doing so will make you a better person.

Certainly, when it comes to teenagers, I think there is considerable wisdom in the notion that a magnificent obsession can be a godsend.

Growing up is a solitary process. As an adult-in-training, you get lots of advice, but unfortunately, no "stand-ins" to undergo the metamorphosis for you. To leave your bedroom cocoon in the morning is to walk into uncharted territory: will your parents blithely hand over the keys to the car or fight your proposed curfew, and will you defy them if they do? Will your classmates praise your new dress or make fun of your new hairstyle (and why should you care what they think anyway)? Will that cute boy you've been eyeing suddenly strike up a conversation or haul out a pack of smokes and offer you one, and can you refuse without seeming like a nerd ... or do you even want to refuse? Amid all the sundry possibilities, it is easy to lose your way.

For teenagers, I believe the value of a "magnificent obsession" is, at its simplest, the value of an anchor in a storm—a secure lifeline. To it, teenagers can attach their hopes and dreams and through it they can discover their inner worth. And as "magnificent obsessions" go, a passion for drama is a particularly good choice. After all, to become a player in this particular game is to sample other characters and other lives, to find templates for your own existence, and to do this with a group of other people committed to helping each other learn from this experience. When it comes to helping young people get through the make-or-break teenage years with their egos intact, spirits high, horizons broadened, and humanity awakened, involvement with dramatic production can be invaluable. I speak from personal experience.

Just as my daughter is now doing, I spent my own teenage years engaged in a frenzy of thespian adventures, although I began slightly later than she did. My experiences centered on an extracurricular drama program at Saint John High in New Brunswick. This endeavor was the defining experience of my adolescent years. To a great extent, it has determined who I am today, and perhaps what I am passing on to my children. How else can I account for two theatre-loving offspring, the above-mentioned thirteen-year-old actress-daughter, and an incongruous seventeen-year-old son who despises literature but is passionately devoted to Shakespeare?

I entered Saint John High School in the fall of 1964 and soon found out about the Drama Club. At the time, I was no stranger to performing in front of an audience—in fact, I'd been doing it most of my life and was a bit of a celebrity in my home town. However, all of it was singing solo. I had never done any group performances or serious acting.

My musical career began at age five when I won a spot on a locally produced television program. I had been entertaining my own family for years—my parents had discovered my nice singing voice when I was barely out of toddlerhood and loved to hear me sing almost as much as I loved to sing. In particular, I used to give command performances of "Tina the Ballerina." "Tina the Ballerina" was a children's record, a favorite of mine, which interwove a simple narrative with songs. I would put the record on at low volume and use it rather like a karaoke to give my own rendition of this material. It seems that I was forever hounding my mother about singing on radio or television like other little kids I observed on a variety of entertainment programs popular during that era. One day, I overheard my mother talking about the upcoming auditions for a new weekly children's talent show that was being started by the local television station, CHSJ, and I insisted on trying out for a spot. When the auditions took place, I not only won a spot on the premiere telecast, but the producers and the live audience responded so enthusiastically that I was invited to become a regular. I performed on *Time For Juniors* every week thereafter until I was fourteen and became very much a "star" in my city and its surrounding community.

Strangely enough, while this experience made me comfortable in front of an audience, it did nothing to make me comfortable with my peers. In fact, it marginalized me as "different," someone to target. I brushed up against a lot of jealousy and arbitrary character assassination, often by kids who didn't even know me. I was forever encountering two sisters, identical twins, on my walk to school. These girls, who were strangers to me, used to walk a few feet behind me and talk in loud voices about how "stuck-up" I was. I never knew what to do about it, how to introduce myself, how to tell them I wasn't stuck up—I just didn't know them! Things weren't much better with my classmates, from whom I was often at the receiving end of jibes and petty resentments ("You're the teacher's pet because you're on TV!").

I was by nature a thin-skinned child and the taunts hurt. Mostly, I coped by trying to pretend to myself that I didn't care, but often I would stroll casually past a group of popular girls, secretly observing them, trying to figure out how I could become one of them. They were always flitting and fluttering about and inevitably made me think of butterflies. I even wrote a poem about this once. All I remember is the first line, "The Butterfly Girls don't notice me…" The Butterfly Girls were all very pretty and wore trendy clothes whereas I was rather plain and unfashionable. Sometimes, I would go home and stand for hours in front of the mirror, playing with my hair, changing my clothes, trying to find ways to make myself more attractive in the hope these things would improve my social status. But nothing worked for me. I always felt like an outsider, a misfit, never quite able to fit in with all the other kids I knew—they weren't on television, I was. They were average, "normal" kids, I wasn't.

By the time I arrived at Saint John High School at the age of fifteen, I was a self-conscious and awkward teenager, lonely and desperate for friends. Nevertheless, I didn't join the school Drama Club to find a social group that would welcome me. Nothing in my experience so far had predisposed me to believe that this was likely to happen. I joined because based on all my performing experience, I thought I'd be reasonably good at it, and like most people, I like to do what I do well. Besides, I simply loved performing. Television was the one "place" where I was popular: people recognized me wherever I went, strangers would stop right on the street to offer compliments. Outside of my family, the audience was the only group of people I could depend on year in and year out to massage my ego and make me feel good about myself.

One of the most powerful images I have of my entire time in the Drama Club—or for that matter, my entire high school experience—centers around my first audition. When I arrived at the announced location, I discovered that another girl from my English class was trying out for the same role that I was. This girl happened to be standing next to me when we found out that we had both got it (to perform on alternate nights). She turned to me with such obvious delight in her face that it was impossible to think that she was simply being "nice." She grabbed my hand spontaneously and said, "Oh, isn't that great? Maybe we can learn our lines together?" Now, a more-or-less unknown teenager making such a modest overture of friendship might not seem like much to most people, but to one unaccustomed to such overtures, it was like receiving a bouquet of roses from a secret admirer. I'm sure I danced all the way home from school that day, if not in body, at least in spirit.

In the end, Judy and I didn't learn our lines together, but she became my very first true friend, ultimately my best friend. Within days of meeting this girl, I came across two boys from the cast who were making plans to see a new movie in town, and who promptly invited me to join them. And more relationships quickly followed, within days of the start of rehearsals—or so it seemed—and without my doing anything! It seemed like the "outsider" existence I was so resigned to had vanished in the space of a few weeks. Suddenly, I went from having no friends to having dozens. I think my "magnificent obsession" with drama began with that first hand that reached out to grab mine at the audition and the other outstretched hands that followed. I was drawn to the unique, inclusive theatre community to portray characters as rare breeds of human folk. This community was a magnanimous, tolerant group who reached out and embraced people that society at large often rejected. People like me. The bottom line for me was that drama provided me with a place to belong in what I continued to regard as a generally unfriendly world. I was an "insider" here. I remained afraid that anywhere else, I would revert to being an "outsider."

I know that other students besides myself responded consciously or unconsciously to these kinds of humanitarian values and were attracted to the Drama Club because of it. Indeed, in the case of a few students I can think of, I'm sure such values were more or less the only reason they joined, because these kids were not—at least on the surface—obvious theatre-buffs. I remember one boy in particular, I'll call him John Smith, who was the sort of fellow that, unfortunately, many teachers tended to write off. John and I were in many of the same classes throughout high school. He always sat in the back of the room and if he wasn't failing, he was just on the verge. If academics weren't his forte, neither was acting. He was simply dreadful! Yet, he auditioned for plays year after year. He generally ended up with a bit part, servant or soldier or some such character, said things like "Prithee help me!" and died before the third act. He didn't mingle much, but came to all the rehearsals without fail, and usually sat by himself. I was far too socially inept to try to interact with anyone so withdrawn and never got to know him very well, but from what I could tell, he seemed quite content in his own way. I think he liked just being there. Perhaps what mattered to him was knowing that he was genuinely welcome on his own terms, and that the choice to sit apart was his, not ours.

In my own case, my acceptance into the drama group was something that I couldn't initially believe. Frankly, I distrusted it, especially because it had been so easy and I had done so little to make it happen.

All I had done, after all, was join a club. I hadn't changed my personality or my life. Why were these people being so nice to me? I tended to be strictly reactive in stoking relationships, even when it came to simple matters. For example, it took me a long time to ask anyone to join me for lunch at school; mostly, I contrived to hang around people from the cast at the appropriate hour, and wait for someone to invite me. But as time passed, and people continued to act friendly and include me in plans to hang out together outside of school and drama, I began to relax and take more initiative. A few months after I became part of the drama "gang," I helped set up an informal group activity. We gathered together one Friday night to sample each other's favorite albums and just shoot the breeze. The "record club," as it came to be called, was quite a success, and soon became a regular weekend event at alternating homes.

In some cases, the ties between us were quite superficial: the simple camaraderie of a group of like-minded people, a comparable dynamic, I assume, to that among members of sports teams. But in other cases, the bonds were much more complex, involving shared interests, intimacies and emotional support. My best friend, Judy, and I were both somewhat overprotected first daughters whose parents were reluctant to let us roam as freely as most other kids. Since neither of us was the rebellious type, we came together to gripe about our lives, talk girl-talk and exchange secret confidences. She was achingly beautiful in an open-faced, wide-eyed, California-girl kind of way, with a sunny-side-up personality. I simply idolized her. Girls delighted in her company and boys always flocked around her. She was everything I wanted to be! I told her this once and she gave me a big hug and said I was great just the way I was, that I just needed to believe it. And I did start to believe it, sort of. I glowed with the light she gave me, as in a kind of sun-moon relationship. I figured I must have something to offer if this popular girl wanted me for her friend, when she could pick and choose! Shining with borrowed self-esteem may not be ideal, but it is a start, and surely better than not shining at all. And thanks to the Drama Club, I now had a whole group of chums, so my inclination to count my value by my number of friends got a hefty boost.

It is always important for children to feel good about themselves, but it is particularly important during the teenage years, when the need to belong and the powerful tides of peer pressure can swamp the vulnerable. With my poor self-image, I sometimes wonder what would have happened to me had I not become involved with something as constructive as drama production and gotten to know people whose friendship encouraged me to develop a more positive view of myself. Given the nurturing and caring family that raised me, I suspect that in my case, whatever mischief I might have got myself into, I would have eventually got myself out, but I'm not sure the same was true for others in the Drama Club whose circumstances were less favorable.

I remember one particularly tortured crew member, our costume and props girl—a tall, gangly, scarecrow of a person who always referred to her mother bitterly as the "old lady" and her father even more bitterly as the "old man" or "the bastard." She lived down the street from me and often ended up at my house, alternately balling her eyes out or hurling invective at her parents—refusing to be particularly specific about their crimes, apart from saying that they neither wanted nor cared about her. Her problems with her home life went so far beyond simple intergenerational conflict that, reflecting on it now, I wonder if she was abused, either physically or sexually—but this was not an era in which these kinds of matters were discussed, even among sympathetic girlfriends. Given her function within the club, there was no need for her to come to rehearsals until the final weeks leading up to the performances, but she came nearly every day, perhaps to avoid going home as much as anything else. She threw herself into the after-theatre social life of our gang with equal dedication. I don't know that being part of the Drama Club helped her deal with her life in the long run—she left town after graduation and I lost track of her—but at least in the short term, during the especially vulnerable adolescent years, it kept her off the streets and out of trouble.

One of the aspects that made drama magical enough to entice me and the others mentioned above was the way people interacted with each other, fed off one another, kept inventing and re-inventing the work at hand, sometimes unexpectedly. Nothing was ever fixed, not even in performance. So infinite were the variables, so complex the creative process, that each time I played out a scene, it could be slightly different than the time before and reveal another layer of truth about a character or situation. In this way the dramatic world interfaces with the real world. In real life, people modify each other's behavior in all kinds of subtle ways. Given exactly the same circumstances, you may react in one way to your husband and quite another to your son or a friend. How you react depends upon the emotional baggage you bring to the situation, the personalities involved, and countless other things. The same is true of actors and acting. In my own case, the way this process inevitably played itself out is that initially, I would develop my part on my own, interpret my character, practice my lines out loud in a way that felt right. But then when it came time to make that character come alive in a scene with other actors, I would discover that they didn't say their lines quite the way I anticipated. So I would make adjustments to make the relationships work. And I had to keep adjusting, constantly, every time I performed the scene, because inevitably, just like in real life, the dynamics between me and my fellow players shifted constantly, however slightly. In a way, I knew what to expect, because it was all scripted and because I not only knew the basic characters but also how people were interpreting them. Yet, in another way, I never knew.

Ultimately, my "magnificent obsession" was formed somewhere between the lure of the friendships and the magic of the dramatic experience. My magnificent obsession may have begun with friendship, but what ultimately fueled it was the passion I developed for the entire experience of participating in drama. As I had suspected, I had a certain raw talent for acting. Naturally, this was very rewarding, and contributed to my enthusiasm for performing.

Two of the three dramatic plays I was in were Shakespearean. Now, if theatre production was new to me, Shakespeare was even newer. I had been required to memorize a sonnet or two in school over the years, and even to study passages from certain plays as part of my English literature curriculum, but essentially my exposure had been minimal. And while I hadn't disliked anything that I had studied, I hadn't become enthusiastic about any of it either.

For the average schoolchild, there are so many obvious difficulties in accessing Shakespeare—foremost among these, the language. It's hard to get excited about a writer who requires translation just to be understood at the most rudimentary level. Take Cordelia's speech in *King Lear.* She has just rescued the mad old king, her father, from a dreadful storm to which he has deliberately exposed himself, after being neglected and abused by his two elder daughters, her sisters:

> Had you not been their father, these white flakes
> Had challenged pity of them. Was this a face
> To be opposed against the warring winds?
> To stand against the deep dread-bolted thunder?
> In the most terrible and nimble stroke
> Of quick, cross lightning? to watch—poor perdu!—
> With this thin helm? Mine enemy's dog,
> Though he had bit me, should have stood that night
> Against my fire; and wast thou fain, poor father,
> To hovel thee with swine, and rogues forlorn,
> In short and musty straw? Alack, alack!
> 'Tis wonder that thy life and wits at once
> Had not concluded all.
> —*King Lear*, Act IV, Scene VII, 36–48

By the time the reader has toggled back and forth between the lines themselves and the exhaustive explanatory notes at the bottom of the page which explain that "white flakes" means "white hair or snowy locks," "challenge" means "claim," "opposed" means "exposed" and so on, everything beyond the crass, literal message of the text has been lost. But to be on stage and speak this passage, to reach over and touch the "white flakes" of the old man beside you, to experience the heart-wrenching pain of a daughter grieving over her insane father, to work through the passion and anger she feels against the two sisters who have caused this terrible thing to happen, is to connect with people living in Elizabethan times and reach into the very centre of the human condition.

I do not cite these particular lines because they are the best example of the barrier between the average reader and Shakespeare, but because I, myself, spoke those lines. I played the part of Cordelia in *King Lear*. And I vividly remember practicing that passage in my room, saying the lines over and over again, letting the emotion of the passage inform my understanding. For me, the difference between merely comprehending a Shakespearean text and experiencing it in a theatrical context was the difference between seeing notes on a page and hearing the music.

When I finally did hear the music, I turned into a kind of frenzied Shakespeare "groupie." I devoured the sonnets, tragedies, and comedies holus bolus, made an eclectic sweep through the histories, and then started on the critics—all within a few months' time. It seemed to me that there was no topic, none at all, that Shakespeare did not examine with profound insight—perhaps in a sonnet, perhaps in a dramatic scene, or perhaps in an entire play. From love to hate and everything in between, one way or the other, through the Shakespearean "Book of Knowledge" I explored the complete alphabet of human emotion and experience and examined the lessons as they applied to my own life.

In *King Lear,* among other concerns, Shakespeare focuses on the responsibilities of children toward foolish and culpable parents. It is an issue that confronts all of us at various points in our lives, often for the first time as teenagers. As children, we tend to think of our moms and dads as infallible, undoubtedly "the best mom and dad in the world." As we grow up, and particularly as we enter the teenage years, we come to the awful realization that they are quite imperfect. In my own case, while my relationship with my mother remained relatively smooth as I passed through my teenage years, my relationship with my father grew increasingly contentious. It was nothing major, mostly differences of personality and temperament, but in fact, that was precisely the crux of my guilt as I compared my own behavior, unfavorably, to that of my character, Cordelia. In the face of quite terrible treatment by her father, she responded with love and compassion, whereas in the face of quite trivial "errors" on the part of my own father, I often responded petulantly. Unfortunately, to know one's own shortcomings is not necessarily to overcome them. I can't pretend that I suddenly turned into the dutiful daughter, or even that I mended my ways much at all. But I was certainly unsettled, and that is where all change begins.

Among the many things that attracted me to Shakespeare's writing was his extraordinary use of language. The plays were also poems, and I had always loved poetry. Poetry was like music after all. It was language with beats and rhythms and melody; it was onomatopoeia and alliteration and other kinds of sonorous verbal play. And no one does this better than Shakespeare. I remember discovering in some readings I undertook to prepare for my role, that Coleridge described *King Lear* as Shakespeare's "greatest effort as a poet," and similarly that Shelley called it "the most perfect specimen of dramatic poetry existing in the world." As an enthusiastic actress and fan, not a poet or scholar, I agreed. In no time at all, without any kind of conscious effort or intention to do this, I knew the entire play by heart. To this day, I can recite many of the passages. My favorite was when Lear, in a moment of lucidity between bouts of madness, sends Kent and the Fool out of the storm, and stops to "pray" before taking sanctuary himself:

> Poor naked wretches, wheresoe'er you are,
> That bide the pelting of this pitiless storm,
> How shall your houseless heads and unfed sides,
> Your loop'd and window'd raggedness, defend you
> From seasons such as these? O, I have ta'en
> Too little care of this! Take physic, pomp;
> Expose thyself to feel what wretches feel,
> That thou mayst shake the superflux to them,
> And show the heavens more just.
> —*King Lear*, Act III, Scene IV, 32–40

At the time, I thought it was one of the most moving pieces of writing I had ever read, and I can't think of a reason to change that opinion today.

Here is a vain, selfish monarch who has always believed that his "pomp" could insulate him from mental and physical distress and who has been indifferent to such distress in others. Suddenly, we find him not only entirely humbled by his suffering but also, for the first time, showing compassion for the "houseless heads" of others. It is an exquisite moment made even better by the elaborate overlaying of images and metaphors of the body as a shelter. Even recited by inexperienced actors, the power of the passage is overwhelming.

As a young and immature actress, perhaps the hardest problem I faced in interpreting Cordelia's character was figuring out why she refused to pander to the old man's vanity. To a sixteen-year old, this wasn't exactly obvious—quite the reverse. Clearly, she knew it would be easier to "play the game," clearly she knew what risks she was taking:

Why did she do it? Was I just supposed to accept her behavior as a sort of dramatic device for moving the plot along, or was there more to it?

I remember mulling this over one day, sitting at the kitchen table at home, when my eye landed on a nearby newspaper. There were several columns that day about the civil rights struggle going on south of the border in the United States, and about some protesters who had been injured in some march or other. And the parallel dawned on me. These marchers were all Cordelias—people who couldn't be bought, couldn't be silenced, couldn't pass up the chance to fight for what they believe, no matter what the consequences. Everyone knows a few Cordelias, or is one. There are Cordelias in every era and in every culture. In *King Lear,* she is the play's conscience. She is the conscience in all of us.

From the moment that I defined for myself who Cordelia is, I slipped into the character as comfortably as into an old shoe. But my next part was much more difficult to slip into—in fact, it was the most challenging of any that I undertook. I played Abigail Williams, the bad girl in Arthur Miller's *The Crucible.* Ostensibly about the witch hunts in seventeenth-century Salem, Massachusetts, but really about the contemporary witch hunts spearheaded by U.S. Senator Joseph McCarthy against so-called "communists," this play had considerable resonance for me. Miller's direct target may have been one specific set of events, but as a Jewish girl well versed in the horrors of the Holocaust, I understood all too well Miller's larger point about the evils and politics of scapegoating.

But while I understood the point of the play perfectly, accessing the role of an overheated, sexually precocious and manipulative young woman who casually denounced people to suit her own ends was quite another matter. I was, as they say, a late bloomer—at sixteen years of age, I had never even been out on a date! Therefore, in preparing for the part, I tried to find events in my own background that were in some way comparable, and use these to create the character. But here, I hit another difficulty. I couldn't find very much. I was a normal, postpubescent, teenager with raging hormones, and I certainly understood sexual desire. What I didn't understand was being desired. No one had ever demonstrated they wanted me at all, never mind wanted me so badly, madly, and uncontrollably that they were willing to break every taboo to have me. Of course, I knew girls like that, girls who had enormous power over men and who used it to get what they wanted. But I found it hard to imagine what being so desirable must feel like on the inside. From where I stood, these girls were like aliens from another planet. I understood manipulative behavior a little better, but not well enough. I was the eldest of three children, and like most first children, I knew lots of tricks for managing my younger brother and sister, but these were pretty trivial compared to the scheme orchestrated by Abigail Williams for exerting control over her lover and her society!

Of course, understanding a dramatic character is just the first and easiest step in acting any role convincingly, not the final step in the process. (If it were, the best actors would be the best critics.) The next step and by far the most difficult task is to convert that character from an intellectual idea into a flesh and blood presence. Naturally, the fact that I had trouble relating to my character compounded the subsequent difficulties I faced in trying to make her live on stage! Professional actors rely on a mixture of intuition, empathy, and acquired technical skills for mastering dramatic roles that are beyond their own experiences. However, I did not have either the emotional maturity to imagine what I had not experienced or the technical skills to assist me with my performance—but I didn't know it at the time. On the day of the first performance, I remember thinking that, all things considered, I had done a terrific job of overcoming the numerous obstacles I faced in dealing with the mysterious Abigail Williams. In retrospect, I know I didn't. I made the mistake many inexperienced performers make in this kind of situation: I overacted wildly.

In terms of educational value, I benefited far more from my participation in the dramatic plays than I did from being in any of the musicals. But in terms of simple, uncomplicated pleasure, the production that stole my heart was *West Side Story,* Leonard Bernstein's contemporary musical version of the Romeo and Juliet tale, in which I played the romantic heroine, Maria. Perhaps it stole my heart because a musical is simply more fun—and what kid doesn't like to have fun? Perhaps it was because it involved my primary talent, singing, or perhaps because it played on my childhood attachment to musical theatre.

I was raised on musical theatre: if other kids sang Buddy Holly or Elvis Presley songs in the shower, I sang Jerome Kern or Richard Rogers melodies. I sang show tunes each week on *Time For Juniors.* I knew the lyrics to almost every song in every major "hit," as well as most of the minor ones.

*West Side Story* had always been one of my favorites. To win the role of Maria was a dream come true. Compared to the struggle of preparing for my dramatic roles, assuming the character of Maria was a breeze. Falling in love—what teenager couldn't relate to that? Star-crossed lovers: wasn't that a necessary part of teenage angst? Certainly, the basic plot held all manner of relevance for me personally. One of the reasons I didn't date was the fact that my parents disapproved strongly of my going out with non-Jewish boys, even casually.

Since I lived in a small Jewish community with only about five Jewish boys of suitable age—all of whom I had known since childhood and thought of, more or less, much like extended family—my romantic possibilities were virtually non-existent. I often worried about the future, when I would leave my father and mother to go away to university. Surely, I would encounter hordes of men, some of whom might like me. With no parental watchdogs around, what would I do if I liked some of them back, and they weren't Jewish? What would I do if I fell in love with one? How would my parents react? I didn't have any clear answers, but needless to say, the *West Side Story* version of *Romeo and Juliet* seemed like a fitting cautionary tale.

Despite the fact that I found my character and the story easy to relate to, there were a couple of things I found difficult about the play. These had to do with certain supplementary requirements of the role of the sort that teenagers naturally find embarrassing. The first problem was The Kiss. One of the love scenes required it. Now, the boy who played the part of my boyfriend, Tony, was a nice enough fellow, but he was several years my junior and I was in no way attracted to him, either physically or emotionally. Therefore my response to the prospect of a long, lingering smooch was "Ugh!" It was a very extreme reaction, and one reason may have been the context of such an event in my own life. Since I hadn't started dating, this encounter would inevitably be my very first "boy-girl" kiss. It was against a background of sentimental movie-land images and scenarios running through my mind that I had always fantasized about my first kiss and how utterly perfect it would be.

Since I didn't want to kiss this boy, it was assuredly not going to work out the way it was supposed to. The whole thing was ruined for me. To add insult to injury, I had to do it in public, before an audience, with all those strangers watching—even more horrible, with fellow students watching and maybe even laughing at me!

The Kiss was bad enough, but far worse was a scene which compelled me to appear on stage wearing just a slip. I had a dreadful body image, harkening back to my childhood and my sense that I wasn't a Butterfly Girl. I was older now, of course, and through my involvement in the Drama Club I had finally achieved a measure of the social acceptance that I associated with the Butterfly Girls, but I was no closer to the ideal of female beauty that they represented. In fact, I was probably further from the mark, having become slightly chubby, so the idea of appearing semi-clothed in public was agonizing. I must have driven my poor mother crazy. Convinced, for some reason, that the right slip would make me look good, I would select one from a shop, buy it, gradually become dissatisfied with my choice, then buy another and go through the same cycle again. I think I must have gone through about six of them before my mother finally said enough! No matter how hard I tried to lose myself in my character Maria, I would shoot back to reality as Lani whenever The Kiss and The Slip Scene took place. The old admonition "grin and bear it" pretty much sums up how I dealt with these scenes.

I entered high school a bit of an "ugly duckling." Now if Hollywood was writing the script, by the time I left, the ugly duckling would have turned into a swan. Needless to say, life is not Hollywood. I didn't vanquish my self-image difficulties or my fears of being rejected by other people, but at least I didn't end up forever crippled by them. The friendships I made through the Drama Club gave me much more confidence in social situations than I had before I joined, and in that sense, allowed me to go forward, albeit tentatively. If I didn't quite turn into a swan, at least I gained a pair of wings. Just a few months after I graduated, I left home for Montreal to go to university. The first day I moved into residence, I knocked on the doors of the girls whose rooms were nearest my own and introduced myself. I was very nervous, but the point is that nervous or not, I did it. Now, this may not sound very remarkable, but if anyone had told me when I entered high school that just three years later, I would be seeking out and inviting personal relationships instead of waiting and hoping for people to invite me, I would never have believed it. More than anything else, it was my experience in the Drama Club that led to this kind of personal growth. My magnificent obsession gave me a career goal. I entered a theatre arts program at university, determined to become a professional performer. And then, a few years later, I took a look around me and faced up to reality. I realized that at least half the young people in my program were more talented than I was. My chances of succeeding as a performer in either musical comedy or dramatic theatre were slim. I wasn't Julie Andrews or Barbara Streisand, neither was I Glenda Jackson or Maggie Smith— and I was unwilling to settle for a life of chorus lines and bit parts in third-rate productions. It was a tough moment for me—few things in life are harder than letting go of your dreams. For a while, I completely lost my sense of purpose. I skipped classes for a week or maybe even longer, spent my days sipping coffee in assorted Montreal bistros and my nights listening to music in folk bars until the wee hours of the morning. Finally, I went back and finished out the year as best I could, mostly because I couldn't think of anything else that made sense and I couldn't hang out in cafes and nightclubs indefinitely.

Ironically, it was something I had learned through my involvement in drama that made me realize why I had to leave it—something that I had gradually come to understand about myself. I needed the "kick" I got from being the centre of attention on stage, from having people admire and praise me. And since I lacked star qualities as an actress and was unlikely to find the kind of success I craved, I was going to have to find some other career that could provide me with a similar kind of "kick." When my magnificent obsession had begun in my first year of high school, I had found it emotionally satisfying simply to be part of that life, part of that scene. But now, this just wasn't enough for me any longer. I wanted, and needed, more. I was an overachiever and couldn't accept mediocrity. I needed to be really good at something and to be recognized as such.

I zigzagged from theatre arts into English literature and got a series of degrees. But the idea of teaching—which is what such studies usually lead to—never really appealed to me, while the idea of performing in *some* capacity still attracted me. What was I to do? Perhaps I could take my academic knowledge of things literary and artistic, combine it with my modest theatrical talent, and parlay all of this into some kind of on-air work in broadcast journalism.

The broadcast-journalism part of my career plan worked out fine but the on-air part just never did. Fortunately, I discovered that I *liked* working behind the scenes and that I did have a "dramatic" flair for it. Today I am a television producer with the Canadian Broadcasting Corporation, based in Toronto. While I am never satisfied with my achievements, I think I have found the kind of "kick" I was looking for. As a producer on *The National/Magazine,* a network program generally regarded to be Canada's most important news and information program, I am more or less at the top of my field.

My love of live theatre has never left me. My husband and I are both movie fans and manage to take in a new film every week, regular as clockwork, but my heart doesn't pound with excitement and anticipation when I enter a movie theatre. I go to see live productions far less often—there are fewer available, and what does exist is far more expensive—but I never enter a theatre without getting chills up my spine. It is hard for me to put my finger on what exactly produces this reaction. I think a lot of it is the associations I bring to it. A few years ago, I took my children to see a production of *Guys and Dolls.* I booked early, and somehow managed to get seats in the second row. Just before the lights went down, I could see bodies rustling behind the curtains and thought, or imagined, I could hear some of the actors laughing and chattering. It took me back to high school, and the moments backstage before the curtain is raised.

Typically, our director would be running around, alternately helping slap pancake make-up on cast members, pointing out last minute problems to the crew and reminding the actors of things to do or not to do. I would be sneaking peeks at the audience, trying to spot family and friends and see who else I recognized. Inevitably, a crisis or three would arise and somehow be averted. One night, my hem came down seconds before the opening curtain and was hastily patched with sticky tape and safety pins (one of which opened during the performance and kept jabbing me whenever I walked too quickly and the skirt swirled). Another night, I broke a heel and the only pair that could be found was a size too large. So I did the dancing numbers in bare feet and kind of shuffled through the rest of the show. One thing has always remained constant for me, however, no matter what went wrong or right during the evening: the electricity in the air when the curtain rose and the spotlight hit. I knew everyone was looking at me and I connected with them. There's no other feeling like it in this world! That's what makes live performances so special: the symbiotic relationship between the performers and the audience, the charge that passes from one to the other that gives the whole experience a color and texture and feeling that goes far beyond the production itself.

One of the legacies of my years in the Drama Club seems to be that I am passing on my enthusiasm for live theatre to my own children. I have never consciously tried to do this—I'm not that kind of parent. However, my husband dislikes this type of entertainment, and refuses to accompany me to the theatre except on rare occasions when we are on vacation in places like New York and London (where he calls it "doing the tourist thing"). I simply started taking my children along with me to the theatre for company, in place of my husband. And they quite took to it, to the point that now they are often the ones who come to me with requests to see some play or other that is in town.

My daughter, as already mentioned, has taken things one step further. She came to me out of the blue one day, and asked me to enroll her in a drama class, and things accelerated from there. I was thrilled about her enthusiasm for acting in and of itself, but not about her subsequent interest in obtaining an agent and going professional. I couldn't help projecting my own childhood experience upon her and worrying that she, too, would find herself turned into an "outsider." I dragged my feet for a long time, hoping she would stop asking. She didn't, and eventually I decided that I was being unfair. It was one thing for me to stand guard and another to stand in the way. My daughter was entitled to pursue her passion just as far as her imagination and her talent would take her, just as I had once tried to do. So far, my fears have proved groundless. But then again, so far, she hasn't become famous, either!

My son's passion for Shakespeare bewilders me. As I said, I made no deliberate efforts to engage him in this regard (and in any case, who would have thought to try? This is a kid who hates all books except for trashy action-adventure novels and the like). We initially came to discuss Shakespeare when he began to study it at school, and somehow, he simply got turned on to it. He's not particularly articulate about what exactly appeals to him—he usually mumbles something about liking the old-fashioned English—but his interest is genuine. He doesn't go out of his way to read any of the plays, but loves to see them performed. He insists on going to every film and theatrical production that comes along, and every summer makes us take him to the Shakespeare festival in Stratford, Ontario.

Just a few weeks ago, I was working at home when my son came in from school, bringing in the mail as he came. "Mom!' he shouted at the top of his lungs, just in case I had suddenly suffered a major hearing loss since he saw me at breakfast, "the brochure has come from the Stratford Festival about the new season!"

"So, what's on the agenda?" I asked, coming into the room.

"*As You Like It*, *The Merchant of Venice*, and *King Lear*."

"*King Lear*!" I exclaimed excitedly.

"Is that a good one?" he asked.

Yes, it's a good one. In and of itself, and because it connects me with my past. I do not have any regrets about my involvement in drama, either at the high school or university level. I have never thought of it as "wasted" because I devoted so much time and energy to something that didn't lead where I wanted to go. To this day, I remain sad about the fact that my hopes for a professional career didn't pan out. It's a natural sentiment. But above all, I feel terribly indebted to this experience for helping me grow up gracefully, for broadening my understanding of the world I live in, for allowing me to dream, and for waking me up gently when it was time.

*Lani Selick was a television producer for the Canadian Broadcasting Corporation for thirty years before retiring in 2010. She has won several awards for her work, including a Gemini (since renamed the Canadian Screen Award). Today she lives in Toronto with her husband of forty-six years and travels the world, as often as funds and circumstances permit, in quest of further life adventures. She has two children and two grandchildren. She is a lifelong art addict, music groupie, balletomaniac and theatre voyeur—a wonderstruck lover of all things creative to which she credits her formative high-school years singing, dancing, performing ... plus the many mentors who brought her to this place.*

# Eight Characters in Search of a Self

Robert Brym

CANADA

After dinner, my parents assembled all the relatives in the living room. I then entered through a narrow hallway. Although I was barely four years old, I was unafraid. I wore a white shirt and dark brown corduroy pants. "*Sha, sha*," my father urged ("hush, hush"). When the room fell still, I sang a Yiddish song about young boys, "fresh out of their eggs," playing under the boughs of saplings. Whether I sang well or poorly I do not recall. I know I sang confidently, mimicking the expansive arm movements of performers I had seen on the *Ed Sullivan Show*. I also remember being surprised that I momentarily captured the attention of my normally raucous two- and three-year-old cousins. When I finished, there was murmured approval and cheek-pinching and lipstick-staining kisses. Then we drank tea and milk and indulged in my mother's pastries. My first public performance was a success.

Although I seemed to take naturally to performance, there was actually little natural about it. My father taught me a repertoire and promoted bravado. My mother's unflagging love instilled self-confidence. Therefore, it only *seemed* natural to me that, at the age of five, I should jump, uninvited, onto the stage of a talent show at the synagogue and burst spontaneously into song. Why certain audience members thought I was obnoxious I couldn't imagine. And although some public school teachers apparently disapproved because I was Jewish, it even seemed natural to me that I should be asked to play the lead role of Santa Claus in my Grade 2 class play, advancing to the role of Narrator for the Grade 4 Christmas pageant, presented in the auditorium before the whole primary school.

Whether reading from the Book of Matthew or singing *Unter di grininke baymelekh*, performance always gave me a great pleasure. I enjoyed the attention and the prestige, to be sure. But it was also fun to escape the everyday world through an act of imagination and to pretend to be someone else; and it was somehow exhilarating to be able to influence the emotional state of so many people all at once. For a decade—between the ages of five and fifteen—the real world grew malevolent. I felt less an actor than the object of other people's actions. But performance offered temporary escape and hinted at better possibilities that would be fully realized only in high school.

In the 1950s and 1960s, Saint John was largely a working-class city of 100,000 people. With only a small middle class, it lacked a university (the University of New Brunswick's Saint John campus opened only in 1964), a professional theatre, and even a bookstore. And while in other Canadian cities of similar size, such as St. John's, Newfoundland, there was a rich folk tradition of music, theatre, and dance that drew sustenance from preindustrial times, I was never aware of any such heritage in Saint John.

Although I was born in Saint John, I was a stranger there. My family's culture did not have a great deal in common with that of the 250 or so embourgeoisified and acculturated members of the Jewish community, and very little in common with that of the city's mainly English Protestant and Irish Catholic Gentile population.

My father, a tailor, had grown up in Poland, where he was a young activist in the Labour-Zionist movement. He trained as an agricultural labourer in preparation for work on a *kibbutz*. He never made it to Palestine because in the pre-war years the British Mandate sharply restricted the entry of Jews so as not to upset the Arab majority. He escaped Poland just as the Nazis entered and spent the war years in a workers' battalion attached to the Soviet Red Army, driving camels in Kazakhstan, sewing uniforms in a Ural Mountain *kolkhoz*, and surviving the bombing of Smolensk and the siege of Stalingrad. Following the war and two years in an American-controlled detention camp in Germany, he embarked for the city where his only North American relative, a first cousin, happened to reside: Saint John.

My mother had arrived twenty years earlier from Lithuania. With her father dead and her mother seriously ill, her eldest brother had decided to send his three sisters to be raised by aunts in North America, one in Boston, one in Moncton, and one in Saint John. My mother finished primary school and served her aunt's family dutifully for twenty years. In 1947 she met my father. Two years later they married. Because my father knew virtually no English, their household language—soon my mother tongue—was Yiddish.

I cannot emphasize strongly enough how bizarre it was to be the only child immersed in Eastern European working-class Yiddish culture in Saint John, New Brunswick, in the 1950s and 1960s. There I was in one of Canada's most ethnically homogeneous cities, long an outpost of British colonialism, whose fame rested chiefly on its having been founded by loyalists to the Crown fleeing northward from the American Revolution. Deference to authority seemed forever after to be one of the most valued attributes of its good citizens. I, in contrast, heard bedtime stories in a strange tongue about other worlds in which rebellion against authority was a prominent theme, stories about my father rejecting the antiquated religiosity of his parents, joining a radical political movement, and even organizing a sit-down strike against the American military, who provided insufficient rations to the inmates of his detention camp after the war.

Nor did my family culture resonate with that of the city's Jews. Their families had arrived long before the war and their roots to Eastern Europe were now drying out. They seemed to me to look down on the three "green" immigrant tailors who settled in Saint John after the war, even though these poor men, no longer young, had firsthand knowledge of the greatest tragedy ever to befall the Jews and of a living and breathing Polish-Jewish culture in which 3.3 million souls participated, a culture with its own newspapers, literature, theatre, and art. Yiddish culture was an important part of my identity, but that was of no interest to anyone outside my immediate family and was undoubtedly the cause of some condescension—and worse.

At first carefully sheltered in the confines of my family, I became dimly aware that I was an oddity only at about the age of five. That is when I simultaneously started playing with Gentile children in our lower-middle-class and working-class neighbourhood, and mixing with middle-class and upper-middle-class Jewish children at synagogue and Sunday school. Looking back, I would say that my ethnicity made me marginal to my social class while my social class made me marginal to my ethnic group. But at the time, of course, the real sources of my misery were utterly mysterious to me.

In Queen Square, across the street from our house, I was repeatedly taunted for killing Christ. On at least one occasion, I was beaten for my role in the murder. Paul C., two years my senior, pushed and slapped me repeatedly. I cried out that I didn't even know Christ, let alone harm him; but my protests made no impact on the young Torquemada. One should not be surprised. The Catholic Church was still teaching that the Jews were responsible for deicide. It was common knowledge that we were miserly and sly. Some Saint Johners even believed that Jews had horns.[1] Fed such beliefs, could one reasonably expect my persecutors to be humane and supportive of difference?

Forty years later, the memory of those bullies is as fresh as a bloody nose. I remember equally vividly my reaction to them. I was the youngest child in the neighbourhood, unathletic, small, a minority of one. I felt mute and powerless. I could not fight back. Instead, I came to see the good sense in my parents' warnings. For them, antisemitism was part of the natural order of things. They admonished me to avoid intimate relations with non-Jews because of the harm they were likely to cause me. I remember falling asleep to the doleful moan of the fog horns in Saint John harbour, thinking about my parents' instructions in the light of my own experience, constructing a psychological barrier of fear, anger, and loathing between me and the Gentile world, a barrier that took many years to break down.

I felt equally distant from the children of the Jewish middle- and upper-middle classes. They sometimes treated me condescendingly because my family was not well off and my background was different from theirs. I do not know how much of this I imagined and how much was real, but I felt that they often snickered at my unfashionable clothes, my address, my parents' accents, the lilt and Yiddish exuberance in my voice. They, however, formed the overwhelming majority,

---

1. The belief apparently derives from a mistranslation that occurred when the Bible was translated from Hebrew to Greek and that was retained in the subsequent Latin and English translations. According to the Bible, when Moses descended Mt. Sinai, rays of light shone from his head. The Hebrew words for "ray" and "horn" have the same consonant root; they are distinguished only by vowels, and the Torah is written without vowels. The Greek translator mistakenly rendered "rays" as "horns." Consequently, Michelangelo gave Moses horns in his famous sculpture, and the belief became widespread that Jews have horns, surviving even unto the suburbs of Saint John in the 1960s.

so their values dominated; I denied my heritage and tried to accept their values as my own. As a result, I both envied and despised them, convinced that I could never achieve what they had. They owned summer cottages in nearby Pamdenec, stylish clothes, and new cars. I was embarrassed by our rusty 1957 Dodge and my parents' dowdy attire. Significantly, by the time I was ten, I informed my parents that I no longer wished to speak Yiddish in public.

My primary and junior high schools, as well as my Hebrew school, did little to help me deal with my ethnic and class marginality. Quite the opposite. The schools just made me feel lonelier, more powerless, and more frightened. Evidently, most of my teachers did not consider it their responsibility to help me figure out who I was, what I was good at, and what I should do with my life. I remember only one teacher before high school, a Mrs. Selby in Grade 4, who was highly emotionally supportive, praising my school work and informing my mother that she would one day be proud of me. Most of my other teachers seemed content to impart certain rudimentary information and ensure our conformity and docility, even if that required the use of injustice and violence. Most of us were, after all, destined to become subordinates in the adult work world and had to be trained accordingly.

I recall one lesson with particular vividness. During a junior high school field trip to the New Brunswick Museum, Linda Campbell and I were standing behind our balding fortyish science teacher when Linda was overcome by demons. She pulled a water pistol from her purse, sprayed the science teacher's pate, quickly tossed the weapon into her purse, and stared intently at the adjacent exhibit of the solar system. The teacher, enraged, turned, saw me suppressing a laugh, and punched me in the stomach. I fell to the ground, unable to breathe. He did not come to my aid. He left me writhing on the floor even after he was told by my angry classmates that I had done nothing.

When I returned home I demanded that my father contact the District School Board and have the teacher fired. (It never occurred to me that he could also be charged for assaulting a minor.) My father, the great anti-authoritarian, demurred on the grounds that the teacher was a married man with children who would be ruined if he lost his job. Many years later I understood that my father's—anyone's—anti-authoritarianism is not just a function of personality but of circumstance. People rebel not just when they suffer injustice or deprivation but when they have the numbers, the organization, and the resources to support them. What my father had in Europe he lacked in Saint John; he was now as intimidated as I was. But I comprehended none of that then. I was unspeakably angry with and disappointed in my father. Even he, it now seemed, was helping to render me mute. Thus, I initially contemplated returning to school the next day with a baseball bat in order to show my science teacher exactly how justice feels when delivered by a stout piece of lumber. But in the event, when I arrived at school the next morning, we just locked eyes for a few seconds. I then took my seat, repressed my anger, and tried to concentrate on my schoolwork.

The brightest spot in those junior high school years was musical comedy. Some time in the early '60s, the Saint John Jewish community hired Moshe Kotler, a chain-smoking expatriate Israeli with a BA in English from the University of Tel Aviv, to teach Hebrew school. He was a mediocre teacher but he wrote musical comedies for one or two Jewish holidays each year, hilarious musicals with riotous lyrics set to popular tunes. Kotler was eventually let go, less because of his temper, I believe, than because of his disregard for the status structure of the Jewish community: it was one thing to throw a chalkboard eraser at a child, quite another when the child's father happened to be the president of the synagogue. But on stage Kotler treated me with rough dignity, giving me the choicest parts and telling me at one point that of all the kids in the Hebrew school I was the only one with any acting talent. Not surprisingly, performing became the most enjoyable part of my life. The rest of the world diminished me, but, for reasons that were still unclear, performing had the capacity to transform me and make me happy.

Thus, the misery was not unrelenting; but it was misery nonetheless. At the age of fourteen, on the eve of my entry to high school, my identity was up for grabs. I lacked voice. I was a cauldron of anger. It was uncertain whether I was competent at anything, with the exception of performing. For a year or two I had been waking up each morning with mild stomach cramps, sick at the thought of having to go to school. I managed to maintain an A-minus average not because I was motivated to study—I wasn't—but because such paltry intellectual demands were placed on me.

Around the age of fourteen or fifteen, I recall thinking how desperately I wanted to hold my own opinions, to know where I stood in the world, to adhere to a set of principles that could serve as consistent guides to life. But my experience to date had done little to help me resolve the one burning question that every adolescent must answer: Who am I? Instead of being able to rely on adults for clarification, I looked around and saw only cowed heads. "The little man," New Brunswick poet Alden Nowlan once quoted his Nova Scotian father as saying, "had better learn to keep his mouth shut and his arse low." That was just the posture assumed by me and most of my classmates.

In Grade 9, in preparation for high school placement, we took an IQ test. A month or two later a visiting psychologist called me to his temporary office in our school. "Robert," he said, "you can be anything you want." I was genuinely and profoundly shocked. At first I didn't believe him and actually asked him if he was sure he had the right file. All these years hardly anybody had told me that I was any good at anything. Now this kind blond stranger assured me that I could achieve whatever I set my mind to. I was elated with the message but wondered what it had to do with a recalcitrant reality that thwarted me at virtually every step. Perhaps, I reckoned, it was just one of those little nuggets, like certain Yiddish songs my father had sung at my bedside, that could comfort me in moments of deep emotional need. On the evidence, there were bound to be plenty.

While still in Grade 9, I attended the Saint John High School production of *The Pirates of Penzance*. I was thrilled by the colour, the vitality, and the hilarity of the operetta. Scores of actors in period costumes rented from Malabar's in Montreal. Part of the New Brunswick Symphony Orchestra in the pit. Loud, clear, happy, confident voices. Not a missed line. A wildly enthusiastic audience. Surely this was professional theatre. Surely this was something I would enjoy doing when the time came.

Shortly after arriving at Saint John High School, I heard that Mr. Garrod, an English teacher, was holding auditions for Arthur Miller's *The Crucible*. I read for Mr. Garrod and was awarded the secondary role of Reverend Hale. I thus became part of the high school's chief extracurricular enterprise. Due solely to Mr. Garrod's initiative and industry, hundreds of us were mobilized annually to participate in two and sometimes three plays. Students sold tickets, built props, applied make-up, worked the lights, acted, sang, and danced. There was a "Room 3" production in the fall—a Shakespearean comedy or a modern classic—performed before an audience of about 100 people for four nights. In Grades 11 and 12 I played Oliver in Shakespeare's *As You Like It* and the Gentleman Caller in Tennessee Williams's *The Glass Menagerie*. Then there was a gala Broadway musical in May. Four spring evenings each year we filled the 1,200-seat auditorium and provided Saint John with its major cultural event of the season. My roles included Tony in *West Side Story* (which also went on the road to the Playhouse in Fredericton), Tommy Albright in *Brigadoon* and Lieutenant Cable in *South Pacific*. In Grade 11, I played Tevye in a summer camp production of *Fiddler on the Roof*, which toured Halifax and Saint John. In my last year of high school we staged T. S. Eliot's *Murder in the Cathedral* in the local Anglican cathedral. I played Becket, Archbishop of Canterbury, much to the outrage of a local bishop when he discovered I was a Jew. (Mr. Garrod listened politely to his complaint and then did what he pleased.) Altogether, I played eight roles, most of them leads, in three years of high school.

I can date precisely the pivot of my adolescence: Friday, December 16, 1966. I was fifteen years old, halfway through tenth grade at Saint John High School. At 4 p.m. I was a nobody and felt it. Half an hour later I was being buffeted up King Street, delighting in the slight sting of snowflakes melting on my upturned face, knowing I had been swept up in a sea change.

About two hundred students sat expectantly in the auditorium that last day of school before the winter vacation as Mr. Garrod prepared to announce the cast of *West Side Story*. I was hoping for a modest speaking part, and was therefore not surprised when Mr. Garrod failed to read my name as a chorus member. But as the list of remaining secondary characters grew shorter I became despondent. Soon only the leads remained. I knew that an unknown kid in Grade 10 could not possibly be asked to take the part of Tony and perform the most prestigious social function in the school. And even if the seemingly impossible did occur, it could not happen to me. For ten years, I had been made to feel an outsider in both class and ethnic terms. Besides,

I had it on the authority of several teachers that I would never amount to anything.

Then the thunderclap. "Tony—Robert Brym. Have a good vacation and we get to work in the new year."

"Who's Robert Brym?" stage-whispered Ann, a pretty Gentile cheerleader whose father was a bank manager. Pamela, a highly intelligent and even more attractive Jewish girl whose father was a doctor, simply shook her head in disbelief and raised her eyebrows. I was as dumbfounded as Pamela, although somewhat more confident that I was up to the task. Nor did I really know the answer to Ann's question.

From a developmental point of view, playing Tony in *West Side Story* was by far the most important event of my youth. The role acted as the first section of a bridge across my adolescence. It served this function by elevating my social status, making me more self-confident, helping me to begin discovering parts of myself that I had not known before, and teaching me that I could act rather than merely be acted upon.

Consider first the question of status, which was raised most acutely in my relationships with girls. I didn't realize it at the time, but Ann—the girl in the auditorium who asked "Who's Robert Brym?"—was expressing more than idle curiosity. With the beginning of rehearsals in January, Ann became my girlfriend. Suddenly, as if by some miracle, I was getting to kiss and fondle a popular blonde upper-class girl who was a full grade ahead of me, the kind of girl who used to be the object only of my fantasies. The romance lasted for several months. It was only on closing night, at the cast and crew party for *West Side Story*, that Ann informed me that she could not continue seeing me. When I asked why, Ann confessed tearfully that her father forbade her to go out with Jews. My *naïveté* prevented me from asking Ann how he found out I was Jewish, since we had never had the pleasure of meeting, or how she was able to keep from him the horrible truth about my origins precisely from the first practice until the cast party. It was only a year or so later that the answer dawned on me.

I regarded Pamela as a bigger prize and I had to accumulate the status attached to all eight of my dramatic roles before she became interested in me towards the end of Grade 12. In the spring of 1969 we would walk to Queen Square during lunch hour, hold hands, and kiss. I took enormous pleasure in that, not least because Queen Square was the site of my *auto-da-fé* a decade earlier and I was now thumbing my nose at my persecutors, as it were. Once Pam came over to my house after school, on a day I knew my parents would not be at home. "This is where you *live*?" she asked as she entered our humble living room. "Yes," I replied, "but we're about to get new carpets." I hated myself as soon as the words left my lips—I knew that I should have asked her to leave at once—but I also understood that if I was going to get her on the couch I would have to see things her way. And so I left the Garden of Eden with the sad but useful knowledge that others might want me less for my self than for the roles I performed.

The interesting thing is, I didn't really mind. On the contrary, if some popular girls found me desirable largely because of my dramatic roles, that was an insult I was only too happy to endure. Given my low sense of self-esteem, I needed a boost in status, and if I could reciprocate, then the exchange seemed entirely fair. All of which, I suppose, corroborates Michel Foucault's observation that sex is more about the exchange of images than the exchange of bodily fluids.

Playing Tony also made me more self-confident. More than thirty years later, I can still smell the salt-and-oil blend of greasepaint and sweat that I exuded minutes before *West Side Story* opened. Who was I fooling? There was a high note in "Maria" I could never hit. The orchestra would drown out my voice. I would never be able to convey romance and passion given an icy leading lady who had insisted during rehearsals that we refrain from consummating the sole kiss called for by the script. The audience would certainly laugh during the scene I had to play with my shirt off. The sheer number of people in the audience would mesmerize me and cause me to forget my lines. These and myriad other anxieties swept over me minutes before opening curtain. But I understood they had to be silenced. I knew that if I allowed my fears to paralyze me, I would be far more humiliated than if any one or a combination of them transpired. If I froze on stage, if I reverted to that quivering little boy from Queen Square, all would be lost. Instead I focused on the fact that here was an opportunity to become something else, something better. And so I forced myself to become Tony—poised, chivalrous, romantic, tragic. And, to a degree, I succeeded. Like those old American social-psychology experiments which show that role-acting can cause attitudinal change (making a speech in favour of civil rights caused the experimental subjects to develop more pro-civil rights attitudes), I learned self-confidence by taking deep breaths, willing my heart to stop hammering, and forcing myself to assume a dramatic role.

It is also clear that my roles helped me to begin seeing aspects of myself that had previously been hidden from me. For example, I remember being deeply impressed by Tony's conciliatory role in *West Side Story*. I was an angry child. My typical responses to interpersonal conflict were silent fuming or verbal aggression, the choice of response depending largely on how threatening my opponent was. Conciliation was a reaction I had never seriously considered. But here was the heroic example of Tony, a young man caught in an inner city gang war between the Puerto Rican Sharks and the Jets of Irish and Polish origin. A former Shark himself, Tony falls in love with Maria, a Puerto Rican girl whose brother is the leader of the Sharks. Tony attempts to affect a truce between the two gangs. He ultimately fails, but his love for Maria suggests that a better world is possible, that submission and aggression are not the only possible reactions to conflict. Unfortunately, I have still not fully internalized Tony's message. I did, however, first realize the importance of trying to do so when I played him at the age of fifteen. Tony taught me that I might be capable of a virtue I hadn't even recognized before. Playing the role of Tony literally extended my self.

The war between Jets and Sharks was an ethnic conflict, and therein laid the germ of another important lesson. Although I had some Gentile friends before high school, I was pretty well convinced by the age of fifteen that the gulf between Jews and Gentiles was fundamentally unbridgeable. Drama showed me I was wrong because it established new criteria for judging a person's worth. What mattered in drama was not my ethnicity or my class but my dependability and my competence as an actor. Thus, through participation in the drama programme I came to be accepted by others on the basis of merit, regardless of my ethnic and class origins. Ironically, in the period between playing Reverend Hale in *The Crucible* and Becket, Archbishop of Canterbury, in *Murder in the Cathedral*, I discovered that the Gentile world was not as threatening as I originally thought. I began to feel more comfortable outside my psychological ghetto and even to admire what I saw there.

In fact, my two best friends in high school turned out to be non-

Jews. Rod Stears was the best athlete in the school. He was, however, far more interested in photography than in competitive sport. Nor did studying engage him; his marks were always low and he never finished Grade 12. Peter McKelvey, in contrast, was an honours student who lived for natural science. He had an almost tactile sense of natural processes. I think his happiest moment in high school occurred when his parents chipped in enough money to allow him to buy a metal lathe, which he worked on for countless hours in his garage. These two boys—Rod is now a professional photographer, Peter an environmental engineer—had substantively little in common with me or with each other. They were, however, competent and independent in their ways and they accepted me on my own terms, as I did them. I admired them profoundly and came to feel more at ease in the non-Jewish world because of them. At some level, the fact that Mr. Garrod, my fellow actors, and my audiences judged me by universalistic criteria in my dramatic roles enabled me to feel comfortable with people who were different from me. This in turn enabled me to befriend non-Jews and then to trust some of them completely.

Finally, while many of the forces in my environment conspired to mute me and make me feel that I was merely an object acted upon by other people, performing gave me voice and taught me agency. My last dramatic role in high school—Becket, Archbishop of Canterbury—drove home the point that I could, indeed must, act not just in plays, but in the world.

The role of Becket was wholly alien to me and I had to work strenuously to master it. I had great trouble understanding the twelfth-century historical context of *Murder in the Cathedral*, T.S. Eliot's difficult language, and, most of all, the motivations underlying Becket's actions. Becket was, after all, willing to defy the King of England in order to defend the church unequivocally. He was uncompromising even though he knew his stand would lead inexorably to martyrdom. For a seventeen-year-old schoolboy in 1969, it took a great leap of imagination to comprehend how someone could be willing to die for his spiritual principles, and a real extension of self to play the role in a convincing way. The review of *Murder in the Cathedral* in our Grade 12 yearbook says my portrayal of Becket was impressive but too monotonically forceful, lacking nuance. The criticism is valid. However, I saw no way of playing the role other than as a force of nature. I could relate to Becket only by seeing him as a man whose sense of moral and religious rectitude eventually rendered him as intransigent as a hurricane. Significantly, however, because it was Becket who created the hurricane of his own free will, I somehow felt free (or is it more accurate to say "saved"?) when the four knights plunged their swords into me; Becket alone had decided his fate in spite of the strictures of earthly power. What a lesson in existentialism acting turned out to be! I felt different after playing Becket, stronger.

Thus, although I was not conscious of it at the time, it is evident now that the drama programme provided a social matrix within which my self was encouraged to crystallize and strengthen. The evidence is mundane but telling. For example, in junior high school I was taught French and math by a Miss C., a sadistic woman who finally completed her BA at the age of about sixty by taking courses summer after summer at the university in Fredericton. Proud daughter of backwoods New Brunswick, she informed me on more than one occasion, each time with apparent delight, that I would amount to nothing. As luck would have it, Miss C. received her undergraduate degree and thus became eligible to teach in high school in the very year I entered Saint John High. But while I was tormented by her in Grade 9, I could laugh her off in Grade 10, when she was my math teacher, because now, thanks to my success in drama, I knew better than she did what I was made of.

By Grade 11, I was beginning to be able to hold my own in the face of public opinion. One day in chemistry class I learned that water and sulphur dioxide combine to form sulphurous acid. It immediately occurred to me that I lived a hundred metres downwind from an Irving pulp and paper mill that spewed sulphur dioxide into the air. Like many Saint Johners, I awoke every morning literally coughing acid. Weeks after I made the (to me) stunning connection in chemistry class, our annual model parliament was held. I tried to make a political issue out of the mass poisoning by Mr. Irving. I got nowhere with my conservative classmates, who tended to regard Mr. Irving as the only reason there were any jobs in the province. Indeed, my radicalism caused a momentary reaction: the principal had to whisk me off the stage because some students were making a move to do so on their own. I was terribly embarrassed by the incident, and the political question of why the students reacted so negatively remained with me for many years. But I had at least stood up and said what had to be said, and I was proud of myself for having done that.[1]

I did not extract a greatly enhanced understanding of human nature from some of the dramatic roles I played in high school. I now feel this was partly because Mr. Garrod spent too little time helping me to fully appreciate their larger significance. He could depend on me to get things right—or, in the case of my singing, at least okay—without much coaching, and so he invested most of his time on other matters. I did not resent his neglect then or now, partly because I always regarded the rewards of drama as more emotional and social than artistic and intellectual, partly because Mr. Garrod was always so warmly supportive of me in other ways. I once related an anecdote to him. I don't remember its content. I don't remember when the incident occurred. I do remember Mr. Garrod's simple reaction: "Bob, how *interesting*," he said. His validation of my experience made my day and I still remember my pleasure thirty-five years later. His remark was incalculably more valuable than a dozen disquisitions on Shakespeare and his times. If I wanted to know more about the Elizabethan world picture I could read Tillyard. What Andrew gave me could not be found in any library.

If drama in high school did less than it could have to help me appreciate the human condition, it was nonetheless useful because it was the one thing I could work hard at, enjoy, take pride in, and receive recognition for. In the classroom I picked up as many disjointed bits of knowledge as I needed to maintain my low A average, but I was rarely enthusiastic about what went on between 9 a.m. and 4 p.m. because as far as I could see it had little relevance to life. After 4 p.m. I came alive because my performances gave me dignity, self-esteem, and agency. This, in turn, enabled me to make sense of the world, to see reality on my own terms, to become me.

One of the tragedies of modern public schooling in Canada is that it provides too few opportunities for students to make sense of the

1. In the late 1980s I read in a newspaper report that Saint Johners suffer elevated rates of lung cancer and other diseases of the respiratory system due to the mill. I also discovered that Mr. Irving was rated by *Forbes* magazine as one of the world's richest men.

world, think well of themselves, and develop competencies. Indeed, certain zealots are trying to gut schools of precisely those programmes in arts and athletics that most often provide such opportunities. They believe that Canadian public schools have turned soft if not rotten. They argue that the youth of Japan and South Korea spend long hours concentrating on the basics of language, math, and science, while their Canadian counterparts spend fewer hours in school and study more drama and other non-basic subjects that are of little practical value. The putative decline in Canadian economic competitiveness is often attributed in part to the deterioration of public education—specifically, the failure to emphasize subjects that "really" matter. From this point of view, cutbacks in education budgets are a blessing. They represent an opportunity to return to basics, increase hours of instruction in core subjects, implement standardized testing, and maintain stricter discipline. In the long run, such policies will supposedly enhance Canadian economic brawn.

Whatever the merits of budget cutbacks, my own experience suggests that public schools need less drama and other non-core subjects the way a turkey needs an axe. Mr. Garrod's drama programme at Saint John High School helped to mould my character and prepare me for adult life. Drama did not just make me, it saved me. The story of how it did so is, I think, especially instructive in an era when the value of drama in public education has been obscured by people armed with impressive-sounding shibboleths, such as "accountability" and "back to the basics," but little idea of the value of a strong sense of self or of the kind of school programmes needed for healthy self-development. I wince to think what I would have become—or not become—without Mr. Garrod's drama programme. With it, my transition through adolescence was just about complete.

More than that: the drama programme prepared me for adult life. By helping me to define the boundaries of my self and my place in the world, drama allowed me to begin resolving my deepest emotional problems, which were, as I have illustrated, bound up with authority, class, and ethnicity. Once I reached university, the search for answers took an intellectual form. I spent more than fifteen years trying to figure out the social conditions that promote and inhibit rebellion against authority, class conflict, and ethnic assimilation into dominant cultures. I studied these problems in the apparently remote contexts of Russia in the 1890s and rural Canada before World War II, and I employed analytical constructs and methods far removed from my youthful understandings of the way the world worked. Nonetheless, the source of my interest in these subjects was always immediate and personal. At an emotional level, the drama programme helped me to formulate and pose the questions that framed my first researches and thus enabled me to become an academic.

Towards the end of my last year in high school, each graduating student was asked to prepare a yearbook blurb headed by a brief quotation that summed up his or her character. I chose an epigram from Nietzsche: "Man is a gregarious animal, more so in his mind than in his body. He may like to go alone for a walk, but he hates to stand alone in his opinions." This was my emancipation proclamation. I was refusing to become an other-directed mass man. In three short years the drama programme had enabled me to gain self-esteem, demonstrate competence at a concrete task, and recognize the possibility of achieving individuality. I never acted in another play after high school (although I relish performing in the theatre of the large lecture hall), and I only occasionally go to the theatre now. What I learned from drama was not art but life.

*Robert (Bob) Brym was born in Saint John, New Brunswick, in 1951 and graduated from Saint John High School in 1968. He studied at Dalhousie University and the Hebrew University of Jerusalem before completing his Ph.D. in Sociology at the University of Toronto in 1976. After spending two years at Memorial University in St. John's, Newfoundland, he joined the faculty at the University of Toronto, where he is now S.D. Clark Professor of Sociology and an Associate of the Centre for Jewish Studies. Bob has published widely on political behaviour in the Soviet Union/Russia, the Middle East, and Canada. He has received numerous awards for his research and teaching, most recently the British Journal of Sociology prize. In 2008, he became a Fellow of the Royal Society of Canada. Bob is joyfully married to Rhonda Lenton, also a sociologist. They have three accomplished adult daughters, all married, the eldest of whom has two remarkable daughters of her own. The first draft of Bob's essay was completed in 1997. Several iterations later, much improved thanks to constructive criticisms generously offered by Andrew Garrod, it was laid to rest on Bob's hard drive, where it remained undisturbed for the better part of a decade. Bob finally mustered the courage to exhume it and send it to the* Canadian Journal of Sociology, *where it was published under a different title in 2006.*

# Fiddler on the Stage

Selina Leem
THE MARSHALL ISLANDS

Passing through the unpainted cement gates and onto the breezy campus of the Marshall Islands High School, with a hint of salt water in the air, I became one of MIHS's many students. The year was 2011. For the next two-plus years, I watched MIHS students and those from other schools come to our school library to audition for Professor Andrew Garrod's plays. I was lucky that, in 2013, I had enough money to purchase a ticket to watch his production of *West Side Story*, which was starring Lulani Ritok, a favorite Marshallese actress, as well as John Riklon, a local celebrity. The performance was held at the International Convention Center, and as Ritok climbed up what looked to be a makeshift balcony belting out her lines, my first thought was, "Wow, Barbie." I was entranced.

As someone who grew up watching Barbie movies, Barbie's singing voice I always considered ethereal. The besotted and enchanted feelings I always get whenever I watch Barbie sing in any of her movies overwhelmed me when watching Ritok sing. Her voice had that delicate, clear, and reaching quality that I associated with Barbie. Except this time, it was coming from the periphery of self with the visual in front of me and audio amplification from the speakers set strategically in the rectangular performance space of ICC.

I watched the cast, as I had those I saw going in to audition, amazed at how brave and adventurous they were. I had friends who said those who went to audition and participate were wannabes—meaning attention-seekers who desired to be something more than what they were. Quite a discouraging thought, really. I allowed their thoughts and comments to keep me from doing something different—basically,

I let their insecurities waylay me. Finally, I reached my junior year. Taking note of how inconsistent I had been, I became indifferent to my classmates' struggle with presenting in front of the class. After all, we all knew each other. However, when my turn came, I still became bashful and got someone else to do it, or I slipped on my persona of confidence—my fake-it-till-you-make-it alter ego. This made me feel ingenuine, and I did not like the feeling. I decided I needed to live up to my intent. After all, others said I sang well, though my younger sister insisted that I did not. She was the cherry on top when she criticized my singing, which she did constantly. Underneath my nonchalant attitude, she really got to me.

Trying out for a play seemed the perfect answer to all my inner dialogues and conflicts. Even with my debilitating lack of confidence, I wanted to make a statement that being or wanting to be different was not wrong. Proving my sister and those who talked behind people's backs—and myself—wrong became a driving point. There would be singing lessons with trained experts who will give me feedback. I will be pushed beyond my comfort zone by having to reconfigure my mannerisms, speech, thinking, and facial expressions to become a fictional character that was far showier than my usual staid self. I will dance publicly with purpose and not be looked at weirdly. I especially wanted this because I love to dance—with my siblings or my friends or even by myself.

Audition day came and, as I made my way to the library alongside my more outgoing friends, a burst of devil-may-care energy filled me. At least I would not be alone as I sat waiting for my turn. I would graduate from MIHS feeling more complete just knowing I had tried out for a Broadway musical. Surely they needed a lot of dancers, villagers, or backup vocals, and I expected to get at least a supporting role. On the registration form, I had put in that I was auditioning for a minor role, no speaking, just singing and dancing. After all, I had zero acting experience. If I was to be an embarrassment, let it not be *that* embarrassment. My entire acting repertoire consisted of the countless times I spent in my grandparent's small bathroom reading my books aloud, paying close attention to the details of the scene, the way the characters acted. I knew I would one day attempt to act it out. This was a side of me that nobody outside my family knew, not even my closest friends.

They knew Selina, but they did not know Tzeitel Selina, the girl who monitored her expressions and body movements in the mirror until she was satisfied that they looked natural enough to be used when the situation called for it.

Keeping in mind the skills I had perfected in front of the mirror, I looked over the script we were given and drew a mental image of me acting them out. The image was of me but was not acting like me. I had to make that disassociation; otherwise my insecurities would ruin the flow of the story. Then we were told that anybody could volunteer to begin. I was surprised at that, expecting nobody to volunteer. Between our traditions and our personalities and having been encouraged to be humble, not to draw attention to ourselves, to put others before us, or simply being shy, when someone asks for a volunteer, there's always a long silence before someone outspoken and brave steps in. On that day, the more daring and experienced among us stepped forward and broke the ice. Feeling warmed up and encouraged, people became more eager to showcase their talents. After some time, I raised my hand at the same time as a student from the Cooperative School. I prayed, "Please let him not be my acting partner." But, he was. I have always felt inferior to private school students, with their perfect English and celebrity magazine talk, so I was intimidated all the more by this pairing.

As usual, now caught in a vulnerable situation, my walls came up to protect me. I slipped on my mask, my alter ego, so that I looked composed and self-assured. While reading the scene out loud with my new partner, I imagined watching myself in the mirror as I practiced the look on my face, the emotion in my eyes, and my tone. What was I conveying? Was I conveying the message in the script? In the scene, the boy was my Perchik. As I looked up at his looming figure, did he see love and desire in my eyes? As I entangled my body with his, did he feel it as trust and comfort? I did not know much about the play and the stage directions were few, so I had free will as to how I played Hodel. I was now the Hodel I enacted in my head. When Perchik and Hodel held hands for their dance, I as Hodel noted my partner's shaking hands. When Perchik drew Hodel closer, she heard his thumping heart. I nearly broke character then because I wanted to laugh. I wondered if it was his nerves, or if he was uncomfortable acting intimate with someone he just met, or both. It might be wrong to say this, but I felt empowered at that moment. I had thought I would be the one shaking. He and I laughed about it when auditions were over.

I did not know how to take having done the scene without much trouble, especially in a public setting in full view of many friends and peers. There was also the matter that the Marshall Islands society is conservative, so public displays of affection occurred seldom and were frowned upon. And there was my having zero experience in the dating department. Nonetheless, I had slipped into the character easily and everybody else had faded. I kept my eyes on my partner and on the script I was holding. I had the benefit of being a fast reader and having a good memory. While my partner was reading his lines, I could read ahead and memorize the next line immediately, so that when my partner was done talking I could keep my eyes focused on him and speak my next lines to him without breaking eye contact. And I was able to pull this off while containing my laughter at his shaking hands.

It was the most exhilarating experience I have ever had. When the audition ended, my friends bombarded me with questions about who my boyfriend was, all the while complimenting my acting. I just laughed, smiled, and told them to read a romance novel.

Several days later, the callbacks were posted. I did not know what a callback was, but my name was on the list, so I attended. We were instructed to act out another scene. I was bewildered. Why was I called? This time we had to do the scene in both English and Marshallese. The production would, after all, be bilingual, with the lyrics in English and the dialogue in Marshallese. We were asked to sing as well, which scared me. I was not asked to sing in the first audition, nor had I prepared myself for such a scenario. Running through my head was *Someone's Watching Over Me,* a song from a movie I had recently watched. I felt that the song's lyrics—"I found myself today" "I won't give up" "When I'm standing in the dark I'll still believe"—captured how I was feeling during that callback, and in general what I was going through personally. I cringed because I was sure I was off key, but I gave a sensitive and genuine performance, for the song revealed more than I was usually willing to express.

Acting for me was a lot easier than singing, except when we had to do it in Marshallese. When acting, I thought in English because all the books I read were in English and were very descriptive. So, I had to make myself speak the words in Marshallese while applying the same tone and expressions I would use in English. It made my own language seem very strange to me, but I also realized how much more intimate and potent the scene became when I was saying it in Marshallese. The words I was speaking to my partner were something I had never heard used in Marshallese.

Days later, everybody who had auditioned got called again. Then my name was called—and I had gotten a lead role. I was to play Tzeitel, the eldest daughter of Tevye, the male lead. Tzeitel is very much the independent-minded eldest daughter, fond of her siblings but willing to take charge of them. However, I was not really paying attention because I had signed up for a small role. One of my friends shook me and said, "Selina, you got a lead role. That is you. There is no other Selina here." My face went numb. I looked at them and at Professor Garrod in disbelief. But how? I had gone and gotten what I least expected—a lead role. So much pressure!

What I found most rewarding about being in the play was building up my character. I practiced the Tzeitel role in both English and Marshallese, and a very different character emerged from performing in the two languages. Playing Tzeitel in English felt more natural. I was delivering lines where she was begging, exuberant, and in love, which flowed more smoothly in English. It was easy to capture the right tone and the way I spoke her words. I hear English speakers express their feelings freely on TV and in the world around me. Their voices change with their emotions, going from a high to low voice, whispering, exasperated. Tzeitel expressed more emotions in one sentence than I would normally hear in Marshallese. As I mentioned earlier, in our conservative society, the Marshallese often repress their inner emotions. We are loud in anger but subdued in expressing everything else. I did not grow up in a household or with friends who said "I love you" or begged their father to bless their love to another who was not betrothed to them. The rigidity or lack of feeling I exercise in my daily Marshallese was transferring to my Tzeitel lines, so I would practice the lines in English and then try to apply the same tone to my lines in Marshallese. This made me more at ease and comfortable delivering my lines in Marshallese, as if they were always meant to be that way.

Then there was the hot seat, where you were asked questions as the character and had to reply as the character would. What is your name? What do you like? Whom do you like? Would you give up anything for your significant other? This really helps the actors get into their roles, as it makes you stop thinking as yourself and you start thinking and feeling like your character. It also helps your character become more familiar to you, rather than just being lines you read from a script. Your character now has a background, a foundation.

However, you can also apply personal experience to give a more convincing and heartfelt performance, such as in the scene where Tzeitel begs her father not to marry her to Lazar Wolf, the butcher. She is very much in love with another man, Motel, the tailor, but her father wants her to marry the much older butcher. I imagined that she would be desperate, frantic, enraged. I tried thinking of a time when I was very stressed out and felt like the world was coming to an end. How did I feel at that moment? Fear and sadness. Hence, I threw myself into the role, getting down on my knees whilst I hung onto my father's hands, pleading and crying. This was my life, Tzeitel's life, but unfortunately it was not mine to dictate and decide. It all rested in the hands of my father.

I liked the fact that the production was to be bilingual, as we have a mix of people in our audiences. The bilingual performance guaranteed that it would be understood and well enjoyed by all. Many of the foreigners who would attend were probably familiar with *Fiddler on the Roof,* but for most Marshallese, a production entirely in English would be confusing. When the lines were delivered in Marshallese, they would understand and could follow along, and foreigners who already knew the play could still follow along. With the songs sung in English, the Marshallese in the audience could still enjoy and appreciate the beauty of the music, as we are a musically gifted people.

For many of the Marshallese actors and actresses, speaking their lines in their own language was a comfort. The cast was a mix of public and private school students, and many of the public school students might not have been as comfortable delivering their lines in English as their private school mates. No one was made fun of or made to feel inferior for having a thick Marshallese accent. In their mother tongue, they dived in and were able to express themselves fluently and magnificently.

Relationships on stage and off turned out to be complicated for the cast members. Each individual complemented another, and as a group delivering their best, wonders were born. Dramas were also born—not just on stage but behind the scenes. It amazed me how superbly a cast could deliver their parts on stage and then let all the good spirits evaporate almost instantly once they stepped off. Once off stage, the actors went back to not speaking to each other or talking about each other to other people.

With two people playing one role, as is often the case with leading parts in Professor Garrod's casting, comparisons will always be made between the two. One will always be seen as better—if not by the director then by the cast members. That takes an extreme toll on the person who is considered the inferior. It eats away at their self-esteem and self-confidence. It is so easy for people to talk unkindly, rather than to offer advice or help.

It made me realize that drama is drama. Drama onstage and drama offstage. I have always watched plays and movies and never considered what happens behind the stage or screen. Now being part of it, it was a whole new world to me and one that drew my increasing respect, for despite all the issues we had as a cast, we still performed with zest on stage. As we were rushing around and reminding everybody that they were due on stage, we made sure no one was left behind. When we realized another person forgot their line, we made something up in the moment. It was true teamwork.

After acting in *Fiddler,* I felt a new surge of confidence. I was less intimidated by the private school students and found that they actually could be nice, chill, and cool people. My circle of friends opened up to include more than just my classmates and others in my school. I also was able to approach people more comfortably, rather than waiting to be approached first. It felt natural. All the socializing I had to do in *Fiddler,* getting to know everybody and observing how people acted and responded—it all rubbed off on me. I also saw how much of an impact it had on the social and emotional aspects of my life.

When I entered the United World College (UWC) Robert Bosch College in Freiburg, Germany, after graduating from MIHS, I decided to take the International Baccalaureate Theatre course. I never would have considered taking the class before acting in *Fiddler.* To me, studying at UWC had always been about education and taking subjects that would get me a job as quickly as possible. With the arts, it was a gamble—and I do not gamble. However, I went ahead and took the theatre course. It turned out to be my favorite course and the one I was most successful at. As the class explored the different types of theatre, it got more personal than I had expected. My inner wounds were opening up—and healing. Frustrations that I had held in were freed as I morphed into other characters.

For me, theatre became a space of expression, with freedom and without judgement, only critical feedback. It provided me with immense support. In all my other classes, my level of performance depended on who the teacher was and who my classmates were. When the classmates and teachers changed, I had to relearn the class dynamics all over again. I was most comfortable in my theatre class because I stuck with the same classmates all the way to my last year at UWC. I was so comfortable having the same teacher and the same classmates, it was like having a family that I had built trust in and with whom I was able to be more vulnerable than I usually allowed myself in other classes. I had gained a family that was insightful, witty, and powerful.

Years later, as a poet, writer, climate warrior, and anti-nuclear advocate, I have to be on stage often to deliver a speech, give a presentation, or perform a poem. When I miss a line or a slide, my training from the play with Professor Garrod or from my theatre classes is my saving grace. I hear Professor Garrod telling me, "Even if you make a mistake, only you and your team knows about it. No one in the audience will know." And that enables me to keep the flow going, rather than disrupt it in obvious discomfort or disappointment. Professor Garrod and my theatre classes taught me that, when I do not feel confident on stage, I must slip my game face on. If the audience's eyes intimidate me, I look above their head. I read my lines ahead so I do not spend too much time with my head down, reading from the paper. I always face the audience, and never turn my back. Before I speak, I plant my feet on the floor to ground me, and I modulate my voice and my gut to project most fully. It's like having a suit of armor ready for the stage, and I could not feel more blessed, more grateful for it.

*Having won a scholarship to attend her last two years of high school in the international boarding school, UWC Robert Bosch College in Freiburg, Germany, Leem finished up her junior year at the Marshall Islands High School and embarked August 2016 to Europe for the most transformational and formative years of her life. During her senior year, at the age of eighteen, she was the youngest delegate to attend the COP21 as part of the Marshall Islands delegate team. On the final day, she delivered the closing statement with the then Ambassador for Climate Change, the late Tony deBrum, urging leaders to take climate actions. Since then she has become a climate warrior for her country, attending international climate conferences as a speaker or spoken word artist, giving interviews and writing articles for multiple media outlets, and recently was invited to be a speaker at the 2021 TED Countdown Summit in Edinburgh, Scotland. Leem is based in Washington, D.C., where she is studying and working as a translator or transcriber for Marshallese when she takes off her climate warrior cap. As for the future, she does not want to think that far for she already has enough on her present plate to attend to.*

# Forgetting Myself

Wilmer Joel

THE MARSHALL ISLANDS

I grew up in the Marshall Islands, part of a culture where storytelling plays a significant role in preserving our people's way of life. When I was a child, there was no theatre to bring these stories to life. Instead, we children sat on a handcrafted mattress listening to our grandparents' traditional stories and relied on our imaginations to experience the story visually. Our grandparents didn't realize that their great-grand-children would one day experience theatre, a modern form of story-telling that brings the story to life. The Marshall Islands are located in the North Pacific; the country encompasses twenty-nine low-ly-ing coral atolls and five coral islands. My country was once a testing ground for one of humanity's deadliest experiments, nuclear testing. The United States of America conducted sixty-seven nuclear tests on four different islands for twelve years "for the good of mankind and to end all world war."

A new threat to the Marshalls is now arising, not from humans but from Mother Nature itself: climate change. Ours is one of the most vulnerable countries in the world, and we have been very vocal on climate change on the world's greatest stages. The fight to ensure that we achieve nuclear and climate justice has been going on for many de-cades. Despite these challenges, the Marshallese people love entertain-ment, especially classic theatre. I have loved watching theatrical per-formances since I was a little boy. In the capital city of Majuro, movies always have been very popular, but live theatre is not that prominent because most of the performance venues have a limited number of seats and cannot accommodate large audiences for plays or musicals.

The first play I saw was *Fiddler on the Roof,* directed by Professor

Andrew Garrod and presented by Youth Bridge Global at the International Conference Center in Majuro in 2014. Before it started, I was clueless about what was going to happen on that empty stage. When the overture was played, I began to understand that I was going to watch a performance that was like some sort of concert. I remember how excited I was to see the fiddler kicking off the play by fiddling with his violin. But then I said to myself, "This is not a concert, this is just people talking to each other, how boring." However, as I began to pay closer attention to the dialogue and the action, I discovered that this was a new and different type of entertainment than I was used to. I realized what the word "theatre" meant; it was like watching a movie, but happening up close and right in front of you. While I was watching the cast, I promised myself that I would be on that stage someday.

That promise was not fulfilled until late January 2018, when I auditioned for Meredith Wilson's *The Music Man*. Wilson was an American composer, musician, and playwright who is well remembered for two of his Broadway hits, *The Music Man* and *It's Beginning to Look a Lot Like Christmas*. I heard from a close friend that auditions were being held in the library of Marshall Islands High School, our country's largest, with more than a thousand students. I wanted to try something new, so I went to the audition to see what was going on. I felt confident as I entered the library and wanted to prove to myself that I was ready for anything. The song I auditioned with was an Elvis Presley classic, "Can't Help Falling in Love with You." After that we did some dance steps, which I tried to keep up with, but it was tricky for me. I was fortunate to be cast as Charlie Cowell, the antagonist of the musical.

A year later I went to audition for Rodgers and Hammerstein's *Carousel*, a more serious and interesting musical. Most of the cast members were teenagers and kids, though there was a significant number of adults participating. For my *Carousel* audition I sang a well-known Christmas carol, "Angels We Have Heard on High."

My character in *The Music Man*, Charlie Cowell, was an anvil salesman. In *Carousel* I was chosen to play mill owner David Bascombe. I felt a huge responsibility for the roles I was given, but I also was living my childhood dream. There were some challenges I had to adapt to while playing these two characters. Cowell's personality is a bit suggestive toward women, which was a challenge, because I was quite innocent at that time. Bascombe, on the other hand, was a vastly wealthy old man who owned a cotton mill factory. I had to think a lot about how to channel an old person at my young age. It was also challenging for me to memorize my lines. To help with this problem, I made up my own lines that were similar to the script, so I was able to remember them easily. Given that the dialogue in the script was bilingual, I found the translation to be very helpful, especially speaking in my native language, so my people would understand the play better.

After a few weeks of rehearsals, the casts of both musicals formed a genuine bond. Friendships were forged that I will always cherish, for we felt like family. The rehearsals were a rigorous process that we had to commit to, and that's where I learned the importance of communication and teamwork. These are two attributes I find useful in my current occupation as a journalist for the *Marshall Islands Journal,* the only independent newspaper in the country.

The very first scene I remember rehearsing was the train scene in *The Music Man.* It was mind-blowing and also demanding, because the dialogue is fast-paced, almost like a form of rapping. All of us involved had to add a bounce to our steps, as if we were on a train. The choreography was created and directed by professional choreographer Nina Roy, a fantastic individual who patiently worked with us on the dance routines. Another scene I loved to rehearse was "Blow High, Blow Low" in *Carousel,* a thrilling dance sequence that required well-coordinated movements. Ilona Bito, a seasoned dancer, choreographed that scene, which was one of the most difficult in *Carousel.*

I enjoyed singing many of the songs in both musicals, but I have two personal favorites that I hold dear to my heart, "Seventy-Six Trombones" and "You'll Never Walk Alone." Although they are very different, both songs gave me a feeling of inspiration and an appreciation for music. Singing those songs was often a challenge for the cast and me, because we thought we could sing however we liked. Thank goodness we had two talented music directors, Summer Cody and Jacob Donoghue, to correct our misconception. Another vital person was the assistant music director, the late Jerre Bennett. He had worked for the Public Instructional Center, where he printed our scripts and the pamphlets for the play. I usually stopped by his office to chat and took advice from him on how to portray my characters. I kept in touch with him even after the plays were over, until the final days of his life.

When we held our rehearsals at the venue where we would be performing, it was very hectic. The atmosphere was tenser than our rehearsals at the school library. Stage sets were being erected, the painters were completing the final touches of their work, sound systems and lighting were being checked, and the costumes were fully fitted. Professor Garrod and his production team were asking more of us than ever before. Thankfully, our beloved producer Bonny Taggart made sure we were taken care of and well-fed.

When we arrived at the last two days of practice, the technical and costume rehearsals, we found it was very hot under the lights, for we were wearing suits. Then the intensive rehearsing was over and the time had finally come for us to perform—*it was show time!* We all gathered in a huddle and said a prayer before we went on stage. I remember looking out from behind the stage set and seeing the crowd waiting to watch the play. I told myself to remain cool and not be nervous. In *The Music Man,* as soon as the overture ended and the lights came up, my fellow salesman and I took our cue to go on stage. It was as if I had entered a new realm, because as soon as I started saying my lines I forgot that I was myself. There were some scenes in *The Music Man* that I hadn't expected to get a lot of reaction from the crowd, and I was surprised when they did. One such scene was when I was acting salaciously toward the female lead, Marian Paroo.

Additionally, the audience also enjoyed a clash between my character Cowell and the male lead, Harold Hill, alternated by Duke Gaston and Jobod Silk. The lights went off after that scene ended, and we almost tripped trying to get down the stage after the lights were extinguished, which was pitch black for the scene off the stage. I was glad that, as always, the stage crew was on it, and they lit our way providing lights with their flashlights for the actors throughout the play. The crew members were the backbone of the play. They're the ones setting set up the props for the actors and actresses. One reminded us when to take them on stage; a crew member was assigned to make sure I held my briefcase, for which I am grateful. A year later, when I played David Bascombe in *Carousel,* I had the same experience of forgetting myself on stage. One scene the audience seemed to enjoy a great deal in *Carousel* was when we performed the challenging dance routine,

"Blow High, Blow Low." While we were doing that number, I noticed Marshall Islands President David Kabua watching with his wife and their granddaughter in obvious enjoyment. Their presence really boosted the players' morale, and I thought we did an outstanding job on that one. The scene in which Billy Bigelow commits suicide with a knife received the opposite reaction to what we expected. Instead of feeling remorseful and sorry, most of the audience was laughing at the death of Bigelow. The woman playing the role of Julie Jordan then sang the play's climactic song, "You'll Never Walk Alone," which shifted the crowd's mood from laughing to crying.

I thought our overall performance in both of these plays was exceptional. However, we were only able to perform *Carousel* three of the six nights because of a suspected COVID case in Majuro. When I was told about the cancellation, I didn't believe it at first. When Professor Garrod confirmed it, I was overcome by so many emotions. Almost everyone was heartbroken by the news. The professor and his team had to catch the first flight back to their home countries.

Being in these plays has been the highlight of my life, and I will never forget the experience. It has transformed many of our lives for the better. Where we were once divided because of the schools we came from, we became a family after getting to know one another during the rehearsals. Never in my wildest dreams did I ever think I would be part of something this life-changing. I've been in other local plays, but nothing tops my experience with Professor Garrod and Youth Bridge Global. What mattered to me in those plays wasn't the costumes, lights, or makeup; it was seeing the audience's reaction. Every time I walk along the street, I am recognized for the characters I played. It really makes my day when I hear a fan tell me they enjoyed my performance because I knew I did something that brought people joy. The unique thing about our island is that we treat each other equally. You can even fist-bump the president without being worried that his bodyguards will tackle you.

In a Western society heavily influenced by Hollywood, fans go wild whenever they see a celebrity. Fans here are the opposite; they are not obsessed with anyone famous or of great renown. They just ask for a picture, say "hello," and continue on their way. Sadly, the youth here are sometimes seen as nothing but a problem by our society. We are often perceived as baby-makers, juvenile delinquents, and drug dealers. However, having programs like theatre breaks these biases and unleashes the participating youths' potential so they can become people who will contribute to the welfare of society.

I mentioned earlier that I forgot myself while playing the characters. It is true, and I was not the only one; the other cast members and the audience forgot themselves too. The cast forgot that they were shy, quiet, innocent students. When they were on stage, they brought their characters to life from start to finish. The audience in turn forgot we were good-for-nothing rascals in the community and were able to see us in a positive light.

One of the most important skills I and others learned while doing the plays was the ability to forget ourselves. For once we got to be someone we were not, we were able to escape reality and jump into another dimension. When we saw the world through the lens of our characters, it exposed a different side of us that those who were watching could enjoy.

*Wilmer Joel is an award-winning filmmaker, intern journalist, poet, social media influencer, and photographer. He is currently a senior and student body president at Marshall Islands High School. He was the school newspaper's editor-in-chief for the newsletter called "The Current." He is also a board member of a Marshallese nonprofit youth organization that lets youths express their feelings and thoughts about the effects of climate change on human health, and translates the feelings and thoughts into forms of art called Jo-Jikum. He loves to read, make videos, write, and listen to music. This essay was written in 2022.*

# What the Bastard Taught Me: Recollections of *King Lear*

Mark Blagrave

CANADA

'Tis the infirmity of his age; yet he hath ever but slenderly
known himself.
—*King Lear*, Act I, Scene II, 292–93

There are photographs, of course—black and white; beautifully shot by one of the staff. They capture the surface and a layer just below: the things a sensitive outsider might have seen, one who knew exactly where to look, and how. These are no mere snapshots, although in one a careless job of cropping has left one head without a top. They are portraits: portraits of the court of King Lear, and of us as we were then in it. It is all there in the pages of the yearbook—the politics of Lear's situation encapsulated in the carefully composed stage picture of the first act; the ambition of Goneril caught forever through a low camera angle, with a much-shorter Albany just out of focus in the background; the pathos of the Fool and of Cordelia (were they one and the same? we debated that late at nights); the nakedness of Edgar. I appear in two, my brief black tunic affording full display of furry arms and legs, thick, you can see even in the photos, with pancake make-up. In one I am Edmund, the Bastard son of Gloucester, conning his brother Edgar out of his inheritance; in the second, Edmund, the would-be ruler of a kingdom, dying with four heads huddled above him, his underpants miraculously just invisible above the hem-line. Looking at the photographs, twenty-five years later, I see myself and not myself, and am reminded (once again) of how much I discovered for the first time that year at Saint John High School. I am reminded of the riddle: when is a person most himself but not himself? Answer: when he (she, it) is acting. Andrew Garrod's Shakespeare showed me that, and although I have rediscovered it (as every actor must) dozens of times since, there is no denying the special mystique of the "first time."

> His breeding, Sir, hath been at my charge: I have so often blush'd
> to acknowledge him, that now I am braz'd to't.
> —*King Lear*, Act I, Scene II, 8–10

Then there are the photographs that do not exist, the pictures (snapshots these would be, I suppose) of my adolescence. We were not a picture-taking family—a policy born in equal parts out of aesthetic principle, philosophical modesty, and sheer technophobia. Outside of photographs of my sixteen-year-old self in roles on stage, the record is, as they say, silent. Who was I? I did not, when I inhabited the role of Edmund in 1973, share the Bastard's anxiety over his parentage. Now, however, in trying to reconstruct what made me who I was then, I feel with him. Who was I, and how had I gotten there? The basic background, of course, I can construct. Saint John High School was my fifth school in five years, a fact motivated in equal parts by my parents' earnest desire to keep me out of temptation's way and by what may have been a mid-life crisis that saw them moving from Ontario to Bermuda and back again, and finally to New Brunswick. I had, in those five years, developed the skills of a chameleon—I could always persuade people by the end of six months that I had been wherever it was forever. Acting, then, was a necessary social skill, a survival technique, as it is for most people—all the more so for me because my "maverick" existence had been led in a series of Anglican rectories. Being a minister's child was no more cool in 1973 than it has ever been. Saint John presented my chameleon act with its greatest challenge to date. It was ugly, dirty, poor, depressing, and stuck, it seemed to me then, in some kind of time warp. I fell in love with it in a matter of months, not for its colour and its character and its ghosts (all of which have since seduced me) but for what it often seemed in 1973 to be doing its best to hide: its commitment, in the face of considerable odds, to the arts. Saint John High School should, by rights, have been a dump, at best a struggling inner-city medium-security institution. Rothesay High would have appeared the more logical choice of school for a boy moving from Canada's wealthiest town to one of its wealthiest suburban villages (Rothesay Collegiate was out—I had run away from and been miserable in one of its Ontario equivalents). Driving by both buildings and judging solely on the basis of their outsides and their settings, the decision might have seemed obvious, but, fortunately, someone had the goodness to share with us uninitiated the truth about what lay beneath the surfaces. Saint John High was, thanks to the efforts of such transplanted Englishmen as Dennis Knibb and Brian Roberts and Andrew Garrod, the *only* school for a sixteen-year-old who fancied himself a serious student, a poet, and an actor.

> My train are men of choice and rarest parts,
> That all particulars of duty know,
> And in the most exact regard support
> The worships of their name.
> —*King Lear*, Act I, Scene IV, 261–64

There should be group portraits somewhere, off the stage I mean, memorializing the sense of belonging to one another that I can still dimly recollect after twenty-five years. High schools then, as much as now I suppose, lent themselves to fragmentation into groups. We would have been the "artsy-fartsies," I realize now, although there was, as I recall it, little of the pretension (the flamboyant dressing, the emotional outbursts) that often goes with that label. Neither do I recall being much aware of the existence of other groups, though there must have been jocks and nerds and whatever other timeless divisions make up a high school. We were, within our "group," a heterogeneous mix; that was part of its allure—you could belong and remain yourself too. There were the three or four all-round best students in Grade Twelve, who would go on (they knew this already) to careers as physicians and scientists and lawyers; there were the visual artists, several of whom would later make their living through their art; there were younger students whose exuberance and general eccentricity bought them a place in the circle. What we shared, I think, was a genuine, unposed interest in things artistic and intellectual, and, more important perhaps, a kind of reverence and special affection for those teachers who fed that interest. The school's course offerings in Music, Art, and Communications (part theatre arts, part media) were extraordinary, and we knew that, and took full advantage. In Andrew Garrod's drama productions, all of these things coalesced.

> … the quality of nothing hath
> not such need to hide itself. Let's see: come;
> if it be nothing, I shall not need spectacles.
> —*King Lear*, Act I, Scene II, 33–35)

From the auditions on, the cast of *King Lear* was a kind of community. In holding open auditions, where everyone could see everyone else's efforts, Mr. Garrod may have been exposing his students to more potential humiliation than they would ever suffer again in trying for a role elsewhere, but he was undoubtedly fostering a sense of community. We had to listen while peers who refused to let the punctuation do its job tortured unlikely inflections out of innocent lines. For some, we felt sorry; for others only contempt—all of it covered by a polite and apparently respectful silence. This habit would prove useful again and again during the process of production. On a more positive note, there were the truly wonderful auditions, which spurred their successors to heights they would not have achieved in a room alone with the director. A spirit of competition that may not have been very different from that of athletic try-outs infused the process. I see now that much of the one-upmanship must have taken the form of acting-from-the-outside—of making things bigger or broader or more English—but at the time its key and vital role was to help us find reserves of confidence we did not know we had. My own was not an audition distinguished by its reasoned approach to a role. I had, in fact, studied a speech of Edmund's quite carefully in advance, noting things to do with my voice, subtle touches that would carry the meaning. In the event, my whole experience was one of flushed face, throbbing ears, rushing blood. Only after I sat down and the adrenalin had subsided did I recall all of the things I had meant to do. I'm not sure whether that is a unique experience, but I doubt it.

Casting, too, was done publicly, maintaining into the next phase the sense of community about the production. As students huddled around the bulletin board where the cast list was posted, the elation and the disappointments were all inevitably public. There was considerable politics. Friends were not slow to point out to me, for instance, that I, as newcomer, had had the luck to be cast in a role in which a veteran had seen himself. That he should have been cast as my nemesis was probably unintentional, but it very likely gave us both something to work with on the stage. Among the women, there must have been an even more complicated dynamic. The number of very talented female actors greatly exceeded available roles (as is the common problem with producing Shakespeare almost anywhere), and so they shared. We had two Cordelias, two Gonerils, two Regans. Knowing that, through a mere accident of Shakespeare's historical period, they would only hold the stage half as many nights as their male opposite numbers cannot have been an easy pill. Neither can it have been easy to sit by and watch as another person walked through your blocking and spoke your lines (whether better or worse). But these were all the little rivalries and jealousies that gave the community life and interest.

> The fitchew not the soiled horse goes to't
> With a more riotous appetite.
> —*King Lear*, Act IV, Scene VI, 121–22)

Sex also kept the community interesting—the promise of sex, if not the actual act itself. It crackled like electricity in the air, the tension, the awareness. Offstage, it was the seemingly accidental touches, the sitting a little closer than necessary in class, the thousands of miscellaneous bytes of teenage body language. Onstage, it was a matter of seducing one another, and the audience—theatre can be that simple, and that difficult; and perhaps nobody is better equipped to discover that than adolescents. Backstage, it was a sense of comfortable belonging and an active concentration in support of our partners still on stage.

> Allow not nature more than nature needs,
> Man's life is cheap as beast's.
> —*King Lear*, Act II, Scene IV, 264–65

In addition to politics and sex, the play provided a social and an intellectual life for the group. We met at Andrew Garrod's apartment (a remarkable book-lined oasis in the derelict Ten Eych Hotel), joined by Richard Thorne (who did the lighting) and Sandra Keirstead (who was wardrobe mistress), to discuss articles we had read about *King Lear*. The readings were difficult and sometimes controversial. We reported to one another on what the critics had had to say over the years about the characters we were to play. We wrestled with Jan Kott's (then quite new) view of *Lear* as Absurdist drama, as well as with A.C. Bradley's more conventional Hegelian readings, and the remarkable thing was that we did not stop to consider whether we were out of our depth. Mr. Garrod, aided by Mr. Thorne and Miss Keirstead, led us as though we were a university seminar group and not the high school cast of the annual Shakespeare production. Nobody patronized anybody as I remember it, and we all grew enormously as a result. In rehearsals and production, the lines quoted in those articles provoked an added prickle at the backs of our necks. Gloucester's "leap" from the cliffs of Dover on a flat stage brought Kott rushing back; and Lear's "I am bound upon a wheel of fire that mine own tears do scald like molten lead" reverberated with a fine article by Wilson Knight.

The choice of *King Lear* for a high school production is not an obvious one. The roles, in particular the lead, appear too large and mature; the tone too relentlessly dismal; the time-frame nearly inaccessible. Where many schools settle for a continuous round of As *You Like It*s, *Twelfth Night*s, and *Midsummer Night's Dream*s, if they venture into Shakespeare any more at all, Garrod's choices for Saint John High never balked at the prospect of the tragedies. *Hamlet* and *Macbeth*, though, remain a far cry from *Lear*. They are household words where *Lear* is unlikely to be; they have clearly available themes (conscience and ambition) where *Lear* is either a ridiculous warning about making proper arrangements for retirement or an unrelieved vision into the void. It was precisely this latter quality, I think, with its absurdist tinge, that made the choice so right for many of us at that time of our lives and in that era. Encouraged by Jan Kott's *Shakespeare Our Contemporary*, we could see our own lives, our own time—not necessarily in the individual characters' lives, but in the life of the play as a whole.

My tears begin to take his part so much,
They mar my counterfeiting.
—*King Lear*, Act III, Scene VI, 59–60)

I do not think I learned anything about so-called "method acting" (in any of its variant and misrepresented forms) in the production of *King Lear*. That, for me, was the beauty of it. I do not remember worrying about what Edmund would have eaten for breakfast; I do not remember trying in any way to access his pre-historic psyche. We had plenty in common, I am sure: we were both outsiders in a sense, cynics, pretenders, and ruled in large measures by our hormones. All of those things were obvious, and I have no doubt that I used them somehow in creating the role. Of far more lasting importance to me, however, was an inkling that I got as I acted Edmund that acting is about "showing," not "being." Andrew Garrod's approach, through auditions and casting and rehearsals and seminars, seemed to encourage us, in experiencing ourselves as a community, to see the play as a whole, to care about it as a whole product. Its overall impression was, it seemed to me in this context, more important than any one individual's ability to empathize with a role. What mattered was that we could show an audience the characters and what they stood for in the scheme of the play, rather than identifying with them in some way that could only ultimately be gratifying to ourselves. I probably did not think of this at the time as particularly liberating, but I have seen it that way ever since.

I was contracted to them both: all three
Now marry in an instant.
—*King Lear*, Act V, Scene III, 227–228)

There are five pictures that do not, could not, be recorded by any camera, and they must serve to illustrate, in pallid words, what I mean about showing rather than being. They represent at the same time Edmund's five major moments in *King Lear,* and, as a unit, what Andrew Garrod's efforts at Saint John High School made possible for me as an actor and, much later, director.

## Moment One: The Nature Speech

The stage is empty. It is just me and the audience. Seduction. I, at least, am dressed for it. "Thou," … pause, think, flash the eyes … "Nature," … pause again … "art my goddess; to thy laws / My services are bound." For "nature" you could substitute any one of a number of baser words and the sound would remain the same, the imagined sound of a stag in rut. Then, after the sex, the reasoning; the "wherefores" and "whys" with which the speech continues as Edmund questions the arbitrary world in which legitimate Edgar has more rights than he; and then the plan to deceive his father. Finally, the climax: "I grow. I prosper; / Now, gods, stand up for bastards!" On this last line, all the lustfulness of the opening returns, but now it is accompanied with a gesture: I raise my right forearm sharply, elbow tight against my pelvic bone, left hand resting in the crook—"stand up," I say, "for bastards." I hear Andrew's voice somewhere in the back of my head as I do this: words to the effect that this will be a metaphor for "getting a hard-on" at the same time as it is the universal sign for "up yours." The action is stagey, it's theatrical; it's anachronistic; and that is what is so important. It is about communicating things to the audience before it is about trying to persuade them you are a prehistoric Briton.

## Moment Two: The Self-wounding

Again, I am by myself, having persuaded my brother that he must fly our father's supposed wrath. Seduction again, persuasion. The next step is to convince our father of my brother's perfidy. To make my story more credible, I will wound myself, claiming that Edgar has drawn my blood. The difficulty is for *anyone* to draw blood in front of an audience. While I draw my blunt dagger across my forearm, I must squeeze a trail of stage-blood from a ball of cotton-batting that is concealed, held in place by an elastic band, on my bicep under the short sleeve of my tunic. It is a nightmare the first few times, and I find myself wanting to ask to cut the effect, trusting instead in the audience's imagination and the distance between the action and the front row of seats. Finally, though, I begin to get the hang of concentrating on two states of being at once: I must be Edmund wounding himself to deceive his father and Mark reaching up under his sleeve to wring fake blood from a cotton ball. I did not begin to master the technique then, but fostering that dual consciousness is something I have tried to do with my own student actors over the years since.

### Moment Three: The Kiss

Here again, the double concentration is crucial. Edmund has formed alliances with both of the evil sisters, literally screwing his way to the top, it seems. At this particular point in Act IV he bids Goneril adieu with a kiss that must show where their relations stand. In early rehearsals, the kiss is taken as read, only fanning the anxiety over it. There is much joking and banter about it, but it is awkward. We are friends, both Gonerils and I. (The fact that there are two only increases the awkwardness geometrically.) But they both have other people they would rather kiss "that way," and so do I, I suppose. The first time we try it in rehearsal, one of the Gonerils and I, we both chew Dentyne (cinnamon) madly, in preparation. I cannot tell whether it is Edmund or me stirring. From then on it is never clear to me whether Edmund is kissing Goneril (and which Goneril; they kiss differently) or me kissing Michelle or Evelyne. So much for losing yourself in a role.

### Moment Four: The "Duel"

One night while Edgar, the force of light, and Edmund, the force of darkness, are going at one another with the huge broadswords made for the production by Geoffrey and Peter Foss, we miscue and Edgar's sword takes a piece out of my hand (not Edmund's, mine; I have the scar still). I am torn between using the pain to increase the passion of my performance and worrying about how I will get the blood stopped for the following scene. I do both.

### Moment Five: The Dying

Edmund's death is not much more than a piece of necessary housekeeping in *King Lear,* and its final throes are kept offstage. It has none of the pathos of the other deaths that follow, perhaps because it, unlike the others, appears so obviously to be earned. For me as Edmund, though, it is not nothing. Simulating the act of dying on stage without provoking a laugh is never easy. Doing so on the floor in a tunic that is too short even when you are standing up straight is even less easy. Andrew rehearses and rehearses us to get the picture right: Albany triumphant over Edmund's fallen body, Goneril reaching across to her dying lover, and a couple of others to support the shoulders so that my face and voice will not be lost to the audience. Despite his efforts, it never falls out exactly the same way any two performances. The most I learn to hope for is that my underpants don't show—because even the dying Edmund will have to walk around the school the next day. And there is the photograph that will appear in the yearbook.

The wheel is come full circle; I am here.
—*King Lear*, Act V, Scene III, 174

I am drawn back to those photographs in the *Red and Grey*. What can they restore to me of who I was twenty-five years ago, and of how that person was affected by his high school drama experience? As I look at them I see myself and not myself. I see Edmund and not Edmund. I recall how the drama "group" allowed me even then to be both myself and a member of something larger. I realize how Andrew's intellectual soirees encouraged us to see our roles in the larger contexts of the play's meaning, to be in the role but also in the play. And I appreciate how the opportunity of playing, at age sixteen, Edmund, in a play as large and ambitious as *King Lear,* gave me an early glimpse of a habit of double consciousness in acting that I have worked to build upon ever since.

*After completing a Ph.D. at the University of Toronto, Mark Blagrave enjoyed a 35-year career teaching English Literature and Drama Studies at three Canadian universities—the University of New Brunswick Saint John, Mount Allison University, and Huron University College at the University of Western Ontario. In addition to academic articles on theatre history and film, he has published two novels (Silver Salts, 2008, and* Lay Figures, *2020) and a collection of linked stories (Salt in the Wounds, 2014). His plays have been produced professionally and in university theatres in the Maritime Provinces. Mark's essay was written in 1998 when he was forty-two years old.*

PART FOUR

# Coming Full Circle

# Full Circle

Elizabeth Foster Chase
CANADA

When I was a student at Saint John High School in New Brunswick, I never thought that my career would lead me in a full circle back to my beginnings. When I stood on the school's stage as a teenager, learning how to act from Andrew Garrod, I never considered the possibility of one day being in his position, directing a new generation of student actors on my old stomping grounds. Nevertheless, here I am, a professional teacher, amateur actor, and head of the drama program at Saint John. My various roles in plays and musicals prepared me for my current role as director. I learned so many lessons through acting under Mr. Garrod's tutelage; some were obvious, others were not evident to me until I took my seat in the director's chair. Many lessons became clear to me after my love scene with Mr. Garrod, a man twice my age.

When I was in Grade Twelve, we performed a production of *She Stoops to Conquer,* an eighteenth-century comedy by Oliver Goldsmith. I played Kate Hardcastle, a refined young woman who pretends to be a barmaid in order to win the reluctant heart of her intended, Marlowe. My favourite scene was the first meeting between these two, which involved Kate being chased around and over (yes, over) a sofa by her suitor. At one point, Kate is caught (not quite unwillingly) and pinned as Marlowe proceeds to nuzzle her neck and "whisper sweet nothings in her ear."

When the young actor playing Marlowe encountered some difficulty in making this scene a believable one, drawing as he was on his own experience (or should I say inexperience), it finally became necessary for the completely frustrated director to show him how it was done. I soon found myself prone on the stage floor with Mr. Garrod nuzzling and whispering away on top of me.

Though it was a strange situation, it could never have been interpreted as a romantic encounter. Mr. Garrod was trying to read from his playbook at the same time, and our awkward positioning dispelled any possibility of romance or intimacy. As I struggled with my now one-armed suitor, who had his eye on his script and certainly not my neck, he loudly stage-whispered to me to push him away and I stage-whispered back, with great frustration, that I was trying—which I was, with all the strength I could muster.

This brief, odd moment provided important lessons in stagecraft for me, lessons that I try to instill in my students today. First and perhaps most importantly, I realized that adults could interact with teenagers as peers: Mr. Garrod showed confidence in my maturity by putting me in such a situation. I came away from that experience with a newfound admiration for Mr. Garrod and what he did for me—he had treated me as an equal, a true actress with the ability to distinguish her own emotions from that of her character's feelings. This lesson is one that I have made certain to instill in my students today; for many of them, it is their first taste of adulthood.

As a director, I try to maintain the sense that I'm on the same level as my students; I knew I had succeeded when they gave me a nickname. We were rehearsing Shakespeare's *The Comedy of Errors,* and some students were having trouble with their English accents. After some discussion, I advised them to go home and watch *Star Trek.* Patrick Stewart, who plays starship Captain Jean-Luc Picard on the show, is an accomplished Shakespearean actor and speaks with a natural British accent. Shortly thereafter, my incredulous students ("You mean, you're actually telling us to watch *Star Trek?*") stopped calling me Mrs. Chase—"Captain" Chase was born. My nickname led to an extra measure of camaraderie amongst the cast and a relaxed, congenial mood during rehearsals.

That rehearsal with Mr. Garrod also taught me that onstage liaisons are completely separate from offstage relationships. Mr. Garrod was "in character," whispering sweet nothings in my ears at one moment and then effortlessly returned to being my teacher and director when the scene ended. Drama provides a fantastic outlet for actors of any age to safely explore new feelings and emotions, but this is especially true for confused and inexperienced teenagers. To be able to scream with anger and frustration at another person and yet to be able to walk away unscathed from that situation provides a unique opportunity to see what can happen without suffering the consequences.

I carried this lesson with me; my recent performance as Kate in an amateur production of *The Taming of the Shrew* comes to mind. In one scene, Petruchio announces his firm resolve to marry Kate, then grabs and kisses her. In response, she screams with fury at him and her father before storming offstage. I felt infuriated as I shouted at this overbearing man who dared to assume that I would marry him. I felt intense pain as I raged at my father who had never listened to my wishes. I felt agonizing frustration as I ran up the stairway to my room. But I laughed with pride and relief at the success of our performances when I saw those same actors at intermission.

Mr. Garrod taught me one final lesson that has influenced every aspect of my style of directing: the importance of praise cannot be overlooked. With one word of praise, a director immediately can bring on a longing for more from the actors. I remember feeling the swell of pride when Mr. Garrod congratulated me on a performance, and I remember wanting to do all I could to earn such praise. But I don't think that I truly understood its importance until I began to direct. As an adult working with teenagers, the look of appreciation on their faces brings back some vivid memories of my own of struggle to please and finding satisfaction in finally discovering an outlet where I could.

I find that praising my young actors provides a two-fold benefit. It brings them satisfaction to do something well in the eyes of an adult and it brings me satisfaction to provide a venue for the growth of self-esteem in them. Too often, the expectation of adults when dealing with teenagers is that, because of their age and inexperience, they are not mature enough or wise enough to do anything well or appropriately. How many times when meeting a well-mannered youth have we turned to another to remark on how seldom we meet someone so polite and well-behaved? Such a sad commentary on our own expectations, especially when we should remember our own youth and, despite our exuberance, what untapped and often unrecognized potential we had. To find an adult willing to give you a chance, to challenge you, and who praises even the smallest accomplishments, can bring about a willingness and determination to demand nothing but the best from yourself.

As I try to instill these lessons in my students, I continue to marvel at the power of drama. Shy students come out of their shells as they are encouraged and praised by their peers. Students with low self-esteem grow to love themselves and be proud of who they are. Teenagers learn that their opinions and ideas do matter, and that they need not be subordinate to adults simply because of their age. Just as I learned from participating in high school theatre, my own students have learned more during the long hours of rehearsal—about commitment, about patience, about determination, about friendship—than most yet have learned in their whole lives. The circle continues.

*After graduating from Saint John High School in 1974, Elizabeth studied theatre at Dalhousie University in Halifax, Nova Scotia. After completing her degree, she returned to Saint John, where she raised her daughter. Elizabeth's great passion was theatre and, in particular, the works of William Shakespeare. Elizabeth spent untold hours bringing his plays to life—she cared deeply about this pursuit and shared this passion with enthusiastic thespians, young and old. Notably, and owing to the profound impact of her high school theatre experience, she volunteered for many years to direct Shakespearean productions at Saint John High School. Elizabeth was a member of the Board of Directors for Saint John's Imperial Theatre. She was a founding member of the Saint John Shakespeare Society and the Artistic Director of the Saint John Shakespeare Festival. Elizabeth acted in, directed, and produced over thirty plays including twenty-one productions of Shakespeare's canon. Some of her most acclaimed and personally meaningful roles included Kate (*The Taming of the Shrew*), Milady de Winter (*The Three Musketeers*), Eliza Doolittle (*My Fair Lady*), Marquise de Merteuil (*Dangerous Liaisons*), and Cleopatra (*Antony and Cleopatra*). About a year before her passing in 2012, she moved back to Halifax to be closer to her daughter's family. Elizabeth contributed profound creativity and unabashed devotion to her many pursuits—family and theatre above all. This piece was written in 1998.*

# I Am Jobod

Jobod Silk
THE MARSHALL ISLANDS

Throughout my childhood, I was always interested in films and performance. I loved the way that a story was portrayed through the TV screen, especially the cliffhanger scenes that had me riveted to my chair. However, what attracted me the most was the acting. I was fascinated with the way the actors played their roles; it was, to me, as if they behaved like that in real life. I often would search for behind-the-scenes moments on the internet just to see what the actors were like behind the camera. I was appalled every single time; in my curious adolescent mind, it seemed impossible for one actor to embody two or more personalities. Thus, my interest in acting and performing was sparked. However, in my home of the Marshall Islands, the possibility of pursuing a career in acting seemed remote; our government prioritizes sending medical students or those pursuing law or engineering abroad to seek higher education beyond our borders.

The Marshall Islands, which is located just a little above the equator, is an island nation comprising twenty-nine atolls and five islands encircled by the vast Pacific Ocean. We are still a developing nation under a free association with the United States. There are not many job opportunities here, thus the need to send students abroad to master important professional fields. That leaves little room for the arts, which means that, growing up with the goal of becoming an actor, I had no support to pursue my dream. That didn't stop me—I was fortunate that my family and schoolmates recognized my ability to entertain, and they encouraged me to explore those talents.

Another thing I loved about films was the singing. As a Pacific Islander, music flows through my veins, as our traditions are passed down orally through chants, stories, and songs. Musicals stirred the islander in me, and at a young age I began to show an ability to sing. Before I was old enough to comprehend what was happening, my parents, who noticed that I loved to sing nursery rhymes, got a gig for me with Li-Mauwe, a famous female singer in Majuro, the capital city of the Marshall Islands. Although I had only two words to speak in her song, I became a familiar voice to the locals. One Sunday morning, when I was still in my middle school years, I went to my friend's church. I was new there, but the songs were not new to me and I sang along like I was a member of the church. One of the older men pulled me aside and asked me to introduce myself. Now, in Marshallese custom, when introducing oneself it is essential to mention the names of one's parents, grandparents, and clan. The man knew who I was as soon as I told him who my parents were, and he asked if I remembered joining in Li-Mauwe's song. This kind of recognition and attention paved the way for my name to become a familiar one around Majuro.

One summer during my middle school years, my friends and I had a picnic on one of the smaller islets in Majuro. Exhausted from swimming, I decided to take a break, so I took a ukulele and went to sing on the grass. Two other friends of mine, Emina Jorbon and Atina Kaminaga, joined in. We had so much fun jamming and, realizing that we sounded good together as a trio, we decided to film ourselves. We sang a cover of "Love and Honesty" and posted it on Facebook. That post got the most "likes" I had ever received on social media. We were receiving requests to post more songs, and so we did. A few months later, we posted a "selfie" music video of our cover of Leonard Cohen's "Hallelujah." That video went viral even more than the last. Soon after that, however, I transferred to Xavier High School, a boarding school in Chuuk, Micronesia. I met a group of boys on my first day in the dorm and introduced myself as Johnny Silk, from the Marshall Islands. Upon learning that I am Marshallese, the boys asked if I knew who Jobod is—the dude singing on Facebook—and I informed them that that is my nickname. *I am Jobod.*

Word spread around the school that Jobod was one of the new students, and by orientation day a bunch of other students were asking me to sing for them or with them. I loved the attention. Back home, I was always known as my siblings' little brother and did not have an identity for myself. This made me determined to make a name for myself. At Xavier, I sang for and with as many people as I could, in the hope of portraying Jobod as Jobod, and not as his siblings' younger brother. However, for personal reasons, I had to return home by the end of the first semester and enroll once again in my former school, Majuro Baptist Christian Academy. I was welcomed back with open arms. In no time I was jamming with my old friends, including Emina and Atina, during chapel, break time, and even after school. We soon posted our third singing video on Facebook, a cover of "Shut De Do." This cover jammed the Marshallese internet, so people posted it on YouTube without our consent. As it was already done, we couldn't do anything about it. However, it turned out to be to our advantage, because word of our video reached the ears of Tommy Kabua, who at the time was recruiting actors for a play production led by Professor Andrew Garrod, whom we called "Professor," and Youth Bridge Global (YBG), Andrew's nonprofit that encourages dramatic youth performance around the world.

After persistent persuasion from Tommy as well as our friends, our trio decided to audition for the Professor and YBG's production of *Oklahoma!* All three of us got offered a role, but with schoolwork and other extracurricular activities, I eventually was the only one of the three able to join the cast. I was given the role of Will Parker. Will was the comic lead role, a not-too-bright cowboy who was desperately in love with Ado Annie, "the girl who can't say no." As it was my first time in a play, I found it extremely difficult to put myself in another's shoes (might I add that the costume shoes literally did not fit me). I also was unfamiliar with the terms "stage direction" and "projection," and I felt intimidated. As far as I knew, my only talent was that I could sing well. Everyone else looked so natural on the stage, and I felt I needed to do better or else my music videos on Facebook would be "bullshit." So, I pushed myself through rehearsal after rehearsal—working hard on the vocals, the acting, and the choreography. Especially the choreography. I had always been known to have "three left feet" and was not comfortable with dancing. I had trouble keeping up with the choreography, especially since Will had a rather large dancing part, but I made it a priority to prove to my doubters that I could keep up with the rhythm. Therefore, it was my pride and joy to show on stage that I was capable of doing Will's signature rope dance. After every performance I felt deeply satisfied because I showed those who felt I couldn't handle the dancing—especially myself!—that in fact I COULD.

After playing Will in *Oklahoma!*, I was officially addicted to the stage. I enjoyed the rush I got from performing—being on stage, the costumes, the acting, and working with a cast of other students who were much like me. I believe one benefit of developing that cast was that a new community was formed—a community composed of talented Marshallese kids with unsupported dreams who wished to demonstrate the importance of sharing art with our community. This community of performers will eventually be the one that demonstrates the importance of art as a field to pursue and to bring back to our country.

With these thoughts in my mind, I decided to join the next play, should Professor Garrod and his team return. They did not disappoint. The next year, 2018, the team returned with the script for one of the islanders' favorite films, *Grease,* by Jim Jacobs and Warren Casey. With no second thoughts, I auditioned. Since it was my second time auditioning for a YBG production, I was familiar with how things went; however, that did not stop my nerves from going crazy. I really wanted to play Danny Zuko, the bad boy who was afraid of romance, and I tried to show it during the audition. But, when I saw the other kids' talents, I was intimidated. There was no way I would outshine these people. To my surprise, though, I got the role of Danny Zuko, shared with my friend, Bryant Zebedy; although I was ecstatic, I also was hesitant. With its extremely difficult songs and the stamina-testing dance numbers, this demanding role would test my limits. I found "You're the One That I Want" to be most trying, with its demanding high notes and the long and tiring dance routine. However, Bryant was a familiar face in YBG's productions, and he guided me through. In fact, he helped me develop my character as Danny, and as Jobod.

While I had fun performing, I also found it hard to stay in character, because Danny's rude behavior was completely different from my own way of interacting with others. It was a struggle for me to maintain the bad boy behavior Zuko oozes, and his abusive comments made me feel like an asshole. After every scene I was apologizing profusely to Carnie Reimers, who played Sandra Dee, because I felt bad being mean to her in my role as Danny. I realize now, of course, that it was not me being rude but Danny, the person I was impersonating. *I was acting*! However, feeling guilty and needing to apologize only fueled my drive to continue because it told me that, if I felt that way about myself, the audience would probably feel the same, which would mean that I was "selling the act." One thing I often mention to my friends when we reminisce about our time doing *Grease* is the "Hand Jive" dance. It was extremely complex, and I found myself trying to catch my breath while both singing the song and dancing. However, what made me the most nervous about the dance was my duet with Chacha De Gregario, who was played by Berlin Philippo. The fact that the spotlight would be on us as we had to pull off the intricate choreography, all the while out of breath, absolutely wrecked my nerves—especially the part where I had to hold her up in the air. I have to give credit to Berlin and her outstanding dance moves, which also made me shine. If not for her, I would not have been able to pull that off. This demonstrates that, even though one doubts themself, given time, practice, and dedication, their talents can and will improve.

As with the previous play, my favorite part about performing in *Grease* was the curtain call. The fact that we received so much applause made my heart burst with pride and joy, because WE DID THAT. The International Conference Center, where the performances were held, was packed to the point where some people were denied entrance because there were no more seats available, not even standing room. One thousand people attended the performance on our final night. That number alone gave me a real sense of accomplishment, because I really did push myself to excel—so much so that I lost my voice after performance week. I loved to entertain, whether telling stories, singing, or acting, and after *Grease* I definitely felt that acting was my calling.

The next year's musical was *The Music Man,* and boy, when I heard the songs, I was intimidated. I had never done that type of singing before, and the fact that the songs were lengthy and required stamina made me second guess the thought of auditioning. However, I was talked into it, and again, with my increasing confidence, I got the lead role, Professor Harold Hill, which I shared with Duke Gaston. Hill is a conman who travels from city to city, tricks the people into giving him money, and then ditches them in the blink of an eye. However, when he comes into River City in Iowa, he falls in love. I relished playing

Harold Hill, and personally believe my performance in that musical was my best. The fact that Ikue Omwere, my girlfriend at the time, was playing my love interest definitely fueled my adrenalin, I must say. (The original actor in that role was unable to continue, and Ikue took her place.) The biggest challenges I faced playing Hill were definitely the music numbers. The songs were in a low key—just low enough to require me to put more effort into my singing—but the dialogue right after the songs was the most challenging. After singing, I would be out of breath and energy, and I found myself pushing to get through the dialogues that came straight after. I remember struggling to do the "76 Trombones" number one night when the music director played the wrong track, and I also had trouble singing to the beat on "Trouble." It took a lot for me to maintain my concentration on the music while also keeping up with the choreography and staying in character. Although I was glad when the music director put the right track on in the middle of the performance, I felt unsatisfied that I hadn't been able to perform "Trouble" successfully. However, the applause was as strong as ever, and I was relieved and proud because, despite the technical difficulties, I was able to reach the crowd. That was the proudest I had ever been while performing.

The chemistry between Ikue and me was phenomenal. We would practice at school during lunch, or when cleaning up the classroom, or even when walking home. In the middle of a conversation, I would start performing a scene that we had together and we would act it out. That process made our performance on stage more believable. I especially recall that, during the scene where Professor Hill is arrested by the sheriff, Ikue was so caught up in the moment that she started to actually cry. That made me very proud of her.

In 2020, I auditioned for what turned out to be my last play with Professor, *Carousel*. I auditioned and once again got the lead role, Billy Bigalow, the aggressive, abusive carousel barker. I was intimidated by this role because I was uncomfortable with the idea that Billy abuses Julie Jordan, his love interest. That, coupled with the fact that I was in my freshman year of college and doing an internship at a nonprofit, made it really difficult for me to meet expectations at school, work, and rehearsals. During this time, we were nearing Nuclear Victims' Remembrance Day, which is an important event for the Republic of the

Marshall Islands (RMI), and as part of my internship I was required to help organize the event. It was hard to balance that with the demands of rehearsals, and I found myself burnt out. I started forgetting lines and dance steps, missing my cues, and not being mentally present. However, I pushed through and tried my best.

One of my favorite things about *Carousel* was my duets with Carnie, who played Julie. It just felt so natural, like we were having a normal everyday conversation whenever we came on stage together, and the fact that we had Duke as our partner definitely helped. Working with Duke really helped my acting. We would share ideas on how to perform in a certain scene, and we practiced our songs together and made sure we both stayed on top of things.

The most intimidating thing about *Carousel* was Billy's soliloquy, "My Boy Bill." It was nearly eight minutes long and very intense. It starts off hopefully, with Billy visualizing a son in the future and how he would raise his son to be, and then, when he realizes that the baby might be a girl, his mood changes to subtle anger and a sense of desperation to become a better man for his daughter. The fact that the song has so many mood changes was challenging, but the technicalities of the song were even more difficult. It took so much for me not to run out of breath on the long notes, and I struggled with both the high notes and the strong low ones. The ending note of the song was long, high, and filled with so much emotion—it was the most difficult line I have had in any play, and I had to sing it on while my knees, arching my back as if screaming at the sky. I had to practice that effect time and time again.

My favorite song from *Carousel* was "If I Loved You," which is a duet between Billy and Julie. I loved the way we switched back and forth between singing and dialogue, and the way Carnie sang her part was inspiring and it pushed me to match her energy. I never thought I was capable of singing the way I did in "If I Loved You," and Jacob, the music director, observed that my singing abilities had improved since the auditions. When he said that, I felt validated, because I had been feeling that I was doing poorly during rehearsals, as I was exhausted from work and school. It was really pleasing to know that my hard work was paying off and that my ability was growing.

YBG's production of *Carousel* in the year 2020 came to an early end when a case of COVID-19 was confirmed in Kwajalein. I was devastated, as were the entire cast and crew. We had put our hearts into this show, but it did not work out the way we wanted and expected it to. Despite that, I felt a sense of pride and gratitude for the time I spent with the production team. I was able to keep discovering new things about myself and learned more about my limits. I had started off bashful and quiet, and felt uneasy raising my voice, even if it was just acting. I had trouble moving my feet to the rhythm. I also had trouble keeping up with my demanding roles as an actor, student, and worker, and therefore learned to budget my time wisely. I made new friends and I became a better team player. Although I only had one night on the stage performing *Carousel*—we had to close after only three nights of an intended six-night run—I was extremely grateful for that experience. I can actually say I have come to love that single performance, as that one night I shared the stage with my friends was one of the best moments I have ever had. Although I did not expect it to be my last on stage, I believe that all the hard work we all put in paid off that night, and for that I will always be grateful.

In 2019, only a day after my graduation from high school, I boarded a plane and headed to Massachusetts to attend a summer intensive training in Shakespearean art. It was my first time ever outside of Micronesia, and the experience was one I will never forget. Duke and I were completely clueless, as we were both new to traveling abroad. We were not used to big airports and different terminals and check-in lanes, so we were really lost. The road to Massachusetts was bumpy, as certain setbacks hindered our trip, but we were fortunately able to reach our destination safely. The atmosphere of the States was foreign to us. Upon coming in contact with the colder weather, I felt quite uncomfortable, as I was used to the warm, humid atmosphere of the Marshall Islands. Professor and our dear friend, Dody, were so kind and generous in helping us acquire proper clothing for the weather, familiarizing us with the unfamiliar location and atmosphere, and feeding us during the hours we spent together. Their support really made me feel more prepared to face the unknown adventures that would greet me at Shakespeare & Company.

Duke and I settled in rather quickly and comfortably at the workshop. We made friends easily and built a community with complete strangers. My fellow actors had no idea what or where the Marshall Islands are, and I was happy to explain this to them. I, in turn, had no idea how important personal pronouns were—the way informants want their gender identity to be recognized through the use of pronouns—and they explained them to me. I went to the workshop knowing nothing of Shakespeare, besides the fact that Taylor Swift's "Love Story" was a reference to *Romeo and Juliet,* and I honestly went there only because I wanted to experience life outside the safe bubble of the Marshalls. However, the things that I experienced at Shakespeare & Company really made a change in me—as an actor, and as an individual.

I recall having a hard time staying in character during a rehearsal. The director asked me to take a walk inside the classroom. Although I found this request odd, I did as I was told. After about twenty seconds of walking, the director asked me to take a seat and listen to the others as they described my walk. They said that I walk with quick paces, my eyes glued to the ground, with a frown on my face and my shoulders hunched. I remember thinking, "Okay, and …?" Then they went on to explain that my walk is a reflection of my personality, or at least their assumption of it, based on how I walk. This really hit home, and it made me realize and acknowledge so many things about myself that I had not been able to before. That motivated me to try to improve not just my walk but also my mental image of myself. The director's comments on my walk opened a portal for me to think about my personal emotions, something not common in the RMI. It allowed me to tap into my emotions and use them to fuel my performance on stage. This was something new to me, and it enabled me to become a better actor.

For my final performance at Shakespeare & Company, I had the wonderful honor of working with the student-actor Acadia Weinberg in a scene from *The Tempest.* Acadia and I initially had no idea who the other was, but they (Acadia's preferred pronoun) made me feel like family. We built a bond that I feel made our scene more realistic and enjoyable. My acting also was enhanced by keeping my mentors' advice in mind. I learned how to walk like the character I was playing, how to breathe like him, and even how to breathe correctly whether I was singing or acting out a monologue or just speaking one line.

My time at Shakespeare & Company provided an opportunity for me to develop new bonds of friendship and to explore my capabilities. These kinds of opportunities do not come easily in the RMI, so having been recommended by Professor for this U.S. acting workshop was a great honor. Not only was I able explore my ability as an actor, I also learned so much more about myself as an individual. How I walk, how I breathe, how to interact with others, even if they are completely different from me, how to handle my vulnerability and use it to my advantage. Had it not been for that summer workshop experience, I would not have grown to be the person I believe myself to be today.

Being part of the plays with Professor and his team really has left a mark on all Marshallese. Professor and his team have had such a strong influence that art is being taken more seriously in my country today. Many of the national activities here on Majuro now include an art event—singing, painting, poetry, weaving—and other forms of art have been introduced, such as upcycling and storytelling. Sadly, due to COVID, this is our second year with no play performances with YBG or Professor Garrod. I recently was giving this some thought, as I had really hoped that the pandemic would die down by now. I felt bad for all the kids with so much potential but no means of exploring and showcasing their talents, especially kids who are as passionate about theatre as I was at their age. I have tried to have performance art incorporated into some of the activities we do at work, but it's difficult to direct and stage a play when you are overseeing all the activities yourself, and it is equally difficult to find someone to do the directing, because not everyone is comfortable being in a leadership position. But, in early 2022, things began looking brighter.

For the 2022 Nuclear Victims' Remembrance Day in early March, the organizing committee agreed to produce a play. The play was written by members of the Nuclear Club at the College of the Marshall Islands. It tells of the role the Marshall Islands played in the nuclear bomb testing era, including stories of what the Marshallese people went through as the subjects of nuclear weapons experiments, their losses and the damage they experienced. It also tells of the current condition of the islands that the bombs were tested on, and of the people who were affected by the radioactive fallout. The one-hour play was to be performed on only one night. As a member of the organizing committee for Nuclear Victims' Remembrance Day, I was put in charge of recruiting actors, looking for directors, and handling the other logistics of producing a play. This made me feel very proud of myself. I started off as a member of a cast in one play, and now I was helping to produce and direct one myself. I hope this makes Professor smile, as he has played an enormous role in this great accomplishment. He brought the idea of putting on a play to the people of the RMI; he then came here to produce and direct the plays, year after year. Then COVID struck and he was forced to leave overnight … he was gone for the rest of that year, and the next year—and this year the RMI itself would be putting on its first national play! I was overjoyed and couldn't wait to see how the play turned out.

As it turned out, Ariana Tibon, commissioner of the National Nuclear Commission, had no idea how to direct a play, let alone how to write one. As I am a member of the committee and had experience in Professor Garrod's productions, she asked me to write, produce, and direct the play for Nuclear Victims' Remembrance Day. I was extremely honored and felt a sense of pride that my time working with YBG was paying off. I was now co-writing, co-producing, and co-directing a play, the first one since Professor's departure, and this time, the play would not be about foreign people's stories, but our own.

As it was the first time we were producing a play on our own, the script took a long time to complete, we had to find sponsors to provide treats for the players after practice, and everything was a mess. The script was finally complete just two weeks before the performance, and we were able to practice the entire play at once. While the actors mostly got their lines down, there was no time to practice using mics, or with the costumes, makeup, and lighting. Everything was done at the last minute, and we were not able to produce the play as eloquently as Professor and his team do theirs. Nevertheless, we pushed through and tried our best, and based on the feedback we got from the community on and off the island, we did magnificently. This is certainly the proudest I have been about anything I've done in my life.

The feedback we got included a request from the president of the Marshall Islands to perform the play once again for him, his ministers and senators, and their families. The second performance of the play was held March 19, about two weeks after our first performance. The extra two weeks of practice enhanced the actors' performance, but the logistics were still an issue. With the death of our dear friend Jerre Bennett, who participated in YBG's productions, we also lost most of the costumes. The production team had to scramble to assemble costumes and props at the last minute. My colleague Ariana Tibon was ill during that period, so I was busy at work preparing for a climate webinar series while also doing the play. That made rehearsals extremely difficult. We also had multiple actors playing different roles because we did not have enough actors, and the prop crew consisted of just five guys. That does not sound like an attractive way to mount a production.

Although I did not feel confident about the play, I was hopeful that the cast and crew would pull through and be able to shine on the stage. And boy, did they SHINE! The audience at both performances was clearly moved, and they congratulated the players over and over again. In fact, the audience was so touched by the performance that we were invited to perform again, this time at Laura Ball Field. This definitely shows me that there is a good chance that theatre is finally finding its place in the RMI, and it makes me very proud.

*Jobod Silk, 21 years old, is Marshallese, born and raised. His family is musical and theatrical, frequently performing songs or small skits during family gatherings. This is where his love for performing and singing comes from. He grew up attending makeshift Sunday school classes with his grandmother, where all the kids around town learned how to read music. From there, Jobod was able to develop his musical abilities. In the summer of 2019, Jobod got the wonderful opportunity, with the help of Professor Garrod, to attend a summer intensive at Shakespeare & Company in Lenox, Massachusetts. Jobod was able to engage with youths from different backgrounds and to develop his acting skills by learning the Linklater methods of acting, walking, and even breathing. By the fall of 2019, after his return to the Marshall Islands, Jobod enrolled in the University of the South Pacific. After one semester and careful consideration, Jobod realized that the College of the Marshall Islands was a better career move. Therefore, in the spring of 2020, Jobod moved to CMI. He also started an internship at the nonprofit Jo-Jikum, an NGO focused on promoting youth engagement in the environmental issues that affect the RMI, such as climate change and our nuclear legacy. By 2021, Jobod got promoted from intern to the position of Youth Coordinator. Since then,*

*Jobod has been responsible for developing projects at Jo-Jikum, most no-tably the annual Climate Change and Health Arts Seminar, which in-troduces the effects climate change has on health to high school students from Majuro and other outer islands. The students have transformed the information they learned into art in the form of paintings, songs, poems, and traditional weavings. Jobod is now awaiting graduation in the summer of 2022, after which he will pursue a bachelor's degree in environmental science at the University of Hilo in Hawaii. This essay was written in 2022.*

# Finding Purpose

Mustafa Stupac
BOSNIA AND HERZEGOVINA

Acting has always been a passion of mine, a feeling I had in my gut that wouldn't let me go, and I just could not ignore it. I wanted to explore the feeling, and somehow I knew the answer was in theatre. If I had ignored it, it might have been one of the biggest mistakes of my life.

I always push myself into new challenges, such as projects that I feel will be a valuable life experience that brings me knowledge, space, and time to learn something new about myself. I like to push myself to the limit so I can see where I am right now and then discover new ways to enrich myself and grow. Every play production I have been in has brought some new, exhilarating experience into my life, and that's why I try out for plays whenever I can.

A few years ago, I was looking for an opportunity to satisfy my hunger for theatre. I wanted to demonstrate and hone my acting abilities, to meet new people, make new friendships, and be exposed to theatre practitioners from all around the world so I could learn more about Shakespeare, theatre, and myself. I also wanted to learn about the production process in general, as I thought this would help me overcome some personal insecurities and, most importantly, enable me to have fun. I was hoping to grow from the theatre experience as both a striving actor and a human being. I hoped to participate in a production that would enable me to reflect on the play, and, when it was over, the part I played in its success. I also was hoping it would open the door for me to future theatre projects. I did find such a production—Shakespeare's *Twelfth Night*, produced by the US nonprofit organization Youth Bridge Global—and it did indeed do all this. I am eternally grateful for that opportunity, and for those that followed.

Though I was born in 1992, just a few months before the war in the

Balkans began, I see my life as blessed and full of opportunities. Growing up playing in the alleys of Cernica, a neighborhood of Mostar, I had a wonderful childhood. Many may not be able to comprehend it, but I did not recognize that the houses and buildings around me had been demolished. They were as they were, and I played ball, rode my bike, and socialized with my peers in the shadows of the ruined buildings. I had wonderful parents who are still my role models in life; I felt loved and I lacked nothing in my life.

I had great friends on my street, and we hung out all day. But, every now and then, I had an incident due to my Muslim name. When I went to play basketball with some friends, I always walked "with eyes on my back" so that no one could attack me from behind. Even today, this habit remains wherever I go, be it in America, Europe, or the Balkans. As if I were a secret agent, I always consider what the situation is around me and whether there might be any chance of an unexpected confrontation. In an environment like ours, you mature faster than in others. To paraphrase Rocky Balboa, "Nothing hits harder than life itself," and you either accept it and get over it, or it will follow you for the rest of your life.

Throughout my life, I have met and socialized with people of different religions and ethnic and national backgrounds. Amongst my close friends, it was never a problem whether someone was a Bosniak, Croat, Serb, or Jew—we are simply not taught to divide people like that. While, to this day, you have a lot of people who only hang out within their ethnic groups—there are not many of them, but they do exist—and I shouldn't avoid offering the reader such information.

As I grew older, I became more interested and passionate about the possibility of acting. The first roles I was given were in Youth Bridge Global's (YBG) productions of Shakespeare's *Twelfth Night* and *Romeo and Juliet,* in which I played Malvolio and Mercutio respectively. Though Malvolio and Mercutio both begin with the letter *M,* end with the letter *o,* and have four syllables in their name, the two characters have nothing in common with each other and absolutely nothing in common with me. I'm not a puritan self-deluded social climber like Malvolio, nor am I a sex-obsessed libertine like Mercutio. These were the most challenging roles I could have taken in the two plays, as they are so different from my own personality.

Still, after immersing myself in these characters, I started to love them for who they were, with all their strengths and vulnerabilities. My job as an actor was to justify their actions and defend their choices, which reflect the core of their beings. Sometimes, after spending so much time working on the roles and having integrated part of yourself into the characters, it's hard to let them go.

Malvolio, Olivia's butler, is a delicious part. He is a killjoy and an upstart, and he is infatuated with Olivia. After reading the play and following Professor Andrew Garrod's instructions, I decided to play Malvolio's character as a typically pretentious and capricious English butler with slightly effeminate movements, which I felt would portray the pompous person I was striving for. These characteristics included my posture, the way I talked and moved, and how I related to other people. All my actions were driven by Malvolio's rigid, presumptuous, humorless, condescending, and absurd traits and characteristics.

Malvolio's susceptibility to being gulled is captured perfectly in the box-tree scene, which presented complications, as there are two over-lapping conversations—one by Malvolio, who is reading a letter aloud, the other among three male actors. Coordination was essential, and the scene was full of unexpected and improvised situations. It was a great experience in concentration and listening. I was attired in silly yellow stockings that made me feel self-important and grand. I had been complimented by actors backstage—including a few friendly butt-pinches from both genders—who were appreciative of the round contours of my bottom. My adrenalin was rushing, I felt exhilarated!

My—and Malvolio's—mission in the scene was to woo and win Olivia. While I was slowly, sensually approaching Olivia and proudly showing her my legs in the tight yellow stockings, I was full of myself. I thought, "This is a done deal!" Of course, this was Malvolio's absurd perspective, but the audience's reaction was uplifting beyond my wild-est expectations, and they really helped me achieve the full potential of my character. With each scene I felt more and more comfortable in Malvolio's skin and increasingly connected to him. In my mind my outlandish actions were justified, and the audience seemed to approve of my excesses. I built the momentum and brought Malvolio to the heights and happiness of his achievement. After this scene, Malvolio's downfall begins. Punished for his hubris, he is arrested and incarcerated, a cruel and terrible shock. His final words in the play, "I'll be revenged on the whole pack of you," elicited tears as much as laughter. I could feel the audience's sympathy; they saw his humanity and truly felt sorry for him. That was my biggest reward, as I felt I had played the character convincingly.

Based on the promise that I apparently showed as Malvolio, YBG arranged a scholarship for me with Shakespeare & Company in Lenox, Massachusetts, where the distinguished training and performance group holds an annual four-week program in Shakespearean acting. I had high expectations, and I was not disappointed. During the weeks with a remarkable group of teachers and actors, I learned a lot about theatre, Shakespeare, and, most importantly, myself. The program brought back memories I had completely forgotten and made me more self-aware. It helped me realize how much of myself I hid from others and even from myself. The best aspect of the program was the colleagues and mentors I met at the workshop. After only three days, the other student actors and I felt we had known each other for years My new friends could not have been more welcoming and kind to me, which I especially appreciated because I was the only non-American in the program. The warm reception I received blew my mind and changed some of the prejudices—fed by American movies—I had about American youth.

The workshop lived up to its description as "intensive." Our thought-fully planned schedule was filled with classes on voice, movement, physical awareness, and other topics, and each day broke us down and built us back up, little by little. The program was physically, psycholog-ically, and emotionally demanding, and all the participants felt drained at some point, but our amazing teachers supported us throughout our four-week stay. They were fully invested in our learning and taught us through guidance, rather than direct instruction, so that in the end we were teaching ourselves. Even though they were in charge, our teach-ers never put themselves above us and always treated us as equals. The Shakespeare & Company program exceeded all of my expectations. It changed my perceptions of American youth, learning, and even of myself, all the while granting me the courage to keep on doing what I love. It also connected me with new friends, with whom I bonded and could share the kinds of things we usually don't say. It was nice to learn that I am not the only one who struggles and that I am not afraid to show I am struggling.

The Shakespeare & Company program was a unique and unforgettable experience, and what I appreciated most was the amazing people that I met there. I think I will always have their support, and since we all went through this extraordinary journey together, we have become a team. I cannot express enough words of gratitude for being able to participate in this program. At Shakespeare & Company I learned many techniques that I wanted to share with my Mostar colleagues. The best opportunity I had to do that was through YBG back in Mostar during the summer of 2016 production of *Romeo and Juliet*. This was the ideal opportunity to practice my new skills and knowledge, and to pass them on to my colleagues. Although I was offered the role of Romeo, I realized the real challenge for me was the complex, physically challenging role of Mercutio. After a long negotiation with the production team, I was given the opportunity to play that character, and I think I justified both the team's and my own expectations. My confidence in saying this springs from my sense that I had grown as an actor through my recent stay with Shakespeare & Company and had acquired acting tools that would enable me to work with my comrades in any production in the capacity of actor or director. Mercutio, Romeo's sex-obsessed and mercurial best friend (as reflected in his name), was as distant from my own values and character as Malvolio had been. Mercutio was perhaps the most challenging role I have ever played, and certainly the one I had the most fun interpreting and performing, due to his fanciful temperament and dynamic personality. To fully capture his exuberance, I had to get out of my own comfort zone, and after each show I was visibly tired and exhausted. Spent though I was, I enjoyed trying to capture the workings of his devious mind. The costume I wore to play Mercutio was probably my favorite. We had set our play in the 1960s, and I was wearing a torn tank top with a massive print of a hand, the middle finger erect. My body was covered with tattoos and my hairstyle was a red-dyed mohawk. They captured my sexually driven character who doesn't think about the consequences of his actions and is unafraid of death. Mercutio had a restless mind, which is why I moved on stage with fast and sudden movements, covering most of the stage in every scene. Playing the role very energetically and with a lot of movement enabled me to express my flamboyant person-ality. I played the role proudly, actually embracing the advice Mercutio gave to Romeo: "You are a lover. Borrow Cupid's wings and soar with them above a common bound." I did indeed feel I was flying above the stage during the entire performance.

Mercutio's long, fanciful Queen Mab speech was a nightly challenge, as it required tumultuous emotion and energy. I took an intensive, stu-dious approach to the scene and tried to fathom the meaning of each word. For me, this was the most important scene for this character because in a very short time you could see his inner turmoil and un-certainty while at the same time he displayed his flamboyant personal-ity. I put a massive effort into this scene, as I wanted above all to keep the audience's attention. Annie Considine, an assistant director, was a huge help and contributed enormously to what I achieved. We had numerous serious conversations about the interpretation of the scene, and her engagement and suggestions enabled me to play the role so much better.

The scene with Tybalt where he and Mercutio get into an intense fight was enjoyable to perform. Working on fight choreography with Ray Rochester, an assistant director, and Alex Payne, the fight director, was something new to me. I did take a class in fighting at Shakespeare & Company, but I had never participated in a fight on stage. Ray and Alex wanted to make the fight look real to the audience without fright-ening them into thinking we actors could be hurt. The biggest compli-ments came from people who asked me if the knives were for real and warned that we should be more careful.

All the scenes with Mercutio were challenging because he is such a vigorous character, and during the performance I could feel my energy level steadily draining. I had to be physically and mentally prepared for the role because I felt exhausted after every performance, and it did take a toll on me. But that doesn't mean I didn't enjoy myself in that performance; in fact, it was probably the most enjoyable charac-ter I played during my whole theatre career. I'm never fully satisfied with my performances. After every show, I reflect on what I can do to make my performance better the next time. I also think about what others can do to make us look like a more cohesive ensemble on the stage. However, the audience reaction is the true measure of our performances, and I feel a certain satisfaction when they praise our work, even if there are some details that need improvement.

I have found deep inner satisfaction through my work with YBG and Shakespeare & Company. They are an amazing group of people to work with, from the friendly participants to the knowledgeable and kind professors. I also found the kind of experience that I was seeking, and it occurred in a wonderful atmosphere that enabled all of us to put our creative forces together to produce a successful play. I will remember these productions for the amazing organization and attention given, right down to the smallest details. I was impressed by the production staff's work ethic and organizational skills, something even professional theatres lack in Bosnia and Herzegovina. Being part of these plays taught me how a serious production should be handled, which gave me a splendid basis for my future projects and for some lovely experiences in the theatre and in life, which I will cherish always because they broadened my horizons.

My desire to be a part of the theatre world continued to grow, and I realized that being involved in the arts is something I want in my life. I accepted that I am a storyteller with a lot of stories I want to tell, and I have decided that being engaged in theatre, video, and filming is what I want to do with my life. In answer to the question about how participating in theatre productions has affected me, my resolution to commit to filming and theatre says it best. This is a life-changing decision, and I will try with all my body and heart to make it happen. There are so many stories about everyday life that I want to tell, and I believe that theatre and film are the right place for me to do it.

One topic I want to shed light on in my creative work is the "two schools under one roof" policy in Mostar, wherein children in the same school are taught two different curricula, based on their ethnicity. This is not the case with theatre workshops that take place outside the school, such as those held at the Mostar Youth Theatre. At an acting workshop there, I met Ilija, and our initial acquaintance turned first into a friendship and then into brotherhood. Ilija is a Croat and I'm Bosniak, but in our friendship that never mattered because we share a passion for theatre, film, and literature, and even our worldviews match fairly well. Since we met, we have done a lot of joint projects, and we support each other. We have gone through a lot of difficult life situations together, including when the world around us collapsed, and when at times it felt impossible to work with Ilija on one of our joint projects, we always overcame the feeling together. We didn't give up on our goals or our projects, we didn't give up on ourselves, and, most important of all, we were always there for each other.

For years, Ilija and I have struggled to move from our respective studies in economics and law to work in theatre and film. Ilija took the first step by enrolling in a directing course at the academy in Sarajevo; in the meantime, I invested in video equipment so we could experiment with all forms of film. We continue to complement each other, and in time I might take a step like Ilija did and go to school. First we will see how much I am able to do as an independent filmmaker, writer, and producer.

After six years of reflection, we have finally invested ourselves 100 percent in this world. We have gathered a fine core team, we are working more than ever before, and we are preparing projects for the next few years. I will not lie, this has been difficult, since we are still financing everything ourselves, but we are taking the right steps. We have talked to several potential financers, and I am full of positive energy when I talk about our work. We rely on ourselves, our personal qualities, and a little bit of luck, because without all of that, nothing in life can be achieved. Ilija and I have gathered a team of people who also work hard, who do not give up on their dreams; even though we are already in our late twenties and early thirties, we believe the real things are yet to come for us.

If it were not for the plays I was in with YBG, as well as my training at Shakespeare & Company, where both Ilija and I studied at different times, I doubt our love for theatre would have deepened and strengthened the decision that this is what we really want to do in life, none of what we have done would have been possible. There are no words for how immensely grateful we are to Professor Garrod, the creator of YBG and director of the productions, and the man who enabled us to attend Shakespeare & Company.

*Mustafa Stupac, who was born in Mostar, has a bachelor's degree in law. In addition to his studies, he has been active in the theatre world. He was part of the Croatian National Theatre drama studio in Mostar, where he eventually starred in two plays that are still in the repertoire. He is also involved in video production and, with his friend Ilija Pujic, wrote his first play,* Neither Here, Nor There, *which is in pre-production. They plan to produce a play and a short film based on that text, with the long-term goal of making their feature debut. Mustafa made his documentary debut, in collaboration with the Berlin Center for Integrative Mediation, with* The Story of Departure and Return. *He is involved in the artistic life of the city of Mostar, where he collaborates with actors, musicians, and poets. Mustafa is working on many projects in all spheres of the arts, including music videos and several short films that will be released in 2022. He currently lives and works in Mostar. This essay was written in 2022.*

# The Courageous Heart Theatre Company

Ilija Pujić

BOSNIA AND HERZEGOVINA

A day doesn't go by that I do not think of or mention Professor Garrod and Youth Bridge Global (YBG). I met Professor Garrod in 2011 while participating in the YBG production of *The Tempest* and again in 2012 while performing in YBG's *As You Like It*. I had heard about this foreign production company that came to Mostar and did plays in the local language and English. Some of my friends had acted in these productions, and they were thrilled with how fulfilling it was. The first production I saw in my hometown was *Much Ado About Nothing* in 2009, one of the best plays I had ever seen. Even though the cast featured Mostarian youth who had little or no acting experience, the overall impression was very professional. One could see the amount of work that had been put into the production and the actors' performances. Moved by these performances, I got my own chance to participate a couple of years later.

At that time, I was writing a novel, and I went to the audition because I wanted to learn more about crafting dialogue. What welcomed me was a serious professional approach to Shakespeare and creating a theatre production. During the summers that I participated in the YBG productions, I enjoyed learning new things and being in a group of people with a similar mindset. In our deep conversations about important topics and the themes of the play, we shared our points of view and our thoughts on society and the youth around us, and we tried to express those ideas and emotions through the given material. The conversations in which we broke down Shakespeare's verse and sought its meaning in the modern world of Mostar broadened our perspective on the world and connected us around the common goal of making our environment a better place to live in.

We put a lot of effort into our speech exercises, our movement work, and, of course, our bonding exercises. As we matured throughout the process, we also developed the ability to speak Shakespeare's words in both our own tongue and in English. But the most important part about the YBG productions was that they connected us young people, who were raised in post-war surroundings and hadn't had a safe environment in which to share their personal thoughts or to have a joint future in once-divided Mostar.

The summer of 2021 marked the ten-year anniversary of my first YBG audition, for the production of *The Tempest* in Mostar, in which I played Ferdinand. The realization that a decade had passed came while I was filming my first short movie, *Richard & Lady Anne*. As my first venture into the acting world had been with a Shakespeare play, it wasn't a big surprise that I made my directing debut using a scene from *Richard III* as my inspiration. One evening during our filming, Goran Stojkic (who played Alonso, father to my Ferdinand) and I were watching the material we had shot that day and talking passionately about our future projects—what we wanted to do to engage our community, to make space for people to express themselves, and to build a platform for the younger generation that was coming up. While talking, we dug deeper into our own character traits and asked ourselves why we are the way we are, why we wanted to make our small city a better place to live. The answer was pretty easy: for both of us, acting in *The Tempest* in the summer of 2011 was a defining moment. Before that summer we were involved in many different things, as every teenager is, and could have gone on to become different people with different occupations. However, in the magical atmosphere of that YBG production, we both began something brand new that was brought to us by working with Professor Andrew Garrod. After that, we began to think of our society on a broader scale and within a bigger picture that somehow was including us.

I remember my audition for *The Tempest* quite well, as I was one of the few males who showed up the first day. Asked to fill in for other roles when someone was auditioning, I stayed for the whole first day and a good portion of the second to help my colleagues audition.

When I came forward for my own audition, I was aiming for the part of Ariel, the spirit imprisoned on the island by the magician Prospero, as I was fascinated with the character's symbolism and ambiguity. I thought the role would correspond with the state of mind I was in at the time. Thankfully, I didn't get that part. I realized how little I knew about acting, and saw that putting yourself in different characters can help you explore and build on your own. By the end of the auditions, I had learned to open myself up to new possibilities. I got caught up in exploring life and questioning the society I lived in, and sought to understand the people and problems in my surroundings. Above all, I learned to give my all in whatever I decided to take on.

Participating as an actor in *The Tempest* and *As You Like It* and as an assistant director in YBG's *Romeo and Juliet* in 2016 shaped my profession, my way of life, and, most importantly, my mentality. I see theatre as a place of healing, of searching for purpose and meaning, and a place to display the human soul. To me, the basis of theatre is human existence. It also is a place where one can voice concerns about the state of society. Participating in theatre enabled me to grow with my city, Mostar. And as I grew stronger, so did Mostar.

Remembering those experiences with YBG, I think it was perfect timing and perfect people. Mostarian society needed healthy people who could help to create a healthy community. Professor Garrod and his team came to Mostar with a project that at first seemed like some summer fun for youth. However, we soon learned that theatre is much more than just fun. The YBG experience connected people from the divided sides of our community and served as a medium for social education after the war. For many of us, those summer days preparing to perform the play were an ideal representation of what Mostar needed to be. Some participants were saying that, when Professor Garrod was in town, Mostar was transformed into a magical place that could be anywhere in Europe or the USA, not in a country that suffered a recent war. Of course, when he went away, that magical atmosphere was weakened, and the youth of Mostar were left to themselves, but each time he returned, the magical atmosphere in Mostar grew stronger, as did its youth. More people responded to the call for auditions, and the new generation of would-be actors were visited by the participants of previous projects. From 2006 to 2016, Mostar's youth grew stronger and helped to create a healthy sense of community that spread across the town. Many former participants of the YBG summer productions continue their work with various community projects.

Looking back, I see that my first audition became a formula for how I wanted to approach living my life. I wasn't the shyest boy on the block, but I wasn't the most open either. Growing up in a society with a narrow perspective and that, in the post-war times, restricted even what streets we were "allowed" to walk on, I wasn't taking too many chances. The audition got me a little bit out of my comfort zone, but with guidance from Professor Garrod, the place I was stepping into seemed to be a whole new world full of exciting adventures. The more I exposed myself, the more I benefitted from it, and for most of the ensuing years I took that approach to life—to give my all, no matter what I was doing. This became an emblem of my work and my approach to it. Sometimes I benefited by achieving in ways that exceeded even my own expectations, at other times I got hit by the harsh reality of giving too much in exchange for nothing, but I don't have any regrets. I've been discovering recently that the amount of passion I invest in my work comes back to me in a satisfying experience. For the first time, I'm seeing in myself the kind of passion and knowledge that resonates with the passion Professor Garrod showed as he guided me on that first long-ago audition day.

In my life and the lives of my friends who were involved in the YBG productions in Mostar, and with Professor Garrod, theatre played an enormous part in our developing into the people we are today—stable adults who continue to create beautiful stories. I remember well, sitting in a circle after every rehearsal of *The Tempest,* as each of us, cast and crew alike, would share our thoughts about the production process or personal stories that affected our preparations for the play. With each day, this group of strangers learned more about each other, and by the first performance, we were true friends. When I'm doing a play or preparing for a movie today, I encourage that kind of sharing and expressing of thoughts among the production members.

But above all, it was meeting Professor Garrod, a truly astonishing human being, that changed my life. The effort and love Professor Garrod puts into his work resonated with me. There are few people in life whom you admire and look up to, and in whom you can recognize your own passion, and possibly, a future vocation. I remember one letter in which I called him a "tutor of life," and I stand by those words to this day.

I never thought I'd get the chance to study acting with Shakespeare & Company (S&Co.) in the US state of Massachusetts. The offer to do so came from Professor James, who was assistant director to Professor Garrod on *As You Like* in Mostar in 2012, in which I played Orlando. After a crowd-pleasing first-night performance, Professor James asked me if I would like to continue to study acting. I was confused by the question, as the theatre school in Mostar had been shut down for quite some time. The YBG productions were the only opportunity in Mostar to learn about acting. When I heard that Professor James and Professor Garrod were thinking of sending me to an intensive four-week acting workshop in the U.S., I was blown away. I never dreamed that the summer joy of hanging out with Professor Garrod and my theatre friends would turn out to be my life calling.

S&Co, located in the Berkshire Mountains, is a natural paradise and an actor's ideal place to study and learn. The program I attended aims to improve the actors' skills and enhance their understanding of Shakespeare's language. It does that masterfully, but far more important is that the training improves you as a person. Shakespeare is not taught as something remote and hard to understand. The instructors make you comfortable with his words, the plots are presented as something happening right now in your own world, and the characters are bursting with emotions that make it impossible for you not to react. The script no longer represents a muddle of words on a page but characters you can interact with as real humans. I dare say that, after a while, you know your fellow actors better than the friends you went to high school with.

Being a war child in Bosnia and Herzegovina, I had difficulty expressing my emotions. The world I grew up in taught me to hide things rather that express them, and I was taught to keep my emotions to myself, which became a way of life for me. It was more than not showing my feelings to others; masking them was a skill that I had carefully crafted to protect myself from my surroundings. At S&Co., I learned how to express my emotions and not be afraid of them or to restrain them. It was liberating. The program teaches you to act and react authentically, and demands that you bring your own emotions to your part. I learned a great deal about myself through this training and did things I didn't think I'd be able to do. For the first time I got to know who I am and what I am worth, and I got a sense of what I had been missing. I felt so much love around me and saw how much love I'm capable of giving. Although expressing my emotions did make me more vulnerable, it also expanded my emotional depth and improved me as an actor and a person.

I was the kind of guy who likes to be positive and to suppress my negative energy. I was always dividing myself into two parts: the kind person who can inspire others and help make the world a better place to live, and the dark person who had experienced some horrible things and was raised on hatred. That part of me was a huge burden. It was a tremendous struggle for me to release that negativity, but in the safe environment of S&Co. I was finally able to. I felt like someone had lifted a huge weight from my chest. All the anger and rage I had collected in my past, all my fear that someone would hurt my loved ones or me, all the fights I had experienced and my fight to survive because of the war mentality in my city during my childhood—I was able to release all of that and I finally felt free!

In one fight class at S&Co. we were learning to give stage slaps. One guy slapped a girl (not for real, just as an exercise) and he was enjoying it. The whole group was terrified; they were crying and upset and wanted to end the practice. I felt like an outcast because I didn't react the way they did. I don't know why. I knew his pleasure was wrong, but I've seen and heard so many worse things that one slap in practice just didn't seem like a reason for so much upset. But I also was sad; I felt that the others had reacted to the slap like normal human beings and I had not. I didn't really even notice it! I hated myself that night and was crying because, for the first time in my life, I realized I was different in a way I felt was wrong.

That night I had a talk with one of the S&Co. faculty members, and he pointed me in the right direction. He explained that there is nothing wrong with me, and that I shouldn't hate myself for what I did in the past or what was done to me. He said I needed to forgive myself, and to accept myself for who I am, both my good side and bad. He assured me that, no matter how huge my anger and rage are, my kindness and compassion are even bigger. He told me that no matter what happens, he believes I am a good person, and no war or any society full of hatred can ever change that. That was the night I started to live my life fully; I was no longer divided, no longer blamed myself. I can finally say who I am and that I love who I am. When I went to S&Co., I thought I would learn a lot about acting, but I never thought I would learn so much about myself. For the first time in my life I actually know who I am and can be who I want to be! I finally can say my name, *Ilija,* knowing fully who I really am. It is the best feeling in the world when you know that your name represents the whole you!

On the day the S&Co. workshop held its final performance, Tina Packer, a founding member of the company and its artistic director, said she wanted me to return to participate in the teacher training program. She told me that the way I speak, my enthusiasm and open heart, and my ability to move people reminded her of herself at the time she created the theatre company. Kevin Coleman, a favorite teacher and an inspiration to many, said they all were glad to have me at the workshop because I encouraged my comrades and they could always count on me. They both boosted my confidence.

Before the final performance began, I was surprised and happy to see Professor James and his wife Heidi in the audience. I felt so loved and supported. I enjoyed the final presentations of all the Shakespearean scenes enormously, and although I can't be objective about how the audience reacted, my work on the balcony scene of *Romeo and Juliet* was a small reflection of the effort I had put in and of what I had learned.

After the workshop, I stayed with friends from the education department at S&Co. Each year, the education department presents the Fall Festival of Shakespeare, during which the team members fan out to a dozen high schools across Massachusetts and direct a selected play. Later the kids from those schools come back to S&Co. for a weekend, and each group presents their play before the other participants. It became my heart's desire to bring this kind of theatre to children in post-war countries and to anyone who has experienced trauma. Theatre could bring hope to so many lives and teach people how to live them fully. The Fall Festival provided a model I thought would work well.

I also knew that Professor Garrod wanted to leave something behind in Mostar that would connect the youth who participated in YGB projects. I decided to pursue my dream of creating a theatre company in Mostar that, like Professor Garrod and YBG, provides a healthy place for youth to hang out and share their stories and dreams. I want to create a healthy theatre community and to leave an impression on those who participate, to get them to ask questions about the world and strive to improve society—and themselves.

After a lot of thinking and talking to friends, I decided to create a theatre company in Mostar and to stage *Julius Caesar,* a play that asks people to question themselves and the society around them. This company will be an opportunity for people who participated in YBG projects to do more acting in the same spirit. It will be a place where they can feel safe, continue their friendships, and build both a theatre company and a community in the YBG spirit. I believe this is a very promising idea for Mostar. I will call the company the Courageous Heart Theatre Company.

Opening myself up through the YBG productions and at S&Co. made me realize who I am and what I was missing by not allowing myself to feel. There is a huge amount of love around us, and I want others to discover this and learn to express their own emotions through theatre. This will be the true mission of the Courageous Heart.

*Ilija Pujić is a professionally trained actor and theatre and film director. He currently is finishing his studies at the Academy of Dramatic Arts in Sarajevo, Bosnia and Herzegovina. Early in his career, he worked as an assistant director with Andrew Garrod on Youth Bridge Global productions of* Twelfth Night *(2014) and* Romeo and Juliet *(2016) in his beloved hometown of Mostar. Ilija is active in the local community, where he collaborates with several organizations to raise awareness of social problems through community-engaged art. For some time, he worked with students at the University of Mostar, where he directed several plays in English with Professor Anđelka Raguž. He encouraged the creation of the first association of students of English in Mostar, which was called Excalibur. His professional work was spotted by Hrvatsko Narodno Kazalište Mostar, and he was engaged as an actor in numerous plays over several seasons. In 2019, Ilija became one of the few individual artists from the Western Balkans to be involved in a European Reshape research and development project. His debut short film,* Richard & Lady Anne, *which was inspired by Shakespeare's* Richard III, *premiered at the Sarajevo Film Festival in 2022. This essay was written in 2021 and 2022.*

# Afterword: Clues For a Constantly Renewed Adventure

David Barnet

At the 1974 Canadian Dominion Drama Festival in St John's, Newfoundland, I saw a production of *Romeo and Juliet* presented by students from Saint John High School (SJHS) in New Brunswick, directed by Andrew Garrod. The performance was stunning! The actors understood the text's intricate detail, and told the story swiftly and robustly. The conflicts of the combating households, the emotional and physical passion of the lovers, and the fights between the Capulets and the Montagues (which seemed to involve whole football teams of young men), were played with such exuberant authenticity, that the packed Arts and Culture Centre audience of 1200 were left standing and cheering. To me, it seemed as if the sixteen-year-old Juliet was as poised and perfect in the role as I remember the young Judi Dench in Franco Zeffirelli's 1960 production at the Old Vic in London.

I was an adjudicator at this Festival, and I asked the students how they had achieved such honesty and clarity in performance: surely, they must have used improvisation (that being my particular interest) in their rehearsals? "What's improvisation?" they replied. "We write essays on the tragic flaw." They were referring to the "tragic flaw" theory of character articulated by A.C. Bradley (my nemesis at grammar school), which Mark Blagrave mentions in his essay. This did not make sense. How could an "academic" investigation contribute to an actor's personal ownership of a text or to spontaneity in performance?

Apparently curious about improvisation, Andrew Garrod invited me to SJHS to apply these techniques to his next production, *A Midsummer's Night Dream*. The students and I had a lot of fun exploring the ideas of Viola Spolin and Keith Johnston, but I don't think I added anything to the production. It was still early in the rehearsals, but already the students were completely familiar with the nuances of the text and deeply identified with their characters.

How a teacher, such as Andrew Garrod, can achieve such a quality of theatre with high school students is a mystery, but there are many clues in these essays. My own teaching quest has been to establish a similar sense of ownership and truth in theatre with liberal arts students at a university.

My students have a variety of agendas, including preparation for careers in academic or professional theatre. I will concentrate, however, on those who, like high school students, explore theatre for a while, en route to somewhere else. They do not fall into a convenient category: "amateur" and "recreational" are considered pejorative. They are not "generalists" since some briefly focus on drama while others have majors from across the university, and are frequently the brightest in their field, whether it be microbiology or environmental engineering. Like students at high school, they can create theatre of great meaning and incorporate into their lives the skills and attitudes learnt through the practice of drama. Much of the theatre they produce is from established texts, such as the work at SJHS. However, of equal significance is the theatre they create themselves, through the group process of collective creation. This performer-created theatre uses improvisation, adaptation, playwriting, and any other technique and performance element that can contribute to the composition of a drama.

The most apparent similarity between high school and university liberal arts students is the freedom from a reliance on acting technique. Instead, they can place their primary focus on the discovery and communication of meaning. Satisfaction comes from their participation in the group's creative process and in the audience's reception of the play. They might ask the natural question, "Did you like my performance?" but essentially, their goal is for the audience to respond to the play as personally as they have.

With these students, inexperience and lack of confidence in the theatrical process encourages an engagement with both the material and the group or "ensemble." Ignorance of theatrical practice, particularly television naturalism, can be a blessing! If they think they "can't act," then they will not "cheat" or "short cut" their way to a performance, nor focus on how effectively they are acting. Instead, they will go to where they are safe, into the text, into meaning, into the understanding of character, into the dynamics of the group. "Meaning" is the argument of the text—whether it is the moral journey of the characters in the world of a Shakespeare play, or the issues of a performer-created drama.

In order for students to have the courage to pursue or create meaning, without the support of significant acting technique, a particular educational and artistic environment must be established. There's nothing unique about this, since it applies equally to high schools, liberal arts programs, or professional acting schools. Based on the evidence of these essays and my own observation, it existed at SJHS when Andrew Garrod taught there. In discussing this environment, I will draw on the writing of the director and teacher Michel Saint-Denis, the principal force behind leading theatre schools in the UK, France, the United States and Canada.

For Michel Saint-Denis, one of the most important elements in a theatre school was the establishment of "a human and artistic milieu, which … will spread a sense of individual responsibility. This milieu, this climate, if it is authentic and generous, could impress students and actors more profoundly than the study of even the most advanced techniques" (1982, p. 84).

Within this milieu, the teacher/director establishes the ensemble. This is a group of actors (and perhaps a director, designers and production staff) working together, trusting and testing each other, and secure in their shared risks and common goal. For Saint-Denis, "it is of prime importance to establish from the beginning the idea of ensemble acting because what, in fact, creates life on the stage is the actor's awareness of his relationships—spiritual, imaginative, perceptive, physical—with other actors" (Saint-Denis 1982, p. 81). "An 'ensemblier,' according to the dictionary, is 'an artist who aims at unity of general effect.' We were 'ensembliers.' We set out to develop initiative, freedom, and a sense of responsibility in the individual, as long as he or she was ready and able to merge his personal qualities into the ensemble" (Saint-Denis 1960, p. 92). This is not a mysterious concept or a fancy name for the group dynamics of any acting company or drama class. An effective ensemble requires certain ingredients, many of which are described in the essays of the SJHS graduates.

Essential to the ensemble is the articulation of a common goal, and the students' commitment to the level of discipline and self-denial required for excellence. For Mark Blagrave, for example, "Andrew Garrod's approach ... seemed to encourage us, in experiencing ourselves as a community, to see the play as a whole, to care about it as a whole product. Its overall impression was ... more important that any one individual's ability to empathize with a role." Gail Taylor: "The ceremony of form calls for excellence, the interactions a kind of grace."

In the ensemble, the risks are shared, and students empathize with and celebrate each other's exploration. This is a supportive process, but it is also rigorous. Philip Palmer: "[I]n the midst of every social activity, there is this quiet process of self-discovery going on. It is not gentle, and I didn't find it easy." My students also tell me not to underestimate the friendships made in this environment: it is not only a forum to practice feelings and ideas, but a place where they are most likely to meet likeminded colleagues. There is a particular strength in a high school or a liberal arts program, when students have eclectic backgrounds and life experiences. In the process of creating theatre, whether scripted or improvised, they will negotiate with different points of view and preconceptions about theatre. They will learn patience, flexibility, and diplomacy, and they will celebrate and synthesize the differences between them, or they will quit.

This learning environment leads to the growth of independence in students. At SJHS, Andrew Garrod assumed that his students "were complete human beings able to make and understand choice. In short, we were treated as adults in a remarkable and liberating way, for moral freedom depends on moral responsibility, and moral responsibility is the essence of adulthood" (Philip Palmer). Julie Guravich writes: "Andrew Garrod's method as a director of young minds was to formulate appropriate questions, providing prompts whenever we became insecure so that we, the players, could work out the answers."

Saint-Denis: "The teacher/director should not force anything on the student/actor. But he must induce the student to use varied means of expression and keep his imagination always well orientated and open. Under these conditions, freedom can thrive. To arrive at *la vie scénique,* the total life of the play on the stage, achievement of this freedom is of first importance" (1982, p. 84).

The first step for many of my students is discovering how to work for themselves and not for my approval. "I don't have to ask you how I'm doing anymore, I know." "I want to play my character; I don't need to please you." "From your teaching we saw the direction, but we found the path and destination ourselves." I remember from my own acting training the tyranny of "I like that" and "that's good" spoken by well-intentioned teachers, but creating in me a dependency on their approbation. One of my students wrote: "As young … students we were all self-directed … and so we required permission more than persuasion. Permission and a cartographer's direction in a personal search."

As the students take a journey through drama, so does the teacher. Andrew Garrod is described as "a fine mimic, athletic and poised, who emitted a kinetic energy. He … gave rehearsals both energy and dignity. Garrod pushed himself as well as his actors" (Philip Palmer). I think that a teacher can only create an environment of risk if the adventure is mutual and the discoveries of both teacher and student are celebrated equally. If the process is reciprocal, it isn't easy: it is rigorous, with flexibility and openness being the hardest tasks.

Mark Blagrave describes another secret about acting that Andrew Garrod instinctively understood, that "acting is about 'showing' not 'being,'" and that the overall impression of the play was "more important that any one individual's ability to empathize with a role." "What mattered was that we could show an audience the characters and what they stood for in the scheme of the play, rather than identifying with the character, in some way that could ultimately be gratifying only to ourselves." Empathy is useful as part of the exploration process but inhibits the narrative if an actor over-identifies with the character. This is particularly true in collective theatre, where the actor cannot draw attention to her own emotional state, and must 'represent' rather than 'be' the character. David Mamet writes in his book on acting, *True and False*: "The very act of striving to create an emotional state in oneself takes one out of the play. It is the ultimate self-consciousness, and though it may be self-consciousness in the service of an ideal, it is no less boring for that" (p. 11).

The point is not to be a "good actor" but to serve the play. Palmer writes "Andrew Garrod didn't school us in acting techniques, such as breathing exercises or improvisations." Some technical skill is useful, otherwise the actor won't be understood, but imagination and curiosity are invaluable. Saint-Denis: "This artistic adventure, which every artist has got to go through, cannot be separated from the human adventure. What one says, what one does, is what one is" (1982, p. 59).

Within this milieu, play happens—the freedom to explore, to have fun. It is almost a cliché that "theatre is 'un jeu' where inspiration and childlike rapture are more important than sweat and fits of temper" (Saint-Denis 1982, p. 88). Yet, in the hurly-burly of production, performance and craft, we sometimes forget the centrality of letting loose the child in the actor. As Gail Taylor writes about her acting at SJHS: "It was the serious adolescent equivalent of childhood's playing, where risk and invention are the whole point."

Within the safety and challenge of the ensemble, risk leads to courage, and students find clarity in the play and in themselves. The exploration of the one brings meaning to the other. Brent Banbury writes, "Play would be the vehicle for my drive to survive, my need to be heard, for the demands of my voice, whatever that voice was."

Burns Macmillan: "In each case, the exploration of the character was, simultaneously, an exploration of myself." Writing about *The Crucible*, Palmer says, "John Proctor alerted me to the possibility of exercising courage, even redemptive courage, where both innocence and virtue have been lost". For Gail Taylor, "drama … was concerned with the exploration of identity, and treated character as faceted, edgy, and in flux. I loved the headlong theatrical slide into the disputed territory of choice-making, the great grapplings of the drama with all that is shadowy as well as radiant and ribald."

Not only do students come to understand themselves through their characters, but they also continue to make sense of their world. Lani Selick, playing Cordelia, saw a civil rights march on television: "These marchers were all Cordelias—people who can't be bought, can't be silenced, can't pass up the chance to fight for what they believe, no matter what the consequences. Everyone knows a Cordelia, or is one. There are Cordelias in every era and in every culture. In *King Lear*, she is the play's *conscience*. She is the conscience of us all."

If a play is to transform the actor, it must itself have particular qualities. The SJHS graduates write particularly positively about Shakespeare, Arthur Miller (*The Crucible*) and Jean Anouilh (*Poor Bitos*). Although the musicals were important to them on many levels, they do not seem to have offered the same moral challenge. Shakespeare for example, has great stories, huge characters and moral conflict, with structure and language that offer a toehold to any young actor with pluck enough for the climb. The Quebecois director Jean-Stephane Roy, in his program notes for *Pericles*, his first English-language Shakespeare production (University of Alberta 2000), writes: "For us, he's freedom. He's the king of imagination, the inventor of Hollywood … he gives us the right to use our passion in the creation act and not just our intelligence. His characters are clear and human. What's great about Shakespeare, he's a national writer in every country, he belongs to everyone and every culture has a special vision of Shakespeare." This seems to sum up the experience of Andrew Garrod's SJHS students in the 1970s. Mark Blagrave describes *Lear* as "an unrelieved vision into the void. It was precisely this … quality … with its absurdist tinge, that made the choice so right for many of us at that time of our lives and in that era."

What did I learn from watching and working with the young actors at SJHS and reading their articulate accounts of their theatre practice with Andrew Garrod? I am currently working with an intergenerational theatre company, actors aged twenty to ninety, that creates its own plays and adapts others (including Shakespeare) based on issues of aging and stories drawn from their own lives. What do these young and older actors have in common? A fearless delight in a playful ensemble, a willingness to engage themselves unreservedly in the pursuit of the moral argument of their plays, and a continuing desire to challenge both their audiences and themselves, regardless of age or circumstance. I think we have always known these things, but sometimes we didn't know that we knew them.

### References

Johnstone, K. (1979). *Impro,* London: Faber and Faber.

Mamet, D. (1997). *True and False.* New York: Vintage Books.

Roy, J-S. (2000). *Pericles* (program notes). Edmonton: Studio Theatre, University of Alberta.

Saint-Denis, M. (1960). *The Rediscovery of Style.* New York: Theatre

Arts Books.

Saint-Denis, M. (1982). *Training for the Theatre.* New York: Theatre Arts Books.

Spolin, V. (1963). *Improvisation for the Theatre.* Evanston: Northwestern University Press.

# Andrew Garrod: A Tribute

Robert Brym

> The job in Saint John I regard as serendipitous. The job in the
> Marshall Islands I regard as serendipitous. Going to Rwanda I
> regard as serendipitous.
> —Andrew Garrod, January 2023

To hear Andrew tell it, his story is one of chance. When I interviewed him in January 2023, he insisted at the outset that "planfulness on my part … wasn't the way I generally functioned." Thus, shortly after graduating from Oxford, Andrew applied to North American high schools for a teaching position. Despite offers from California and New York, he says that the head of the English programme at Saint John High School swayed him with whimsy, remarking that in New Brunswick Andrew would be afforded the opportunity to hunt bear. Decades later, now a professor at Dartmouth College in Hanover, New Hampshire, Andrew attended a dinner for recipients of honorary degrees. He happened to sit beside the Minister of Health for Rwanda. When she learned that Andrew had recently been directing plays for high school students in less developed regions and conflict zones, she invited him to stage *Romeo and Juliet* in her country. And so he did. According to Andrew, all was chance.

These are charming stories, but I don't buy them. I take the view that circumstances past and present lead us to develop predispositions that, in turn, influence the choices we make.

Andrew's father was an Anglican clergyman. His family was infused with principles of righteousness, justice, charity, and service. Before he left the UK at the age of twenty-five, Andrew says he tried to find out as much as he could about Saint John, so he must have known that the city was a small, poor cultural backwater.[1] Most people presented with the opportunities available to Andrew in 1962 would not have selected Saint John. I believe Andrew chose us over New Yorkers and Californians because his upbringing primed him to sense that we had greater need for his talents. And he was right.

Before Andrew, we marched in lockstep like the pupils in Pink Floyd's "Another Brick in the Wall (Part 2)." By providing us with the opportunity to grapple with English literature and drama, Andrew showed us a wider world full of possibilities and limitations, enabling us to see more clearly what we might become.

We thought we were assembling in Andrew's apartment for first readings of plays that we were scheduled to perform. We were usefully deceived. None of us knew it at the time, but Andrew was really in the business of helping us construct moral compasses. The plays were just vehicles in service of that higher goal. Andrew took callow youth, uncertain of their identity and direction, showed them how to accomplish a concrete, collective task in the glare of the public spotlight, and helped to turn them—turn us—into young adults who saw the outlines of our future selves sufficiently clearly that we could move forward with confidence and purpose. A craftsman he was and still is, but a craftsman who gives his raw materials the autonomy to help determine the form they eventually take.

We knew what we lost when Andrew left, which is why it was easy in 2007, fully three decades after he departed Saint John, to galvanize hundreds of former students from near and far to attend a gala in his honour and fund a scholarship in his name at the University of New Brunswick. A decade later, the University of New Brunswick recognized his contribution to youth in the province by awarding him an honorary doctorate.

Following his time at Saint John High School, Andrew went on to complete a doctorate at Harvard. Given that he had devoted himself to raising the ethical awareness of adolescents for sixteen years at Saint John High School, it seems to me there was nothing even remotely serdendipitous in his choice of subject and advisors. He enrolled in Harvard's educational psychology programme and selected as advi-

1. John Leroux, *The Lost City: Ian MacEachern's Photographs of Saint John* (Fredericton, NB: Goose Lane Editions, 2018).

sors Lawrence Kohlberg and Carol Gilligan, two giants in the study of moral development, particularly in children and adolescents.

The main theme underlying Andrew's story reasserted itself once he graduated from Harvard and landed a job at Dartmouth College. Dartmouth provides generous scholarships for promising students from marginalized racial and religious groups, many of them the first in their family to receive a university education. Knowing Andrew's predispositions, I find it utterly unsurprising that these strangers in a largely White, elite, liberal arts college—Black, Native American, Latino/a, Asian, and Muslim—most attracted him. He devoted himself to understanding and getting them to understand their intellectual abilities, interests, ways of seeing the world, and emotional needs. During his twenty-five-year tenure at Dartmouth, Andrew served as chair of the education department and director of teacher education. He won the university's distinguished teaching award twice. With colleagues, Andrew published nine volumes that allowed marginalized students to tell their own life stories.[1] However, his most important accomplishment was the same as in Saint John: assisting students in their moral growth by promoting their self-understanding.

In 2004, another variation of Andrew's story began to unfold. He co-founded Youth Bridge Global with David Yorio. Their aim was to "use drama and art to ... connect youth across cultures and provide educational opportunities to under-resourced regions of the world."[2] And so, with Dartmouth students as his assistants, Andrew dared to

1. Andrew Garrod and Colleen Larimore, eds., *First Person, First Peoples: Native American College Graduates Tell Their Life Stories* (Ithaca, NY: Cornell University Press, 1997); Andrew Garrod, Janie Victoria Ward, Tracy L. Robinson, and Robert Kilkenny, eds., *Souls Looking Back: Life Stories of Growing up Black* (New York: Routledge, 1999); Andrew Garrod and Jay Davis, eds. *Crossing Customs: International Students Write on U.S. College Life and Culture* (New York: Routledge, 1999); Andrew Garrod and Robert Kilkenny, eds. *Balancing Two Worlds: Asian American College Students Tell Their Life* Stories (Ithaca, NY: Cornell University Press, 2007); Andrew Garrod, Robert Kilkenny, and Christina Gómez, eds., *Mi Voz, Mi Vida: Latino College Students Tell Their Life Stories* (Ithaca, NY: Cornell University Press, 2007); Andrew Garrod and Robert Kilkenny, eds., *Growing up Muslim: Muslim College Students in America Tell Their Life Stories* (Ithaca, NY: Cornell University Press, 2014); Andrew Garrod, Robert Kilkenny, and Christina Gómez, eds. *Mixed: Multiracial College Students Tell Their Life Stories* (Ithaca, NY: Cornell University Press, 2013); Andrew Garrod, Robert Kilkenny, and Melanie Benson Taylor, eds., *I Am Where I Come From: Native American College Students Tell Their Life Stories* (Ithaca, NY: Cornell University Press, 2017); Andrew Garrod and Robert Kilkenny, eds., *Adolescent Portraits: Identity, Relationships, and Challenges*, 8th ed. (New York: Routledge, 2022).
2. Youth Bridge Global, 2023, http://www.ybglobal.org/team.

stage *Fiddler on the Roof* in the Marshall Islands; *Much Ado About Nothing* in Bosnia and Herzegovina (with Muslim, Serb, and Catholic youth); *Romeo and Juliet* in Rwanda (with Hutu and Tutsi youth); and so on. It is a remarkable repertoire that continues to grow in Andrew's eighty-sixth year.

In 1969, when I graduated from Saint John High School, Andrew presented me with a large and beautifully illustrated book, *World Theatre*, by Bamber Gascoigne. Andrew inscribed it with the following quotation from T. S. Eliot's *Murder in the Cathedral*, my last play at Saint John High: "But in the life of one man, never the same time returns."

Andrew Garrod, in rehearsal directing Shakespeare in the ruins of the old university library in Mostar, Bosnia and Herzegovina. (Courtesy of Andrew Garrod.)

I returned to Eliot's words several times over the years, finally reaching the conclusion that they are nonsense. All of us who have worked with Andrew know that a moral compass well-constructed lasts a lifetime. In effect, therefore, "the same time" returns every day. That time, and Andrew's example, will always form a part—a foundation stone—of who we are.

# A Selection
## of Photographs

Brent Bambury as Tevye in *Fiddler on the Roof,*
Saint John, 1978

Shane Ervin as Claudio and Brent Bambury as Benedick
in *Much Ado About Nothing,*
Saint John, 1978

Judy Steen as Hero and Philip Palmer as Claudio
in *Much Ado About Nothing,*
Saint John, 1965

Philip Palmer as Proctor, Gary Zatzman as Danforth,
and Al Kushing as Reverend Parris in *The Crucible*,
Saint John, 1966

Brent Bambury as Orlando and Heather Chesley as Rosalind
in *As You Like It*,
Saint John, 1977

Brian Stevenson as Kastril, Heather Chesley as Dame Pliant,
and Rob Keenan as Surly in *The Alchemist*,
Saint John, 1977

Harun Hasanagić as Prospero
in *The Tempest*,
Bosnia and Herzegovina, 2011

Robert Silver as Hamlet
in *Hamlet,*
Saint John, 1972

Robert Silver as Hamlet, Burns MacMillan as King Claudius,
and Wendy Reevey as Gertrude in *Hamlet*,
Saint John, 1972

Bruce Campbell as Nathan Detroit and Robert Silver as Sky Masterson
in *Guys and Dolls*,
Saint John, 1972

Clovis Shyaka as Benvolio
in *Romeo and Juliet*,
Rwanda, 2013

Left:
Richard Green as King Lear
and Gail Taylor as Goneril
in *King Lear*,
Saint John, 1964

Right:
Gail Taylor as Goneril
and Bill Irving as Cornwall
in *King Lear*,
Saint John, 1964

Mary Edwards as First Fairy, Richard Meltzer as Oberon,
and Julie Guravich as Titania
in *A Midsummer Night's Dream*,
Saint John, 1975

Julie Guravich as Juliet and Diane Daigle as the Nurse
in *Romeo and Juliet*,
Saint John, 1974

Brian Disher as a Londoner, Wayne Best as Doolittle,
and Jim Burns as a Londoner in *My Fair Lady*,
Saint John, 1975

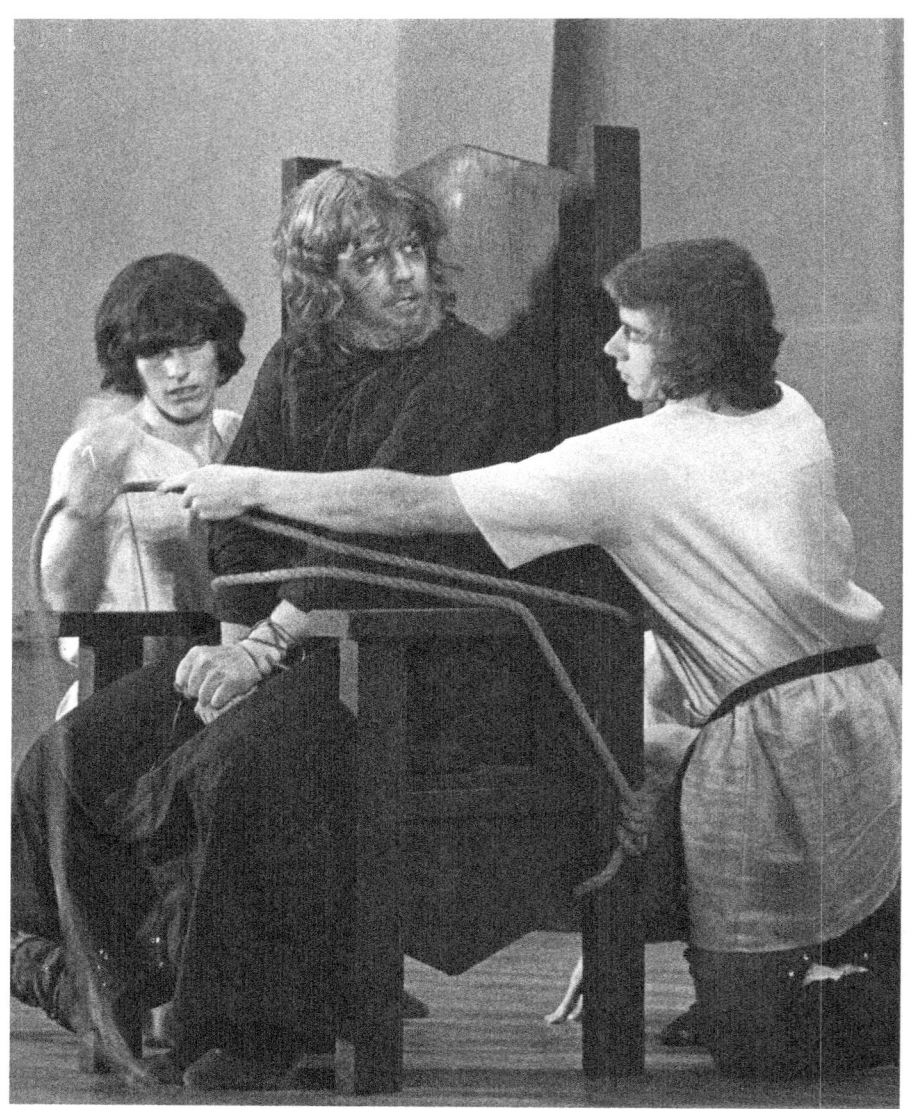

Wayne Best as Servant (left), David MacKenzie as Duke of Gloucester,
and James Rooney as Servant (right) in *King Lear*,
Saint John, 1973

Tristen Horiuchi as Jigger Craigin (left) and Yolanie Jurelang as Mrs. Mullin
in *Carousel*,
Marshall Islands, 2020

Yolanie Jurelang as Eulalie Mackecknie Shinn (left)
and Duke Gaston as Harold Hill (right)
in *The Music Man*,
Marshall Islands, 2019

Erza Syla as Titania with attending fairies
in *A Midsummer Night's Dream*,
Kosovo, 2019

Jusuf Tofaj as Oberon and Erza Syla as Titania
in *A Midsummer Night's Dream*,
Kosovo, 2019

Muhamadi Nshimiyimana as Romeo
in *Romeo and Juliet*,
Rwanda, 2013

Clovis Shyaka as Benvolio and Muhamadi Nshimiyimana as Romeo
in *Romeo and Juliet*,
Rwanda, 2013

Burns MacMillan as Bitos
in *Poor Bitos*,
Saint John, 1971

Lani Selick as Abigail Williams
in *The Crucible*,
Saint John, 1968

Top: Robert Brym as Tony and Lani Selick as Maria in *West Side Story*, Saint John, 1967
Bottom: Jennifer Brittain as Laura Wingfield and Robert Brym as The Gentleman Caller
in *The Glass Menagerie*, Saint John, 1968

Robert Brym as Becket
in *Murder in the Cathedral*,
Saint John, 1968

Erik Abdo as Motel (left) and Selina Leem as Tzeitel
in *Fiddler on the Roof*,
Marshall Islands, 2014

Erik Abdo as Motel (front left), Barron Noah as The Rabbi (middle),
and Selina Leem as Tzeitel
in *Fiddler on the Roof,*
Marshall Islands, 2014

Wilmer Joel as Charlie Cowell (left), Jobod Silk as Harold Hill (right)
in *The Music Man,*
Marshall Islands, 2019

Jensen Malimai as the Policeman (left) and Wilmer Joel as David Bascombe (right)
in Carousel,
Marshall Islands, 2020

Mark Blagrave as Edmund and David MacKenzie as the Duke of Gloucester
in *King Lear*,
Saint John, 1973

Steve Morgan as Edgar and Mark Blagrave as Edmund
in *King Lear*,
Saint John, 1973

Steve Morgan as Professor Higgins and Elizabeth Foster Chase as Eliza Doolittle
in *My Fair Lady,*
Saint John, 1975

Elizabeth Foster Chase as Kate Hardcastle
in *She Stoops to Conquer*,
Saint John, 1972

Jobod Silk as Danny Zuko with fellow Greasers
in *Grease,*
Marshall Islands, 2018

Jobod Silk as Harold Hill with fellow students
in *The Music Man*,
Marshall Islands, 2019

Mustafa Stupac as Mercutio (right) and Goran Knezović as Benvolio (left)
in *Romeo and Juliet,*
Bosnia and Herzegovina, 2016

Žarko Šaravanja as Sir Andrew (back left),
Ante Čović-Stanić as Sir Toby Belch (back middle),
Mustafa Stupac as Malvolio (front and center),
and Nikola Đorđevski as Fabian (back right)
in *Twelfth Night*,
Bosnia and Herzegovina, 2014

Ilija Pujić as Ferdinand in
*The Tempest,*
Bosnia and Herzegovina, 2011

Ilija Pujić as Orlando and Dea Catela as Rosalind
in *As You Like It,*
Bosnia and Herzegovina, 2012

Belma Beglerović as Hero (left), Harun Hasanagić as Leonato (middle),
and Marko Matić as Claudio
in *Much Ado About Nothing*,
Bosnia and Herzegovina, 2009

# About the Editors and the Authors of the Foreword and Afterword

**Andrew Garrod,** a Canadian citizen, is a professor emeritus at Dartmouth College, where he previously chaired the Department of Education, directed the teacher education program, and taught courses in adolescence, moral development, and contemporary issues in U.S. education. For several years, he conducted a research project in Bosnia and Herzegovina on forgiveness, faith development, and moral reasoning. In that same country, he has directed seven bilingual Shakespearean productions that have played in Mostar and elsewhere in the Balkans. He mounted a trilingual production of *Romeo and Juliet* in Kigali, Rwanda, a few years ago and most recently led a production of *A Midsummer Night's Dream* in Pristina, Kosovo. In the Marshall Islands, he has directed numerous bilingual Shakespearean plays and Broadway musicals, and for fifteen years, led a volunteer teaching program in this Central Pacific nation. His most recent co-edited books include *I Am Where I Come From: Native American College Students and Graduates Tell Their Life Stories* and *Growing Up Muslim: Muslim Students in America Tell Their Life Stories.* Recent co-authored articles include "Be Not Afeard; the Isle is Full of Noises: Expanding Youths' Aspirations Through Shakespeare and Musical Productions in the Marshall Islands" and "Constructive Disequilibrium and Transformative Pedagogy: Developing Global Citizens in Faraway Spaces." In 1991 and 2009, he was awarded Dartmouth College's Distinguished Teaching Award. He holds an honorary doctorate in Humane Letters from the University of New Brunswick and is an honorary citizen of the Marshall Islands.

**James Goodwin Rice** is an actor and teacher. He attended the University of Washington, Skidmore College (BA, Theatre) and New York University (MA, Theatre). He is Senior Lecturer of Theatre at Dartmouth College, specializing in acting and voice training since 1997. He studied acting in New York with the twentieth-century masters Sanford Meisner and Uta Hagen. Later he trained with Kristin Linklater and was designated as a teacher of her vocal approach in 1992. Believing that "theatre is rehearsal for living," James' interest is in how actor-based training techniques and autobiographical storytelling facilitate empathy, trust, and community building. In 2012, he met Andrew Garrod, who invited him to join Youth Bridge Global and co-direct Shakespeare's *As You Like It* in Mostar, Bosnia and Herzegovina. Subsequently, he assisted with productions of *Romeo and Juliet* in Kigali, Rwanda (2013) and *Romeo and Juliet* in Mostar, Bosnia and Herzegovina (2016).

**Andrew Nalani,** a Ugandan, has a Ph.D. in Applied Psychology (Psychology and Social Intervention) from NYU Steinhardt. He is currently Assistant Professor of Human and Organizational Development at Peabody College of Vanderbilt University. He takes an interdisciplinary approach to understanding how transformative programs are designed and their influence on positive youth development across cultures and sectors, drawing particularly from theories and methods in developmental and community psychology as well as sociology and organizational studies. At NYU, he worked on the research teams for the Listening Project, SAFE Spaces: Systems Aligning for Equity, and has engaged in innovation in the youth work field through a research-practice partnership with Partners for Youth Empowerment. His work on social-science based pathways to reduce youth inequality received the 2022 Social Policy Article Publication Award from the Society for Research on Adolescence. He was a keynote speaker at the Gates Foundation 2018 Bill and Melinda Gates Foundation Goalkeepers Initiative to advance global goals, a recipient of the 2019 Hollyhock Center's Dana Bass Solomon Fund for emerging leaders and change makers and community builders, and a recipient of Dartmouth's Barret All-Round Achievement Cup. He is a highly skilled group-learning facilitator and draws on several art forms to foster dynamic and effective learning experiences for youth and adults. He holds a Master's in Education from Harvard University (where he received the Leadership in Education Fellowship and the inaugural Anne M. Sweeney Scholarship) and an AB from Dartmouth College.

**Mike Leigh** is a writer-director. He trained at the Royal Academy of Dramatic Art, Camberwell and Central Art Schools in London, and at the London Film School. His first feature film was *Bleak Moments* (1971); this was followed by the full-length television films, *Hard Labour* (1973), *Nuts in May* (1975), *The Kiss of Death* (1976), *Who's Who* (1978), *Grown-Ups* (1980), *Home Sweet Home* (1982), *Meantime* (1983), and *Four Days In July* (1984). Other feature films are *High Hopes* (1988), *Life Is Sweet* (1990), *Naked* (1993), *Secrets and Lies* (1996), *Career Girls* (1997), *Topsy-Turvy* (1999), *All Or Nothing* (2002), *Vera Drake* (2004), *Happy-Go-Lucky* (2008), *Another Year* (2010), *Mr. Turner* (2014), and *Peterloo* (2018). He has written and directed over twenty stage plays. These include *Babies Grow Old* (1974), *Abigail's Party* (1977), *Ecstasy* (1979), *Goose-Pimples* (1981), *Smelling A Rat* (1988), *Greek Tragedy* (1989), *It's A Great Big Shame!* (1993), *Two Thousand Years* (2005), and *Grief* (2011).

**David Barnet** is a professor emeritus in the drama department at the University of Alberta, where he specialized in acting Shakespeare, ensemble performance, and devised theatre, and was department chair for many years. He is a 3M National Teaching Fellow. David was the founding artistic director of Catalyst Theatre and GeriActors & Friends, an intergenerational theatre company now in its twenty-first season. With the GeriActors he has developed numerous productions, including "We Decide," which is based on *King Lear*. Initially in response to COVID, he started a new branch of the company—Audio Geris—which creates radio versions of their productions. His recent creative research includes the CIHR-funded project, Theatre as a Pathway to Healthy Aging, and his book, *GeriActors & Friends: Fearless Acting and the Delight of Intergenerational Theatre*, has been accepted for publication in Canada. He has received international prizes for his productions on radio (CKUA) and network television (CBC). He was the artistic director of the Manitoba Theatre School, an assistant director at the Stratford and Shaw theatre festivals and the National Theatre School, and a frequent adjudicator. In the latter capacity at Canada's Dominion Drama Festival, he first observed the remarkable Shakespeare productions of Andrew Garrod and the Saint John High School students.

Printed in Great Britain
by Amazon

46193266R00205